D1542024

Number 2 in the series *North American Beethoven Studies*, edited by William Meredith

Letters to Beethoven
and Other Correspondence

VOLUME 3 : 1824–1828

Beethoven in May 1824. Chalk drawing by
Stephan Drecker. Source: Historisches Museum
der Stadt Wien.

LETTERS TO

BEETHOVEN

and Other Correspondence

৵ৡ

Translated and Edited by

Theodore Albrecht

VOLUME 3: 1824–1828

Published by the *University of Nebraska Press*,
Lincoln & London, in association
with the *American Beethoven Society* and
the *Ira F. Brilliant Center for
Beethoven Studies*, San Jose State
University

♾ The paper in this book meets the minimum
requirements of American National
Standard for Information Sciences – Permanence
of Paper for Printed Library Materials,
ANSI Z39.48-1984.

Library of Congress
Cataloging-in-Publication Data
Letters to Beethoven and other correspondence /
translated and edited by Theodore Albrecht
p. cm. – (North American Beethoven studies; no.2)
Includes bibliographical references (p.   ) and index.
ISBN 0-8032-1033-7 (cloth: alkaline paper) (v.1)
ISBN 0-8032-1039-6 (cloth: alkaline paper) (v.2)
ISBN 0-8032-1040-x (cloth: alkaline paper) (v.3)
1. Beethoven, Ludwig van, 1770–1827 – Correspondence.
2. Composers – Austria – Correspondence.
I. Albrecht, Theodore. II. Series.
ML410.B4L5338 1996 780'.92–dc20 [B]
95-43793 CIP MN

CONTENTS

LETTERS AND DOCUMENTS

ILLUSTRATIONS

NOTE ON CURRENCY VALUES

The nature of the currencies used in Beethoven's day—spanning from a period of variously enlightened monarchies, through the Napoleonic wars, to an uneasy period when the monarchy was restored in France—is complicated, both in terminology and in purchasing power. In general, however, the following relative values applied to the various denominations (using the Austrian kreuzer [or kreutzer] as the lowest practical value):

1 groschen = ca. 3 kreuzer
1 gulden = 60 kreuzer
1 gulden = 1 florin[1]
1 gulden = ca. 2 shillings (British)
1 ducat (#) = ca. 4½ gulden (or 4½ florins)
2 ducats = ca. 1 louis d'or (French, variable)
8 gulden = 1 friedrich d'or (Prussian)
9 gulden = 1 carolin (German)
10 gulden = ca. £1 (British)

Less frequently encountered in this volume is the Thaler:

1 Reichsthaler = 90 kreuzer
1 Rheinthaler = 120 kreuzer (2 gulden)

After Austria officially went bankrupt as a result of inflation during the Napoleonic Wars, the government initiated a *Finanz-Patent* on February 20, 1811, and ultimately a number of reforms in currency values, with figures given in *Convenzions-münze* (*C.M.*: convention coinage, called "Assimilated Coinage" by Anderson) and in local paper currency, *Wiener Währung* (*W.W.*: called "Viennese Currency" by Anderson).

1. The two terms were virtually interchangeable, sometimes within the same letter or similar document.

Emily Anderson's "Notes on Money Values" in her 1961 *Letters of Beethoven*, I, xlvii–xlviii, provides a concise and generally comprehensible account of the situation, without attempting to equate early currencies with modern purchasing power.

In consultation with Eduard Holzmair, director of the Vienna Coin Cabinet, George Marek (*Beethoven*, pp. xvii–xviii) attempted to equate Austrian currency in Beethoven's day with the approximate American purchasing power of 1969; his success was moderate but short-lived, as inflation became a daily factor in the 1970s.

Mary Sue Morrow covered "Business and Financial Aspects . . ." through roughly 1810 in her *Concert Life in Haydn's Vienna* (1989), pp. 109–139. Similarly, Alice Hanson discussed economic circumstances faced by Vienna's musicians, especially late in Beethoven's lifetime, in her *Musical Life in Biedermeier Vienna* (1985), pp. 3, 14–33. Although it does not consider all aspects of Beethoven's income (notably the Thomson folk song commissions in his middle years), Julia Moore's 1987 dissertation, "Beethoven and Musical Economics," presents the most thorough discussion of this thorny subject to date. Barry Cooper fills the aforementioned lacuna in his chapter "Economics and Logistics: Beethoven's Earnings," in *Beethoven's Folksong Settings* (1994), pp. 93–101. A concise overview of the whole subject appears in Cooper's "Economics," in *Beethoven Compendium,* ed. Barry Cooper (1991), pp. 68–70.

ABBREVIATIONS

As noted in the preface, this collection employs very few abbreviations. Abbreviated citations of published source materials are given as complete names and/or key words in the notes and thus can be located in the bibliography with little difficulty.

Anderson
The Letters of Beethoven, trans. and ed. Emily Anderson, 3 vols. (London: Macmillan; New York: St. Martin's, 1961; reprint, New York: W. W. Norton, 1985). Citations generally by letter number (Anderson No. 35); in the case of prefatory material or the roughly 82 letters in nine appendixes, citations by volume and page numbers (Anderson, III, 1428–1429).

Grove
Grove's Dictionary of Music and Musicians, most commonly the 5th edition, ed. Eric Blom, 9 vols. & suppl. (London: Macmillan, 1954, 1959). Earlier editions, extending back to 1889, are also valuable for details necessarily omitted as the chronology expanded later. See also *New Grove* (below) for the 6th edition.

Hess
Numbers assigned to incomplete, previously unrecognized or recently discovered works in Willy Hess, *Verzeichnis der nicht in der Gesamtausgabe veröffentlichten Werke Ludwig van Beethovens* (Wiesbaden: Breitkopf & Härtel, 1957).

MacArdle & Misch
New Beethoven Letters, trans. and ed. Donald W. MacArdle and Ludwig Misch (Norman: University of Oklahoma Press, 1957). Citations generally by letter number (MacArdle & Misch No. 67).

MGG
Die Musik in Geschichte und Gegenwart, ed. Friedrich Blume, 17 vols. (Basel

and Kassel: Bärenreiter, 1949–1986). Its index (in vol. 17) renders it especially indispensable for verifying details.

New Grove

The New Grove Dictionary of Music and Musicians, ed. Stanley Sadie, 20 vols. (London: Macmillan, 1980). Actually the 6th edition of *Grove* (above), which it does not entirely supersede in many details.

P.P.

Praemissis Praemittendis (premising what is to be premised; i.e., with the necessary introduction, Dear Sir or Dear Madam), a form of heading, address or salutation occasionally used in business letters. Beethoven used this formula less frequently after 1810, but its use in the present collection is almost exclusively confined to the years 1802–1804. Another combination of the same letters is *pp.* (lowercase, usually with a period following), meaning "the aforementioned," "the said," "selfsame" or a similar intensification. Härtel used it occasionally, other business correspondents only rarely. In the present collection, it is translated directly into English or sometimes simply omitted if the context warrants.

WoO

Werk(e) ohne Opuszahl. Work(s) without an opus number, in order of organization in Georg Kinsky, *Das Werk Beethovens: Thematisch-bibliographisches Verzeichnis seiner sämtlichen vollendeten Kompositionen,* completed by Hans Halm (Munich: G. Henle, 1955).

1824

341. The Gesellschaft der Musikfreunde,[1] Vienna, to Beethoven

Vienna; [mid-January] 1824[2]

To the Well-born Herr Ludwig van Beethoven

Dear Sir!

When the Society of the Friends of Music of the Austrian Imperial State invited you four years ago to write an oratorio,[3] a proposal that you accepted as well as its conditions, it [the Society] left to you the choice of the poem and the poet. Soon afterward it learned that Herr Bernard had undertaken the writing of the poem. As often as we turned to you in this long interim and asked if you were already occupied with this work, we heard that you did not yet have the poetry in your hands. We could not expect that a composer of your style should sketch the plan of his musical composition before he had been entrusted with the whole of the poem, and had found it planned and executed according to his wish; we therefore could only turn to Herr Bernard and urge him on. Finally he handed the completed poem in to the Society near the end of October 1823, and stated that he had also delivered a copy to you.[4] Since on the one hand we can only make use of the poem if you, the composer, have actually chosen it for composition, but also have actually finished it; on the other hand, however, the resolve to furnish such a work to the Society has repeatedly been expressed by you, and has been confirmed by the partial payment made upon demand;[5] we consequently request that you let the Society know for certain whether you will set to music the poem furnished by Herr Bernard and at what time we may hope to receive this work, to which every Friend of Music and admirer of your great talent has been looking forward for such a long time with intense expectation.

Receive the assurance of our most distinguished esteem.

1. The name of the Gesellschaft has been translated in the text, as have elements of that name denoting the society treated as proper nouns.

2. Like the Gesellschaft's letter to Joseph Carl Bernard at the same time (No. 342 below), the present letter was written sometime after the society's board met on January 9, 1824, but before Beethoven's reply of January 23 (Anderson No. 1260).

3. Founded in December 1812, the Gesellschaft had approached Beethoven to compose an oratorio as early as 1815 (doubtless after his popular successes at the Congress of Vienna). The actual commission dates from around May 1818, judging from Beethoven's reply in early June 1818 (Anderson No. 903). The matter of the commission and the circumstances under which the present pair of letters was written are discussed at length in Schindler-MacArdle, pp. 270–271, 292–297, 349–350, and in Kalischer (German), V, 3–7, and Kalischer-Shedlock, II, 306–307.

4. *Der Sieg des Kreuzes*, never set by Beethoven. The manuscript was autographed by Stargardt, Berlin, in 1902 and came into the hands of Dr. Erich Prieger, Bonn.

5. On August 18, 1819, the Gesellschaft had paid Beethoven an advance of 400 florins. After the oratorio commission had come to nought, Beethoven probably hoped to repay the Gesellschaft out of the proceeds from the repeat performance of his Ninth Symphony, ultimately held on May 23, 1824 (Pohl, pp. 9–10, 13–14).

Incipit: Als die Gesellschaft der Musikfreunde. . . .

Sources: Draft in the collection of the Gesellschaft der Musikfreunde, Vienna, published in Carl Ferdinand Pohl, *Die Gesellschaft der Musikfreunde des Österreichischen Kaiserstaates und ihr Conservatorium* (Vienna: Wilhelm Braumüller, 1871), pp. 58–59. Thayer's copy published in Thayer-Deiters-Riemann, V, 10–11; Thayer-Forbes, p. 884.

342. The Gesellschaft der Musikfreunde,[1] Vienna, to Joseph Carl Bernard[2]

Vienna; [mid-January] 1824[3]

To the Well-born Herr J. C. Bernard

Dear Sir!

You have delivered to the Society, through the hands of its secretary Privy Councillor Sonnleithner,[4] a copy of the oratorio,[5] which you have designated for composition by Herr Ludwig van Beethoven. You are receiving the present answer so late because the board of directors of the Society met for the first time on the 9th of this month. Of course the Society was very pleased to learn of the completion of this labor, to which it looked forward for several years. Since it had left the choice of the poem to Herr van Beethoven, it [has] requested him to declare, as soon as possible, if he will furnish the composition of this poem, and approximately when he will complete same.

Without wanting to offend the value of your excellent work in the least, we cannot leave unmentioned that the Society can make use of it only when Herr van Beethoven has completed the composition and your poem has been passed by the censor. We are keeping it, meanwhile, and wish that you will join with us in inducing Herr van Beethoven to finish this work, so long awaited by the entire musical world.

Receive the assurance of our most distinguished esteem.

1. The name of the Gesellschaft has been translated in the text of the letter as *Society.*

2. Joseph Carl Bernard (1775–1850), editor of the *Wiener Zeitschrift* from 1818, and for many years in the 1810s a close friend of Beethoven's.

3. Like the Gesellschaft's letter to Beethoven at the same time (No. 341 above), the present letter was written sometime after the society's board meeting on January 9, 1824, and before Beethoven's reply to their letter on January 23 (Anderson No. 1260).

4. Joseph Sonnleithner (1766–1835), himself Beethoven's first librettist for *Fidelio* in 1804–1805.

5. *Der Sieg des Kreuzes,* never set by Beethoven. For further details, see the notes to No. 341 above.

Incipit: Sie haben der Gesellschaft. . . .

Sources: Draft in the collection of the Gesellschaft der Musikfreunde, Vienna, published in Carl Ferdinand Pohl, *Die Gesellschaft der Musikfreunde des Österreichischen Kaiserstaates und ihr Conservatorium* (Vienna: Wilhelm Braumüller, 1871), pp. 59–60; Thayer-Deiters-Riemann, V, 11.

343. Duke Claude-Louis de La Châtre[1] to Beethoven

Tuileries, [Paris]; February 20, 1824[2]

I hasten to inform you, Monsieur, that the King[3] has received with favor the gift of the score of your Mass set to music,[4] and has charged me to send you a gold medal with his effigy.[5] I am pleased to have to send you the evidence of His Majesty's satisfaction, and I take this occasion to offer you the assurance of my great esteem.

The Duke de La Châtre[6]

First Gentleman of the King's Chamber

1. Signature rendered in all versions of Thayer, as well as in Kalischer, as some variant of "Le duc d'Achats." Rendered by Beethoven as the "Duc de Chartres" in his letter to Wegeler of December 7, 1826 (Anderson No. 1542), a version also accepted by Kastner (1910). Present identity and signature follows Bartlitz. La Châtre, roughly fifty kilometers southwest of Bourges, had its origins as a military encampment and in the nineteenth century was closely associated with the author George Sand.

2. Continues the correspondence begun in January or February 1823 with Beethoven's solicitation to subscribe to the *Missa solemnis* and furthered by French letters to Beethoven of April 21 (enclosing April 10), 1823 (No. 317 above). Beethoven's letter to accompany the Mass, probably sent in January or early February, seems not to have survived. See also Schwebel's letter of April 4, 1824 (No. 353 below).

3. Louis XVIII.

4. *Missa solemnis,* Op. 123.

5. For further details, see Thayer-Forbes, pp. 828–829, and Schindler-MacArdle, pp. 242, 345. The medal arrived on April 4, 1824 (see No. 353 below).

6. The signature reads "Le duc de La Châtre."

Incipit: Je m'empresse de vous prevenir. . . .

Sources: Thayer-Deiters-Riemann, V, 369; Thayer-Krehbiel, III, 101; Thayer-Forbes, pp. 828–829 (the last in English); also Kastner (1910), p. 787. Autograph in the Staatsbibliothek zu Berlin–Preussischer Kulturbesitz, Mus. ms. autogr. Beethoven 35, 4; listed in Kalischer, "Beethoven-Autographe," p. 45, and Bartlitz, p. 118.

344. *Musicians and Music Lovers*[1] *to Beethoven*

[Vienna; shortly before February 26, 1824][2]

To Herr Ludwig van Beethoven.

Out of the wide circle of reverent admirers that surrounds your genius in this your second native city, a small number of disciples and lovers of art approach you today to express long-felt wishes, and timidly to proffer a long-suppressed request.

But, since the number of spokesmen is only a small portion of the many who joyfully acknowledge your worth and what you have become for the present time as well as the future, then the wishes and the requests are by no means restricted to the number of those who speak for others of like mind and who, in the name of all to whom art and the realization of their ideals are something more than means and objects of pastime, assert that their wish is also the wish of an unnumbered multitude, their request is echoed loudly or in silence by everyone whose bosom is animated by a sense of the divine in music.

Above all, the wishes of those of our countrymen who venerate art are those that we desire to express here; for although Beethoven's name and his creations belong to all contemporaneous humanity and every country that opens a sensitive heart to art, it is Austria that is best entitled to claim him as her own. Among her inhabitants, appreciation for the great and immortal works that Mozart and Haydn created for all time within the lap of their home has not died, and [these inhabitants] are conscious with joyous pride that the sacred triad, in which these names and yours glow as the symbol of the highest within the spiritual realm of tones, sprang from the soil of the fatherland.

It must have been all the more painful for you to feel that a foreign power[3] has invaded this royal citadel of the noblest, that above the mounds of the dead and around the dwelling place of the only survivor of the band, phantoms are leading the dance who can boast no kinship with the princely spirits of those [royal] houses; that shallowness is abusing the name and insignia of art, and unworthy dalliance with sacred things is beclouding and dissipating appreciation for the pure and eternally beautiful.

For this reason they feel a greater and livelier sense than ever before that the great need of the present moment is a new impulse directed by a powerful hand, a new advent of the ruler in his domain. It is this need that leads them to you today, and following are the petitions that they lay before you on behalf of all to whom these wishes are dear, and in the name of native art.

Do not withhold any longer from the popular enjoyment, do not keep any longer from the oppressed sense of that which is great and perfect, the performance of the latest masterworks of your hand. We know that a grand sacred composition[4] has joined the first one[5] in which you immortalized the emotions of a soul, penetrated and transfigured by the power of faith and superterrestrial light. We know that a new flower grows in the garland of your glorious, still unequaled symphonies.[6] For years, ever since the thunders of the *Victory at Vittoria*[7] ceased to reverberate, we have waited and hoped to see you distribute new gifts from the fullness of your riches to the circle of your friends. Do not disappoint the general expectations any longer! Heighten the effect of your newest creations by giving us the joy of becoming first acquainted with them through you yourself! Do not allow these, your latest offspring, to appear some day, perhaps as foreigners in their place of birth, perhaps introduced by persons who are also strangers to you and your spirit![8] Appear soon among your friends, your admirers, your venerators! This is our first and foremost prayer.

Other claims on your genius have been made public. The desires expressed and offers made to you more than a year ago by the management of the Court Opera and the Society of the Austrian Friends of Music[9] were too long the wish of all admirers of art and your name, and stimulated the hopes and expectations too much not to obtain, far and near, the speediest publicity, and not to awaken the most general interest. Poetry has done her share in giving support to these lovely hopes and wishes. Worthy material from the hand of a valued poet waits to be charmed into life by your imagination.[10] Do not let that intimate call to so noble an aim be made in vain! Do not delay longer leading us back to those departed days when the song of Polyhymnia moved powerfully and delighted the initiates in art and the hearts of the multitude!

Need we tell you with what deep regret your retirement from public life has filled us? Need we assure you that, at a time when all glances were hopefully turned toward you, all perceived with sorrow that *the one* man whom all of us are compelled to acknowledge as foremost among living men in his domain looked on in silence as foreign art took possession of German soil, and the honored home of the German muse, while German works gave pleasure only by echoing the favorite tunes of foreigners;[11] and where the most excellent [musicians] have lived and labored, a second childhood of taste threatens to follow the Golden Age of Art?

You alone are able to ensure a decisive victory to the efforts of the best among us. The Art Society of our country and the German Opera[12] expect from you new blossoms, rejuvenated life and a new sovereignty of the true and beautiful over the dominion to which the prevalent spirit of fashion wishes to subject even the eternal laws of art. Give us hope that the wishes of all who have been drawn to the sound of your harmonies will soon be fulfilled! This is our most urgent second prayer.

May the year that we have begun not come to an end without rejoicing us with the fruits of our petition, and may the coming spring, when it witnesses the unfolding of one of our longed-for gifts, become a twofold blooming time for us and the entire world of art!

Vienna; February, 1824

Prince E. Lichnowsky[13]

Artaria and Co.

V. Hauschka

M. J. Leidesdorf

J. E. von Wayna

Andreas Streicher

Anton Halm

Abbé Stadler

von Felsburg,
   Court Secretary

Count Ferdinand von
   Stockhammer

Count Ferdinand von Palffy

Baron Eduard von Schweiger

Count Czernin

Count Moritz von Fries

I. F. Castelli

Deinhardstein

Ch. Kuffner

Fr. Nehammer,
   State Secretary

Steiner von Felsburg,
   Bank Sequestrator

Count Moritz von Dietrichstein

Ig. Edler von Mosel,
   I.R. Court Councillor

Carl Czerny

Count Moritz von Lichnowsky

Zmeskall

Court Councillor Kiesewetter

Dr. Leopold Sonnleithner

S. A. Steiner and Co.

Anton Diabelli

Lederer

J. N. Bihler

1. Among the signers of this petition, the handwriting in the text most resembles the signature of Leopold Sonnleithner. In many respects, the petition seems a reaction to several references that Beethoven made in the latter part of his letter to the Gesellschaft der Musikfreunde, January 23, 1824 (Anderson No. 1260). In that letter, Beethoven mentioned the *Missa solemnis* and the Ninth Symphony as well as a possible concert in the future; he noted that this information should be passed on to Leopold Sonnleithner and also mentioned that neither his brother Johann nor Anton Schindler had been authorized to negotiate in his (Beethoven's) stead. (See also Thayer-Forbes, p. 884, quoting Carl Ferdinand Pohl, *Die Gesellschaft der Musikfreunde des Österreichischen Kaiserstaates und ihr Conservatorium, auf Grundlage der Gesellschafts-Acten* [Vienna: Wilhelm Braumüller, 1871], pp. 13–14, indicating Sonnleithner's role in proposing such a concert by the society.) The above lends credence to Kojima's assertion (see n. 2, this letter) that Schindler was not party to the petition. Schindler did note that the deputation that delivered it consisted of Court Secretary von Felsburg and J. N. Bihler.

2. At the end of the text, this petition is dated "Vienna, February, 1824." A transcription, along with a detailed account of Beethoven's reaction, appears in

Schindler (see the source note to this letter) and has been repeated and paraphrased, with few modifications, since that time.

Working with recently edited conversation books, however, Shin Augustinus Kojima made new discoveries concerning the document's origins, Beethoven's reaction and Schindler's early acquaintance with its contents. A conversation book entry by Joseph Carl Bernard on May 4 indicates that the petition was "a product of the Ludlamshöhle, a beer house near the Trattnerhof, where Castelli, Kuffner, Deinhardstein, Bäuerle and many others congregate. They wanted to strike a blow against the Italians with it; earlier, they used Weber for the same purpose" (Köhler et al., *Konversationshefte*, VI, 112). Ludlamshöhle, a loosely organized social group of artists, authors and businessmen, met at the *Gasthaus* of J. Haidvogel in the Schlossergasse. Schubert occasionally mixed with this circle before its meetings were forbidden by the police in 1826. Schindler did not mention anything about this in his biography, and it now appears that he had nothing to do with the petition's origins.

Although Adolf B. Bäuerle (1786–1859), editor of the *Wiener Allgemeine Theaterzeitung*, did not sign this petition, he did publish it in his journal, as did Friedrich August Kanne (1778–1833) in the *Wiener Allgemeine musikalische Zeitung* (acts that angered Beethoven); Bäuerle's alleged influence on its conception might explain Beethoven's letter to him of May 1824 (Anderson No. 1295), where the composer writes: "In a few days I shall have the honor of discharging my debt. Please insert the announcement of my concert in your esteemed paper." Since Beethoven intended the proceeds of the repeat performance of the Ninth Symphony on May 23 to go to the Gesellschaft, to repay the advance made him when commissioning *Der Sieg des Kreuzes*, Anderson No. 1295 probably dates from a few days before that concert.

As Kojima notes, Beethoven had advance warning that the petition was coming: seemingly on Wednesday, February 25, an unknown writer (probably Leopold Sonnleithner) asked in a conversation book (leaf 3r; Köhler et al., *Konversationshefte*, V, 179): "Have you received the invitation which I signed yet?" The answer must have been negative. In a later entry (leaf 11v; ibid., V, 179), probably on Friday, February 27, Beethoven's nephew Karl asked: "Have you read through the letter which was sent to you yesterday?" Thus Beethoven probably received the petition on Thursday, February 26, 1824. See Shin Augustinus Kojima, "Die Aufführung der Neunten Symphonie Beethovens — einige neue Tatsachen," in *Bericht über den Internationalen Musikwissenschaftlichen Kongress, Bayreuth, 1981*, ed. Christoph-Hellmut Mahling and Sigrid Wiesmann (Kassel: Bärenreiter, 1984), pp. 390–392.

3. Although Rossini's music was heard there earlier, Vienna had been especially preoccupied with it since *Zelmira* premiered in the Kärntnertor Theater on April 13, 1822. This caused no little apprehension among Beethoven and his circle, to the extent that Beethoven approached Count Brühl, *Intendant* of the Court Theaters in Berlin, about the possibility of producing the *Missa solemnis* and the Symphony

No. 9 in the Prussian capital. When Brühl proved to be interested in the prospect, Beethoven's friends undertook to keep those premieres in Vienna. (See Schindler-MacArdle, pp. 271–273, for further details.)

4. *Missa solemnis*, Op. 123.

5. Mass in C, Op. 86.

6. Symphony No. 9, Op. 125.

7. *Wellington's Victory, or the Battle at Vittoria*, Op. 91, dating from 1813, and evidently considered by some contemporaries as worthy of mention among Beethoven's symphonies.

8. An allusion to the possible consequences in case Beethoven's negotiations with Berlin proved successful.

9. The offer made by the opera probably took place in conjunction with the revival of *Fidelio* on November 3, 1822; the Gesellschaft der Musikfreunde's offer for a commission dated from even earlier and culminated in Beethoven's rejection of Bernard's libretto, *Der Sieg des Kreuzes,* early in 1824. Duport and Barbaja reaffirmed their desire for an opera from Beethoven's pen on April 20, 1824 (No. 358 below).

10. Bernard's libretto for *Der Sieg des Kreuzes.*

11. Possibly an allusion to compositions such as Schubert's Overtures "in the Italian Style," which nonetheless predated the current bout of Rossini fever by several years.

12. Another reference to the Gesellschaft der Musikfreunde and the Court Opera.

13. The signers of the petition may be identified from references in such works as Köhler et al., *Konversationshefte,* and Franz Heinrich Böckh, *Merkwürdigkeiten der Haupt- und Residenz-Stadt Wien . . .* (Vienna: Böckh, 1823). They include, in signature order:

a) Prince Eduard Lichnowsky, nephew of Count Moritz. Until correctly identified by Köhler et al., all authors (starting with Schindler) had transcribed the initial as "C." Prince Carl Lichnowsky had, of course, died in 1814.

b) Artaria, the prominent music publisher.

c) Vincenz Hauschka (1766–1840), finance councillor, founding member of the Gesellschaft der Musikfreunde and friend of Beethoven's.

d) Max Joseph Leidesdorf (1787–1840), composer, partner in the music publishing firm of Sauer and Leidesdorf (Kärntnerstrasse o. 941) from 1822 until he left Vienna in 1827.

e) Joseph von Wayna, wholesale merchant, one of those who invited Beethoven to honorary membership in the Vienna Commercial Society in 1819 (see No. 262 above).

f) Johann Andreas Streicher (1761–1833), piano manufacturer and longtime friend of Beethoven's.

g) Halm (1789–1872), composer, pianist and piano teacher in Vienna since 1815. In 1826, he made a piano four-hands arrangement of the *Grosse Fuge,* Op. 133.

h) Abbé Maximilian Stadler (1748–1833), composer and organist, highly respected among Viennese musicians.

i) Johann Steiner von Felsburg, court secretary of the I.R. Consolidated Court Chancellery. Different from J. J. Steiner von Felsburg (see s below), although both lived at Minoritenplatz No. 38.

j) Stockhammer, high official in the I.R. Treasury.

k) Palffy von Erdöd (1774–1840), manager of the Theater an der Wien, 1813–1825. Shortly after this letter was written, Count Palffy offered Beethoven an attractive "package deal" for the use of the theater and its personnel at his concert. Because Beethoven wanted to substitute certain musicians for others, however, the two could not reach an agreement.

l) Schweiger, possibly related to Joseph von Schweiger (died 1850), a member of Archduke Rudolph's staff.

m) Count Johann Rudolph von Czernin (1757–1845), first chamberlain, patron member of the Gesellschaft der Musikfreunde.

n) Fries (1777–1826), prominent banker, director of the Austrian National Bank and avid art collector.

o) Ignaz Franz Castelli (1781–1862), poet and theatrical dramatist; board member of the Gesellschaft der Musikfreunde and a leader of the Ludlamshöhle society.

p) Johann Ludwig Deinhardstein (1794–1859), dramatic poet, professor of aesthetics at the Theresianum since 1822.

q) Christoph Kuffner (1780–1846), official at the War Ministry, musically talented poet, author of the text of the Choral Fantasia, Op. 80, and of the drama *Tarpeja*, for which Beethoven supplied incidental music, WoO 2, in 1813.

r) Franz Nehammer, one of four secretaries in the Lower Austrian government, amateur violinist in the Gesellschaft der Musikfreunde. (His initials are often erroneously given as J. N.)

s) J. J. Steiner von Felsburg, official in the Austrian National Bank. Different from Johann Steiner von Felsburg (see i above), although both lived at Minoritenplatz No. 38.

t) Dietrichstein (1775–1864), court music administrator (1819–1826), court theater director (1821–1826).

u) Ignaz Franz von Mosel (1772–1844), composer, conductor, vice director of the Court Theaters since 1821; patron member of the Gesellschaft der Musikfreunde.

v) Carl Czerny (1791–1857), pianist, composer, pedagogue, former student of Beethoven's. Around May 20, Beethoven and his circle approached Czerny to appear on the May 23 concert, which repeated the Ninth Symphony. The pianist declined; see his draft letter to Beethoven (ca. May 20, No. 366 below).

w) Lichnowsky (1771–1837), brother of the late Prince Carl, Beethoven's friend and patron.

x) Nikolaus Zmeskall von Domanovecz (1759–1833), Beethoven's longtime friend, now almost totally housebound by gout. He was brought in a sedan chair to the May 7 *Akademie*.

y) Raphael Georg Kiesewetter von Weisenbrunn (1773–1850), high official in the War Ministry, well trained in music, vice president of the Gesellschaft der Musikfreunde (1821–1843). An accomplished amateur music historian, he edited Kandler's German translation of Baini's biography of Palestrina (1834) and wrote monographs on Guido d'Arezzo (1840), secular song in the Middle Ages and Renaissance (1841) and music of the Arabs (1842, with assistance from orientalist Joseph Hammer, now Hammer-Purgstall).

z) Sonnleithner (1797–1873), the nephew of Beethoven's *Fidelio* librettist Joseph Sonnleithner, musical amateur in the Gesellschaft der Musikfreunde and member of the board of the society's concert series. He wrote an account of the rehearsals for and first performance of the Ninth Symphony, "Ad Vocem: Kontrabass-Rezitativ der 9. Symphonie von Beethoven," *Allgemeine musikalische Zeitung*, n.s., 2 (1864), 245–246; translated and edited by Walter Paul et al. as "The Contrabass Recitatives of Beethoven's Ninth Symphony at Its 1824 Premiere," *Journal of the Conductors' Guild* 8, no. 1 (Winter 1987), 38–39; and also by Max Rudolf in *Beethoven Newsletter* (San Jose) 4, no. 3 (Winter 1989), 56–57.

aa) Steiner (1773–1838), music publisher, friend of Beethoven's, member of the Gesellschaft der Musikfreunde.

bb) Diabelli (1781–1858), pianist, composer, music publisher and friend of Beethoven's.

cc) Probably Johann Lederer, amateur violinist in the Gesellschaft der Musikfreunde.

dd) Dr. Johann N[epomuk] Bihler (or Biehler), doctor of pharmaceutics, tutor to various wealthy households.

Incipit: Aus dem weiten Kreise. . . .

Sources: Schindler (1840), pp. 144–148; Schindler-Moscheles, pp. 97–99; Schindler (1860), pt. 2, pp. 60–63; Schindler-MacArdle, pp. 273–275; Thayer-Deiters-Riemann, V, 67–69; Thayer-Krehbiel, III, 153–155 (omits list of names); Thayer-Forbes, pp. 897–899 (restores list of names); Landon, *Beethoven: Documentary Study*, pp. 359–360. The present translation is based on Thayer-Krehbiel, with my own alterations (a practice that MacArdle likewise seems to have employed). Autograph in the Staatsbibliothek zu Berlin–Preussischer Kulturbesitz, Mus. ms. autogr. Beethoven 35, 21; listed in Bartlitz, p. 123. Facsimile in Bory, p. 190; and John Knowles, "Die letzten Jahre," in *Beethoven: Mensch seiner Zeit*, ed. Siegfried Kross (Bonn: Ludwig Röhrscheid, 1980), p. 122.

345. Beethoven to Heinrich Albert Probst,[1] Leipzig

Vienna; March 10, [1824][2]

Dear Sir!

Since you have taken the works that I offered you,[3] you will receive them in the shortest possible time. As soon as the copies are finished, I shall notify you immediately and request that you send instructions for the sum designated for them to an exchange house here and, through it, send me a bill of exchange for which I shall hand over the works, and also have care taken myself, so they [the works] can reach you without great expense. You will not take offense at this, since it is merely to simplify matters. If something gets lost in the mails, I can easily be of assistance in any case, although such a thing need not be feared.

I will gladly arrange the Overture[4] for piano 2-hands or 4-hands for you. I would be very pleased if I could bring out subsequent new works in a manner that would be more convenient for me, without endless paperwork, since lengthy correspondence with distant places robs me of far too much time. I hope that you will not find boastfulness in this, since I have never liked such [a trait].

I have written a grand Solemn Mass,[5] which[6] I could publish even now. Unfortunately, however, I must speak about myself here and tell you that it is certainly the greatest work I have written. The fee would be 1,000 fl[orins], C.M. — A new grand Symphony,[7] which has a finale with entering solo voices and choruses, with words from Schiller's immortal *Lied* "An die Freude," in the same manner as my Piano Fantasia with chorus,[8] but on a far grander scale. The fee would be 600 fl[orins], C.M. With this Symphony, though, comes the condition that it may not appear until July of the coming year, 1825.[9] In return for this long delay, however, I would gladly make a piano score for you without fee; and, in general, if we form a closer association, you will always find me willing to please you.[10]

1. Probst (1791–1846) was born in Dresden and opened his music publishing business in Leipzig on May 1, 1823. In 1831, he sold his firm to Friedrich Kistner and left to join the Parisian publisher Pleyel.

2. This letter, the missing portion of Beethoven's fragmentary letter to Probst, March 10, 1824 (Anderson No. 1269), indicates place, month, and day, but not the year. For further details, see Probst's reply to Beethoven, March 22, 1824 (No. 349 below).

3. Having inquired about the availability of Beethoven's works, probably early in 1824, Probst must have responded almost immediately to Beethoven's reply of February 25, 1824 (Anderson No. 1266). The works offered included the *Opferlied*, Op. 121b, the *Bundeslied*, Op. 122, *Der Kuss*, Op. 128, the *Consecration of the House* Overture, Op. 124, and the Bagatelles, Op. 126.

4. *Consecration of the House*, Op. 124.

5. *Missa solemnis*, Op. 123.

6. The previously untranslated material ends at this point; the completion (otherwise available as Anderson No. 1269) is newly translated here (from Kastner-Kapp No. 1190).

7. Symphony No. 9, Op. 125.

8. Op. 80.

9. Beethoven was envisioning potentially simultaneous publication in several marketing regions, not out of personal dishonesty, but to avoid piracy by other publishers.

10. The signature is lacking.

Incipit: Da Sie die Ihnen von mir vorgeschlagenen Werke übernommen. . . .

Sources: Ludwig van Beethoven, *Sechs Bagatellen für Klavier, Op. 126: Faksimile . . . mit Kommentar*, ed. Sieghard Brandenburg, 2 vols. (Bonn: Beethoven-Haus, 1984), II, 67. Autograph (first half of the letter) in the Stadtarchiv, Bonn, *li* 98/516; acquired in 1974 from Paul Aubert, Lyon; noted in Helms and Staehelin, "Bewegungen . . . 1973–1979," p. 352. My gratitude to Sieghard Brandenburg, Beethoven-Archiv, Bonn, for examining my transcription. The autograph second half of the letter is in the Staatsbibliothek zu Berlin–Preussischer Kulturbesitz.

346. *Prince Nicolas Galitzin to Beethoven*

St. Petersburg; March 11, 1824

Monsieur,

I have not received any news from you for some time,[1] which truly causes me some concern. I fear it might be that your health has changed and has deprived me of the fulfillment of your promises. I know that your affairs are so numerous that foreign requests must be a burden to you. — Please let me know when I can expect the quartets[2] that I await with so much impatience. If you need money, withdraw the sum that you need upon Messrs. Stieglitz & Co. in St. Petersburg, who will pay to your order whatever you want to withdraw from them. — The time will soon be upon us when we should hear your masterpiece.[3] This has been delayed to give the singers time to learn their parts well, which are not easy. Besides, we are counting upon holding about ten general rehearsals[4] so that this work will be performed with all the perfection that its sublimity merits. — Until the present we have held only one orchestra rehearsal without chorus to check the copied parts. But so many errors had gotten in that we have not been able to schedule a subsequent rehearsal, because we had to stop constantly to correct errors. — There were also many omissions in the score. All these difficulties ultimately made us postpone until April 7 the performance for the benefit of the widows of musicians, to which I have dedicated the score.

Please grant me a word of reply and believe me to be the most sincere and most zealous of your admirers and friends.

P[rince] Nicolas Galitzin

P.S. Of all the works that you have composed, there is one that I have never been able to get; that is Op. 56, which I believe is a Concerto for piano, violin and violoncello.[5] I know only the Polonaise arranged for [piano] 4-hands that has been excerpted from this work.[6] May I hope for your extreme good nature in having it sent to me, as soon as you can [do so]?

1. Beethoven's most recent letter seems to have been written on December 13, 1823, to which Galitzin had already replied on December 30.

2. Opp. 127, 130 and 132.

3. *Missa solemnis*, Op. 123.

4. The original reads "répétitions générales," indicating that the prince intended this many rehearsals with all the performers present.

5. Triple Concerto, Op. 56.

6. *Polonaise concertante,* arranged by A[ugust] E[berhard] Müller (Leipzig: A. Kühnel, 1808, plus reprints). Müller's wife, Elisabeth Catharina, played the piano in the first-known public performance of the Triple Concerto, with the Leipzig Gewandhaus Orchestra, in February 1808.

Incipit: Il y a déjà quelque temps. . . .

Sources: Thayer-Deiters-Riemann, V, 558–559 (French); Nohl, "Die Briefe Galitzins," p. 3 (slightly abbreviated German translation). When Thayer and Nohl made their copies, the autograph was in the possession of Beethoven's nephew Karl's widow, Caroline, Vienna, and has since disappeared.

347. *Ferdinand Piringer to Beethoven*

[Vienna;] March 14, 1824

Generalissime omnium compositorum!

The elevated individual indicated above was so kind as to promise me the printed parts of his Pastorale Symphony for the next *Concert spirituel.*[1] I therefore take the liberty to ask most obediently if I may be sent them next Tuesday or Wednesday?

How is it going with the *Akademie?*[2] Has significant progress been made? Which day? Midday or in the evening? What can I do to help?

With greatest pleasure I await your command.

Excellentissimi humillimus servus,

Ferd[inand] Piringer

1. As indicated here, His Excellency Beethoven, the Greatest General of All Composers, had evidently offered his Humble Servant Piringer the loan of the Symphony No. 6 for performance on the *Concerts spirituels* series on April 1, 1824 (an all-Beethoven program). The concerts were spearheaded by Piringer and Johann Geissler. See Köhler et al., *Konversationshefte,* V, 259–260, 283, 311; VI, 16, 373. For another letter with this tone, see Piringer to Beethoven, July 25, 1822 (No. 297 above). Schindler's annotation on the present autograph indicates that Piringer was an exceptionally droll man, who could easily put Beethoven in a jolly mood. He called Mozart "King of all Musicians" and Beethoven "his Generalissimus," maintaining this tone in conversation and written word.

2. These questions concern the complicated preparations for the premiere of the Symphony No. 9, which ultimately took place on May 7.

Incipit: Hochdieselben waren so gütig. . . .

Sources: Autograph in the Staatsbibliothek zu Berlin–Preussischer Kulturbesitz, Mus. ms. autogr. Beethoven 35, 56; listed in Kalischer, "Beethoven-Autographe," p.

51, and Bartlitz, p. 135. Beethoven used much of the remaining blank space on the reverse and exterior for extensive notes to himself about specific points to correct in either copied or printed orchestral parts.

348. The Imperial Royal High Steward's Office (Memorandum)

Vienna; March 16, 1824[1]

No. 380
—————
1824

Van Beethoven, musician, requests permission[2] to hold a musical *Akademie* on the evening of April 7, in the I.R. Redoutensaal.

dated March 13th; rec'd. 16th, 1824.

Decree

Since the permission for holding a musical *Akademie* in the I.R. Redoutensaal does not rest with us, the I.R. Lord High Steward's Office, the petitioner has to apply for the granting of the same to the I.R. High Police Director's Office; then regarding the securing of the hall to the lessee of the I.R. Kärntnertor Theater, Domenico Barbaja.[3]

By the I.R. Lord High Steward's Office

Mayrhofer[4]

Vienna; March 16, 1824

---

1. This memorandum reflects Beethoven's request, dated March 13 (a Saturday), and apparently received on March 16 (a Tuesday).

2. Beethoven's own petition, probably dated March 13, seems to be lost.

3. Domenico Barbaja (ca. 1778–1841) had leased the Kärntnertor Theater since the spring of 1822 and imported Rossini from Italy. Beethoven and his circle generally worked through Barbaja's resident manager, Louis Antoine Duport (1783–1853). The present document gives Barbaja's first name in the German form, *Dominik*.

4. Anton Mayrhofer was registry director of the I.R. Lord High Steward's Office (*k.k. Obersthofmeisteramt*); the first lord high steward was Prince Ferdinand Trautmannsdorf-Weinsberg. Beethoven's letter of March 21, 1824 (Anderson No.

1272), was actually written to Trautmannsdorf, not to Count Moritz Dietrichstein, court musical administrator and director of the Court Theaters (as given in Anderson), because the form of salutation (*Euer Durchlaucht*) was appropriate to a prince but not a count.

Incipit: Van Beethoven Tonkünstler bittet. . . .

Sources: Otto Erich Deutsch, "Zu Beethovens grossen Academien von 1824," *Österreichische Musikzeitschrift* 19 (September 1964), 427–428. Autograph in the Haus-, Hof- und Staatsarchiv, Vienna, Gen. Int. 4/Op. 1824.

349. Heinrich Albert Probst to Beethoven

Leipzig; March 22, 1824[1]

Herr Louis van Beethoven

Vienna

Following your honored letter of the 10th of this month, I look forward to your obliging notice of the completion of the works under consideration. In return, I shall immediately place 100 full-weight Imperial ducats at your disposal with Messrs. Joseph Loydl and Co. in Vienna, which you will then receive against the delivery of all of the following:

> 3 Songs with piano accompaniment, of which two also have a suitable accompaniment for other instruments and can be performed without piano; the third a through-composed arietta;[2]
> 6 Bagatelles for piano solo;[3]
> 1 Grand Overture for full orchestra, along with 2- and 4-hand piano arrangements.[4]

According to your wish, I will gladly postpone the publication of this overture until next July. All the more certain of your kindness, however, I expect the piano arrangements of it at the same time, for as you certainly know, the sale of a work exclusively for orchestra is so limited that it only covers the cost of printing, and therefore I may well count on this mitigation on your part. It will give me sincere pleasure further to continue the business relationship with you in a pleasant manner, and to find the opportunity to serve you in such honorable confidence evermore. I am especially obliged to you for the kind offer you recently made to me of your grand *Missa* and

Symphony,[5] and if our first business deal is entirely arranged to our mutual satisfaction, I shall take the liberty to inform you of my decision about them. In the meantime, I remain with esteem and devotion,

H[einrich] A[lbert] Probst

1. Answers Beethoven's letter of March 10, 1824 (No. 345 above). Beethoven's letter to Probst of February 25, 1824 (Anderson No. 1266), however, provides further background and indicates that the composer was offering Probst a package similar to that sent to (and rejected by) C. F. Peters in 1822–1823. Beethoven's negotiations with Probst came to nothing. Some elements of their correspondence are lost but can be inferred from Beethoven's further letters of July 3 (Anderson No. 1298), July 26 (No. 373 below) and August 28 (Anderson No. 1305) as well as Probst's letters of August 9 and 16, 1824 (Nos. 378 and 379 below).

2. *Opferlied*, Op. 121b, *Bundeslied*, Op. 122, and *Der Kuss*, Op. 128, ultimately published by Schott in 1825.

3. Bagatelles, Op. 126. Since March 1823, when Peters had rejected the Bagatelles, Op. 119, Beethoven had sold that set to Schlesinger and Clementi for simultaneous publication in Paris and London.

4. *Consecration of the House* Overture, Op. 124.

5. *Missa solemnis*, Op. 123, and Symphony No. 9, Op. 125, respectively.

Incipit: Zu Folge Ihrer geehrten Zuschrift. . . .

Sources: Thayer-Deiters-Riemann, V, 103. Autograph in the Staatsbibliothek zu Berlin–Preussischer Kulturbesitz, Mus. ms. autogr. Beethoven 35, 71a; listed in Kalischer, "Beethoven-Autographe," p. 52, and Bartlitz, p. 140.

350. B. Schotts Söhne[1] to Beethoven

Mainz; March 24, 1824[2]

Dear Herr *Kapellmeister!*

We have forwarded your esteemed letter of the 10th of this month to the editorship of the *Cäcilia*[3] for examination, and now hasten to reply to those matters that singularly interest us.

As gladly as we would retain all three of the manuscripts that you most kindly offered us,[4] it is, however, not possible at this time for us to undertake such a large-scale production all at once.[5] We must therefore limit our wish, and request you to transfer the manuscript of the Quartet[6] to the publishing house as our exclusive property. In return, we shall give you the requested 50 ducats in gold upon its receipt; or if you want to withdraw the amount through a business house there immediately upon dispatch of the manuscript to us, then we shall render *prompt* payment. We wish, however, to come into possession of this manuscript very soon.

We certainly attach great importance to your grand Solemn Mass, as well as to your new Symphony, and we would be very sorry to see both works shine as such brilliant stars in a catalog other than ours. We therefore ask you once more, that if you are not inclined to reduce the fee, whether you would consider receiving the fee for them in 4 installments at 6-month intervals. Under these circumstances, we [would] venture to publish these very great and very important works, and would be proud to endow them with every possible beauty and have them engraved immediately in parts in addition to the score.

You will not misconstrue or misunderstand our sincerity, and we look forward to [receiving] an obliging reply soon.

With true regard and complete devotion,

Your obedient servant,

B. Schott[s] Söhne

1. This firm's correspondence with Beethoven, initiated from Mainz sometime before March 10, 1824, was written by Johann Joseph Schott (1782–1855).

2. Answers Beethoven's letter of March 10, 1824 (Anderson No. 1270).

3. Schott's music magazine, edited by Gottfried Weber.

4. The *Missa solemnis*, Op. 123; the Symphony No. 9, Op. 125; and the String Quartet, Op. 127.

5. The German "Ausgabe machen" could also indicate that Schott was not prepared to make such a large financial outlay, a double meaning confirmed later in the letter.

6. Op. 127.

Incipit: Dero verehrtes Schreiben vom 10. dieses. . . .

Sources: Thayer-Deiters-Riemann, V, 106; Staehelin and Brandenburg, *Briefwechsel* (1985), No. 3; excerpted in Nohl, *Beethoven's Leben* (1877), III, 518–519. Autograph in the Staatsbibliothek zu Berlin–Preussischer Kulturbesitz, Mus. ms. autogr. Beethoven 35, 72a; listed in Kalischer, "Beethoven-Autographe," p. 52, and Bartlitz, p. 141.

351. Beethoven to Prince Rudolph Kinsky's Treasury, Prague[1]

Vienna; March 30, 1824[2]

Receipt

for six hundred gulden, the semiannual contribution for subsistence due me, from the last day of September, 1823, until April 1, 1824, which I the undersigned, according to the I[mperial] R[oyal] Bohemian Landrecht's decree, dated Prague, January 18, 1815, No. Exhib. 293, and [as part of] the annual stipend of 1,200 fl[orins] granted to me, have duly received today in cash from Prince Rudolph Kinsky's Pupillary Chief Cashier in Prague.

Vienna, March 30, 1824

That is: 600 fl[orins], *W.W.*

Ludwig van Beethoven

He lives today.

L.S., Pastor[3]

April 5, 1824

Charged through

J. Fischer

Prague, April 9, 1824   by M. Benna

    1. This receipt is a variant of the form used on September 30, 1821 (No. 280 above). It is written in a scribe's hand and signed by Beethoven.

    2. Beethoven received his stipend from Prince Kinsky's estate in semiannual installments.

    3. In the case of a lifetime annuity, such as that from the Kinsky estate, it was customary for a priest or some other reputable person to attest that the recipient was actually alive when the payment was made.

    Incipit: Quittung über Sechshundert Gulden vom ult[imo] Septembr[is] 1823. . . .

    Sources: Transcribed and edited by Otto Biba in Staehelin, "Unbekannte Schrift-stücke," pp. 84–85. In the early 1980s, the autograph was in the private collection of Leo von Chavanne, Vienna.

352. Beethoven to Louis Antoine Duport[1]

[Vienna; ca. March 30 or 31, 1824]

I learned of your kindness in granting me the small hall;[2] *unfortunately,* it is only *suitable for solo players* and for small dances.[3] It is not the thing for me; my works require a large area, a hall to give what are called grand musical performances; naturally one cannot pay great sums for the hall for them [concerts], without the costs being really *significant:* the copying at least 600 florins, for the *authorities* 4,500. Here are already over 5,000 florins, and then *the costs* of a great *number of performers,* and what still remains [for me].[4] As for me, despite the simplicity of my character, it must be admitted that the most illustrious *and the most enlightened patrons and protectors of Art invited me to do so,*[5] but it will not be a misfortune for the capital that I do not give an Akademie. I am very obliged to you *though* for the small hall, and despite all that, I shall not give an *Akademie.*[6] I am always ready to serve[. . . .]

[Seemingly an insert for the second sentence, above:]
naturally with a large chorus, large orchestra, one must expect a large audience, only it is not possible with the small hall. Providence will not patronize me unless I give an Akademie; it is not a kindness to have given me such a hall, for I need[. . . .]

1. Beethoven wrote this letter draft on learning that Duport, administrator of the Kärntnertor Theater, had granted him use of the Kleiner Redoutensaal for the *Akademie* that was to include the Ninth Symphony and the *Missa solemnis.* Beethoven's draft is in rough-and-ready French, with occasional words and phrases (here rendered in italic) still in the German language. The dating follows Köhler.
2. Kleiner Redoutensaal.
3. The original reads "pour petit polonaise."
4. Beethoven expressed much the same sentiment in an undated letter to Schindler (Anderson No. 1281).
5. A reference to the petition, shortly before February 26, 1824 (No. 344 above).
6. Three surviving undated letters from this period (Anderson Nos. 1279, 1282 and 1283) also indicate that there would be no concert. Ultimately, Beethoven gave his *Akademie* in the Kärntnertor Theater on May 7, 1824.

Incipit: J'apprend votre amitie. . . .

Sources: Köhler et al., *Konversationshefte,* V, 256–257; Schindler's background entry on p. 252; partial facsimile facing p. 257 (© Deutscher Verlag für Musik, Leipzig). Autograph in the Staatsbibliothek zu Berlin–Preussischer Kulturbesitz.

353. *Schwebel, French Embassy, to Beethoven*

Vienna; April 4, 1824[1]

Monsieur de Beethoven,

The chargé d'affaires of France hastens to deliver to Monsieur de Beethoven the grand medal of gold[2] that the King,[3] his august master, has deigned to award him. He considers himself fortunate to forward to Monsieur de Beethoven this symbol of His Majesty's benevolence. He requests him [Beethoven] to indicate receipt of it, and to accept on this occasion the assurance of his full esteem.

Schwebel

1. Follows the letter of the duke de La Châtre, February 20, 1824, as well as Schwebel's own earlier letter of April 21, 1823 (Nos. 343 and 317 above, respectively).
2. The medal is illustrated in Ley, *Beethovens Leben in Bildern,* p. 112, and in Köhler et al., *Konversationshefte,* VI, facing p. 320. It was awarded as partial compensation for the French court's subscription to the *Missa solemnis.*
3. Louis XVIII.

Incipit: Le chargé d'affaires de France. . . .

Sources: Ley, *Beethoven als Freund,* p. 222. For background, see Schindler-Mac-Ardle, pp. 242, 345. According to Ley, the document was in the Sammlung von Breuning.

354. *Beethoven to an Unknown Court Official (Draft)*

[Vienna; ca. April 8, 1824][1]

Diploma,[2] since one must think that I do not esteem such things at all, I request that the Gentleman place before [His] Majesty as soon as possible. . . .

1. This draft letter was prompted by the receipt of the medal from Louis XVIII of France (see Schwebel to Beethoven, April 4, 1824, No. 353 above). In the preceding entry in Beethoven's conversation book, his nephew Karl had written: "You could not wear the medal at all; the weight would pull your collar down."

2. The diploma is the honorary membership from the Royal Swedish Musical Academy to Beethoven, dated December 28, 1822, and sent with a letter of January 31, 1823 (Nos. 301 and 306 above). The acceptance of this honor was contingent on the approval of the emperor, which Beethoven had evidently neglected to seek until now, and which was granted, through the intervention of Cabinet Director Anton Martin, on April 21, 1824.

Incipit: Diplom indem man denken muss. . . .

Sources: Köhler et al., *Konversationshefte*, VI, 19, 376 (© Deutscher Verlag für Musik, Leipzig). Autograph in the Staatsbibliothek zu Berlin–Preussischer Kulturbesitz.

355. *Prince Nicolas Galitzin to Beethoven*

St. Petersburg; April 8, 1824

I hasten, Monsieur, to give you the news of the performance of your sublime masterpiece that we introduced to the public here the evening before last.[1] For several months I have been extremely impatient to hear this music performed, all the beauties of which I foresaw in the score. The effect that this music made on the public is indescribable, and I doubt that I exaggerate when I say that, for my part, I have never heard anything so sublime; I do not except even the masterpieces of Mozart, which, with their eternal beauties, have not produced for me the same sensations that you have given me, Monsieur, by the Kyrie and Gloria of your Mass. The masterly harmony and the touching melody of the Benedictus transport the spirit to a truly blissful state. In short, this entire work is a treasury of beauties; one may say that your genius has anticipated the centuries and that some listeners are perhaps not enlightened enough to enjoy all the beauty of this music; but it is posterity that will render homage and that will bless your memory much better than your contemporaries can. Prince Radziwill,[2] who, as you know, is a great lover of music, arrived some days ago from Berlin, and was present at the performance of your Mass, which he did not know yet; he was as delighted with it as I and all those present were. — I hope that your health is restored and that you will give us many more products of your sublime genius. Pardon the nuisance that I often cause you by my letters, but it is the sincere tribute of one of your greatest admirers.

P[rince] Nicolas Galitzin

[Beethoven's address:]
No. 309 Bockgasse. Mathias Holzweg.[3]

1. Galitzin's letter of March 11 (No. 346 above) projects the performance of the *Missa solemnis* for April 7, and contemporary Russian newspapers confirm that it did, in fact, take place on that date. The prince was therefore in error either in dating his letter (in which case he actually wrote it on April 9) or in the French phrase he used, "avant hier soir." Galitzin usually wrote in fluent French but admitted to being slightly conversant with German. A remote possibility exists that he confused the word *hier,* common to both languages, but with different meanings.

Beethoven's next surviving letter to Galitzin, on May 26, 1824 (Anderson No. 1292), seems to indicate that the composer had not yet received Galitzin's news, although the usual mailing time between St. Petersburg and Vienna must have been between three weeks and a month.

2. Prince Anton Heinrich Radziwill (1755–1833), amateur composer and *Stadtholder* of the Grand Duchy of Posen. Beethoven had dedicated the Variations, Op. 108 (published in 1822), to him, as he would the Overture, Op. 115 (published in 1825). The composer had applied to Radziwill early in 1823 to subscribe to the *Missa solemnis* (mentioned in Anderson No. 1135). See the letter from Ludewig Krause, Radziwill's private secretary, to Beethoven, June 28, 1824 (No. 371 below), concerning that subscription.

3. In the fall of 1823, Beethoven had moved to lodgings in the Landstrasse on the corner of Bockgasse (now Beatrixgasse) and Ungargasse.

Incipit: Je m'empresse de vous donner Monsieur. . . .

Sources: Thayer-Deiters-Riemann, V, 559–560 (original French); Thayer-Forbes, p. 925 (English translation). German translation in Nohl, "Die Briefe Galitzins," p. 3, cols. 1–2 (at which time the letter was seemingly in the possession of Karl's widow, Caroline); Schindler (1860), pt. 2, p. 106; and Brenneis, "Fischhof-Manuskript," pp. 79, 81 (regarding the copy in the Staatsbibliothek zu Berlin–Preussischer Kulturbesitz). Excerpt in Schindler-MacArdle, pp. 302, 355. For details on dating, see Boris Schwarz, "More Beethoveniana in Soviet Russia," *Musical Quarterly* 49, no. 2 (1963), 143–149; and Lev Ginsburg, "Ludwig van Beethoven und Nikolai Galitzin," *Beethoven-Jahrbuch* 4 (1962), 60. When Thayer and Nohl made their copies, the autograph was in the possession of Beethoven's nephew Karl's widow, Caroline, Vienna; it has since disappeared.

356. B. Schotts Söhne to Beethoven

Mainz; April 10, 1824

Dear Herr *Kapellmeister!*

Supplementary to our letter of the 24th of last month,[1] we wish to note further to you the certainty that the payments[2] that we offered to you through a banker there should be fulfilled, and that we wish to accomplish this immediately after the agreement on your part. If contrary to expectations, the installments that we proposed to you should be too protracted, just make us another suitable proposal, and we will comply with it as well, since we honor your kind offer and make every endeavor to obtain such works for our publishing house.

We look forward to your well-disposed letter soon, and send all our affection and esteem.

B. Schott[s] Söhne

1. Schott would write still a third letter, on April 19 (No. 357 below), before Beethoven finally replied on May 20 (Anderson No. 1290).

2. Singular in Thayer-Deiters-Riemann; properly plural in *Briefwechsel*.

Incipit: Nachträglich unseres Schreibens vom 24. . . .

Sources: Thayer-Deiters-Riemann, V, 106–107; Staehelin and Brandenburg, *Briefwechsel* (1985), No. 4. Autograph in the Staatsbibliothek zu Berlin–Preussischer Kulturbesitz, Mus. ms. autogr. Beethoven 35, 72b; listed in Kalischer, "Beethoven-Autographe," p. 52, and Bartlitz, pp. 141–142.

357. B. Schotts Söhne to Beethoven

Mainz; April 19, 1924[1]

Herr *Hofkapellmeister*
L. van Beethoven, Vienna

We do not wish to let the suitable opportunity go unused, and refer to our two letters of March 24 and April 10, which, as I hope, you will have received and to which we look forward to your obliging answer.

At the same time we also take the liberty to recommend Herr *Kapellmeister* Rummel,[2] who could make this journey to Vienna with His Highness, the Duke of Nassau, and who, as the bearer of this letter, is a great worshiper of your works. The principal intention of this journey is his urge for improvement in the study of composition, and while his previous works already demonstrated ingenuity, his zeal and great diligence in the world of art create further benefit in the future. For this reason we feel free to recommend this young man very highly to your friendship and goodwill, since you will show him the right path to walk as a disciple of art, and he will make himself worthy of emulating a great master like you.

Meanwhile we declare ourselves prepared to be of every service in return, and sign with the highest esteem and devotion.

B. Schott[s] Söhne

1. As noted in the text, this letter follows Schott's letters of March 24 and April 10 (Nos. 350 and 356 above). Beethoven replied on May 20 (Anderson No. 1290), after still another Schott letter of April 27 (No. 361 below).

2. Christian Rummel (1787–1849), *Kapellmeister* at the court of Duke Wilhelm of Nassau in Wiesbaden.

Incipit: Wir wollen die passende Gelegenheit. . . .

Sources: Thayer-Deiters-Riemann, V, 107; Staehelin and Brandenburg, *Briefwechsel*, No. 5. Autograph in the Staatsbibliothek zu Berlin Preussischer Kulturbesitz, Mus. ms. autogr. Beethoven 35, 72c; listed in Kalischer, "Beethoven-Autographe," p. 52, and Bartlitz, p. 142.

358. Louis Antoine Duport, on Behalf of Domenico Barbaja,[1] to Beethoven

Vienna; April 20, 1824

Monsieur,

I hasten to communicate to you the response of Monsieur Barbaja, which I just received from Naples.

He charges me to assure you that he very much hopes to receive a new opera composed by you, and that he waits only for you to give a definite response in connection with the cost and the time,[2] *if he keeps the lease of the Imperial and Royal Theater near the Italian Gate[3] beyond December 1, 1824.*

I take this occasion to return to you herewith the book that you did me the favor of lending me.

I have the honor, Monsieur, to be

Your very humble and very obedient servant,

L. Duport
for Barbaja

1. Domenico Barbaja (ca. 1778–1841), Italian impresario, who held the lease on the Kärntnertor Theater during most of the period 1821–1828 while maintaining managership of seasons at La Scala in Milan and San Carlo in Naples. He was regarded highly by those with whom he worked, and the composer Giovanni Pacini noted that his word was as good as a written contract.

Louis Antoine Duport (1783–1853), a ballet dancer, directed the Kärntnertor Theater in Barbaja's absence. At this time, the impresario was expected back in Vienna within a week or two, and Duport was also negotiating with Beethoven for the premiere of the Ninth Symphony etc. (ultimately performed on May 7).

2. Details about Beethoven's seeming approach to Barbaja concerning an operatic commission are unclear. The petition of the Musicians and Music Lovers to Beethoven, shortly before February 26, 1824 (No. 344 above), alludes to Beethoven's having been approached by the management for such a project.

3. That is, the Kärntnertor Theater. The province of Kärnten (Carinthia) borders on Italy; the gate faced south.

Incipit: Je m'empresse de vous communiquer la réponse. . . .

Sources: Quoted briefly in Anton Schindler, *Beethoven-Biographie,* ed. Alfred Christlieb Kalischer (Berlin: Schuster & Loeffler, 1909), p. 378n. Autograph in the Staatsbibliothek zu Berlin–Preussischer Kulturbesitz, Mus. ms. autogr. Beethoven 35, 47; listed in Kalischer, "Beethoven-Autographe," pp. 49–50, and Bartlitz, p. 132.

359. Anton Schindler to Louis Antoine Duport[1]

Vienna; April 24, 1824

Dear Sir,

As agent for Herr Ludwig van Beethoven, I have the honor to notify you[2] herewith of his wish, since he intends to hold his grand musical *Akademie* in the I[mperial] R[oyal] Theater near the Kärntnertor, that you will kindly let him have for this purpose all the solo singers, the entire orchestral and choral personnel, as well as the necessary lighting for the sum of 400 fl. C.M.[3] Should the success of this *Akademie* occasion Herr van Beethoven to repeat it once or twice in the next week or at most ten days, he wishes in addition to obtain the I[mperial] R[oyal] Court Theater near the Kärntnertor again under the above conditions. Further, Herr van Beethoven has decided to entrust the leadership of this *Akademie* to Messrs. Umlauf and Schuppanzigh;[4] therefore he also wishes that all that is necessary will be decreed on the part of the administration, so that no difficulties will hereby be made for him by the orchestra.

Herr van Beethoven wishes to give the solo parts to Mademoiselles Sontag and Unger, and to Herr Preisinger,[5] and hopes that the administration will also accede to his wish in this respect.

As a favor to Herr Beethoven, the Musical Society[6] has undertaken to supplement the orchestra with its most superior members, so that, all together, this comes to 24 violins, 10 violas, 12 basses and violoncellos, as well as doubled winds. Therefore it is also necessary to place the whole orchestra on the stage, as is generally the case with large oratorios.

Finally, I have yet to add only that the earlier arrangement with His Excellency, Count von Palffy,[7] has come to nothing because, with the current shortage of capable singers [at the Theater] an der Wien, the solo parts could not be filled according to the wishes of Herr van Beethoven; also His Excellency expressly wished that Herr Clement[8] should direct the orchestra, which Herr van Beethoven had long ago intended for Herr Schuppanzigh,[9] and which he must insist upon for many reasons.

I now request you most urgently to declare yourself in writing about all this immediately, also to reserve the first evening for this *Akademie* as soon as possible, and only not to postpone it past the 3d or 4th of May.[10]

I have the honor to remain

> Your most obedient,

> Anton Schindler

1. "Letter of A. Schindler to Herr Louis Duport, Administrator (in name of Barbaja) of the Imperial Opera Theater, Vienna" (annotation by Thayer). Domenico Barbaja, who leased the Kärntnertor Theater, was in Italy at the moment, leaving dancer-turned-administrator Duport to manage the house in his absence.

2. Schindler uses a formal mode of address throughout the text.

3. The copy is not entirely clear; it could also read "W.W." In the conversation books, one reference is clearly "C.M."

4. Michael Umlauf (1781–1842), son of the composer Ignaz, the conductor who ultimately conducted the premiere of the Symphony No. 9; Ignaz Schuppanzigh (1776–1830), violinist and prominent chamber music performer.

5. Henriette Sontag (1806–1854), soprano; Caroline Unger (1805–1877), contralto; the basso Joseph Preisinger had to give up the part since the tessitura proved too high for him.

6. Gesellschaft der Musikfreunde.

7. Count Ferdinand Palffy (1774–1840), owner of the Theater an der Wien since 1813.

8. Franz Clement (1780–1842), prominent violinist who premiered Beethoven's Violin Concerto in 1806; conductor at the Theater an der Wien, 1818–1824.

9. From this juxtaposition, it becomes clear that the "director" of the orchestra in this case refers to its concertmaster.

10. Thayer evidently miscopied *März* (March) here, a mistake easily made if the archaic spelling *May* (for *Mai*) had an umlaut over the *y* (or was rendered *Maij*), as was often the case.

Incipit: Ich habe die Ehre als Organ. . . .

Sources: Thayer-Deiters-Riemann, V, 82–83, after a copy made by Thayer. Schindler's own handwritten copy in the Staatsbibliothek zu Berlin–Preussischer Kulturbesitz, Mus. ms. autogr. Beethoven 35, 73; listed in Kalischer, "Beethoven-Autographe," p. 53, and Bartlitz, p. 144.

360. Beethoven to Tobias Haslinger

[Vienna; ca. April 24, 1824][1]

For Herr von Tobias Hasslinger[2]
General Adjutant

Worthy Tobias,

No other parts[3] are needed except those for the new best members of the *Verein*.[4] The plates, however, should be corrected according to the parts I am sending you here; otherwise, we shall have to deal with corrections [to the printed materials] again. Piringer[5] has been instructed to select the 8 best violinists, the 2 best violists, the 2 best contrabassists

 6

and the 2 best violoncellists, even if a few wear wigs, for the orchestra is to be strengthened by just this much.

Amicus,

Beethoven

1. This letter appeared as Anderson No. 1277 in an incomplete form. Since the complete text provides important additional information on preparations for the May 7 *Akademie,* it is included here. The contents of the letter reflect some of the same material as in Schindler's letter to Duport, April 24, 1824 (No. 359 above), and it probably dates from around the same time. For a similar item, see Beethoven's note to Schlemmer (?), before November 29, 1814 (No. 193 above).

2. As he often did, Beethoven misspells Haslinger's name, possibly intending a humorous pun on *Hass* (hate).

3. Publishing partner Tobias Haslinger provided printed parts for some of the forces used at the May 7, 1824, *Akademie.* As noted by Schindler, the gross receipts from the May 7 concert were 2,220 florins, against expenses of 1,000 florins (theater) and 800 florins (copying). Beethoven's sheets reckoning these expenses are in the Staatsbibliothek zu Berlin–Preussischer Kulturbesitz, Mus. ms. autogr. Beethoven 35, 75 and 35, 76 (Bartlitz, p. 146).

4. The Gesellschaft der Musikfreunde provided choral singers and amateur in-

strumentalists for the concert, supplementing the forces of the Kärntnertor Theater. For the theater's orchestral personnel, see Beethoven's draft letter of ca. May 9, 1824 (No. 363 below); the theater's chorus members (17 women and 26 men, under Ignaz Dirzka) are listed in Ziegler, *Addressen-Buch von Tonkünstlern*, pp. 75–78. The Gesellschaft's many string players are listed in Ziegler, pp. 134–147; its chorus members (55 women and 112 men, from which members would have been selected for a balanced ensemble) are listed in Ziegler, pp. 121–132.

5. Ferdinand Piringer (1780–1829), government official and a director of the *Concerts Spirituels*. In the division of labor among Beethoven's circle (as reflected in earlier conversation book entries), Piringer had been entrusted with arranging for instrumental personnel.

6. Although Beethoven's notation indicated a higher C, he probably intended that the bassists possess five-string instruments, with the lowest string extending the range downward to C, since these added notes were required in the scores to be played.

Incipit: Es braucht keiner andern Stimmen. . . .

Sources: Otto Erich Deutsch, "Zu Beethovens grossen Akademien von 1824," *Österreichische Musikzeitschrift* 19 (September 1964), 428, with extensive annotation. The letter was auctioned in September 1922 by Karl Ernst Henrici, Berlin, and then disappeared. The auction catalog contained an incomplete and partially inaccurate transcription, copied by Kastner-Kapp No. 1208 and translated as MacArdle & Misch No. 386 and Anderson No. 1277. The letter reappeared by the early 1960s, and conductor Hans Swarowsky provided Deutsch with a photograph of the entire autograph.

361. B. Schotts Söhne to Beethoven

Mainz; April 27, 1824[1]

Herr *Kapellmeister!*

We take the liberty of reporting to you that yesterday we had the pleasure to send off to you, in care of Herr S. A. Steiner & Co. there,[2] a little package that contains the first issue of the new magazine *Cäcilia*. We again recommend this undertaking to your kind acceptance, and wish that you might also oblige the invitation of the editorship, if possible, with even a small contribution.[3]

With great thanks, we shall acknowledge and settle the asked-for fee; we look forward with expectation to each [work].

We most ardently wish a reply to our two letters of March 24 and April 10.

When you transfer the Quartet[4] to us for the understood price, you surely have a friend there in business, who will take care of the dispatch of the manuscript to us here, upon receipt of the fee, and we expect this work of art soon if you therefore want to make no other proposal for the payment there.

Our greatest wish, however, is to be able to regard ourselves as the publisher of all three offered works,[5] about which we still, as always, look forward to a friendly reply of acceptance from you.

We are accustomed to offering the artist somewhat less than the asked-for price, but in order to be able to do what we promised as honorable people, and not to trouble our own business unduly, we made you the offer of payments in installments, which you, however, may determine if the terms proposed are too protracted for you. Upon demand, we shall bear the responsibility for guaranteeing that a banking house in Vienna fulfills your demands.

Please honor this matter with a few lines in reply and remove from us this uncertainty in which we find ourselves.

You will excuse our forwardness; you must attribute it to your offer, which we value highly.

We shall reimburse you for any postage charges caused you, since we can pay them from here only as far as the Austrian border, which is also the case with every letter going there.

We remain with all esteem your most devoted friends and admirers,

B. Schott[s] Söhne

1. A fourth letter to Beethoven in a series also including missives dated March 24, April 10, and April 19 (Nos. 350, 356, and 357 above). Both flattered and annoyed by Schott's persistence, Beethoven replied on May 20, 1824 (Anderson No. 1290).

2. Sigmund Anton Steiner (1773–1838), Viennese publisher.

3. The *Cäcilia*'s editor, Gottfried Weber, evidently hoped that Beethoven would write an article for the periodical.

4. String Quartet, Op. 127.

5. The *Missa solemnis* and the Symphony No. 9, in addition to the quartet.

Incipit: Wir nehmen uns die Freiheit. . . .

Sources: Thayer-Deiters-Riemann, V, 107–108; Staehelin and Brandenburg, *Brief-wechsel*, No. 3. Autograph in the Staatsbibliothek zu Berlin–Preussischer Kulturbe-sitz, Mus. ms. autogr. Beethoven 35, 72d; listed in Kalischer, "Beethoven-Autographe," p. 52, and Bartlitz, p. 142.

362. *Johann Hörr*[1] *to Beethoven*

Penzing; May 1, 1824

Receipt

For 180 fl. C.M., written one hundred eighty Gulden Conventions Münze, which I the undersigned have received from Herr Ludwig van Beethoven as house rent for the summer of 1824 in my house, No. 43, in Penzing, a permanent apartment on the 1st floor,[2] duly paid in cash, herewith attested.

Id est 180 fl. c.m.[3]

Johann Hörr

[Beethoven's pencil annotation:]
"Scoundrel."[4]

1. Johann Hörr was a Viennese tailor who owned a house in Penzing, a village of 194 houses in Beethoven's time, located near the river Wien. For further details of Beethoven's brief and unfortunate stay in Penzing, see Thayer-Forbes, p. 913.

2. American second floor.

3. This remark is written to the left side of the signature, angling upward.

4. Beethoven's word in German was *Schurke,* a near cognate of the English epithet *jerk.*

Incipit: Über 180 fl. C. Mz. Sage. . . .

Sources: Thayer-Deiters-Riemann, V, 101; Thayer-Forbes, p. 913. Autograph in the Staatsbibliothek zu Berlin–Preussischer Kulturbesitz, Mus. ms. autogr. Beethoven 35, 85; listed in Kalischer, "Beethoven-Autographe," p. 57, and Bartlitz, p. 149.

363. *Beethoven to the Orchestra of the Kärntnertor Theater*[1]

[Vienna; probably May 9, 1824][2]

I am obliged to thank most sincerely all those who showed me so much love and cooperation at my *Akademie.* Since I have been invited to give it one more time, I am convinced that I shall not commit an error—since, as a result of the invitation I am giving a second this coming Friday in the

Landständischer Saal[3] — if I request all of the participants once more to take part and to ennoble my work by their assistance. . . .

1. The Kärntnertor Theater's orchestra had constituted the core of the instrumental forces that premiered the Ninth Symphony and gave the Viennese premiere of three movements of the *Missa solemnis* on Friday, May 7, 1824. At a (probably midday) dinner in the Prater on Sunday, May 9, Ignaz Schuppanzigh (concertmaster at the performance) wrote in his customary humorous third-person style in Beethoven's conversation book: "Dear Beethoven! I ask him [you] to draft a little thank-you note to the Orchestra of the Kärntnertor; they will all really like that" (Köhler et al., *Konversationshefte*, VI, 174). Seemingly later in the day, Beethoven jotted the present draft, along with reminders to himself to write editor Adolf B. Bäuerle, editor Joseph Carl Bernard, publisher Tobias Haslinger, theater manager Louis Antoine Duport and conductor Michael Umlauf, probably in much the same vein.

At the end of 1822, the orchestra had included the following personnel (largely in alphabetical order within the sections): *Violins:* Breumann, Georg Helmesberger, Joseph Mayseder (solo), Mathias Meier, Zeno Franz Menzel (the younger), Jacob Rabel, Staufer, Steiner, Strebinger, Tischler, Benedict Tutowitsch, Anton Wranitzky; *Violas:* Johann Barton, Müller, Schreiber, Stichey; *Violoncelli:* Joseph Valentin Dont, Joseph Merk, Weudl (*sic*), Friedrich Wranitzky; *Contrabasses:* Anton Grams, Joseph Melzer (Mölzer) (also contrabassoon), Leitner, Leopold Perschl; *Flutes:* Georg Öhler (also violin), Schall, Zierer; *Oboes:* (Joseph) Khayll, Mollnik; *Clarinets:* Bauer, Joseph Dobihal; *Bassoons:* Nowack, Pattlög (August Mittag?); *Horns:* Camila Belonci (Camillo Bellonci), Friedrich Hradetzky, Johann Janaka, Khayll; *Trumpets:* Beisl, Block, Anton Khayll; *Trombones:* Duschke, Hebel, (Leopold) Segner; and *Timpani:* Anton Hudler. (The members are listed in Ziegler, *Addressen-Buch von Tonkünstlern*, pp. 78–81, with further clarification of a few names in Cox and Cox, *Journals of Smart*, p. 128, and Böckh, *Merkwürdigkeiten*, pp. 363–384.) As noted elsewhere, contrabassist Anton Grams, who had been associated with Beethoven's music at least since the May or June 1804 reading rehearsals of the Symphony No. 3, had died on May 18, 1823, and therefore was not destined to play the Ninth Symphony.

2. When this letter was drafted, the repeat was tentatively projected for the next Friday, May 14. Beethoven may not have sent this letter until the second concert had been firmly rescheduled for May 23.

3. The May 23 concert took place in the Grosser Redoutensaal.

Incipit: Ich halte mich ver[p]flicht[et]. . . .

Sources: Köhler et al., *Konversationshefte*, VI, 176–177 (© Deutscher Verlag für Musik, Leipzig). Autograph in the Staatsbibliothek zu Berlin–Preussischer Kulturbesitz.

364. The Imperial Royal High Steward's Office (Memorandum)

Vienna; May 10, 1824[1]

No. 643

1824

Van Beethoven, musician, requests permission to give an *Akademie* on the evening of the 14th of this month,[2] since it is a *Norma Tag*.[3]

dated May 9; rec'd. 10th, 1824.

ad acta.

1. Deutsch misread the archaic German spelling "May" on the present document as "Marz" (*sic*) the tenth.

The conversation books indicate that, on Sunday, May 9 (two days after the May 7 *Akademie*), Beethoven and his circle had (presumably midday) dinner together and discussed the possibility of a repeat of the Ninth Symphony on Friday, May 14. Later on the ninth, Beethoven drafted a letter to the Kärntnertor Theater Orchestra and jotted a note to himself concerning further letters to be written, one of which was to theater administrator Louis Antoine Duport. The present document, reflecting Beethoven's request of May 9 (to hold a concert on the fourteenth), was therefore penned on May 10. Ultimately the concert was held in the Grosser Redoutensaal on Sunday, May 23 (see Köhler et al., *Konversationshefte*, VI, 176–182).

2. Beethoven and his circle hoped to obtain the Landständischer Saal for the May 14 performance, although the preference is not reflected in this memorandum.

3. A religious/administrative holy day, on which no customary work was done.

Incipit: Van Beethoven, Tonkünstler, bittet. . . .

Sources: Otto Erich Deutsch, "Zu Beethovens grossen Akademien von 1824," *Österreichische Musikzeitschrift* 19 (September 1964), 427–428. Autograph in the Haus-, Hof- und Staatsarchiv, Vienna, Gen. Int. 11/Op. 1824.

365. Beethoven to the Wiener Zeitschrift für Kunst, Literatur, Theater und Mode *(Draft)*

[Vienna; ca. May 13, 1824]

To the *Modejournal:* I request you at least to insert [an announcement] that the *Akademie* that I gave will be given again.[1]

1. In its May 15, 1824, issue, the *Wiener Zeitschrift* combined a review of Beethoven's May 7 concert with an announcement that it would be repeated.

Incipit: Modejournal. Ich bitte sie wenigstens. . . .

Sources: Köhler et al., *Konversationshefte*, VI, 182, 407 (© Deutscher Verlag für Musik, Leipzig). Autograph in the Staatsbibliothek zu Berlin–Preussischer Kulturbesitz.

366. Carl Czerny[1] *to Beethoven*

[Vienna; ca. May 20, 1824][2]

Most honored Herr Beethoven,

Your wish, which honored me beyond my capability to express it, forced me, with all the frankness with which one must speak man to man, to explain to you my opinions as well as my circumstances. I have sacrificed the last 15 years of my life giving lessons in order to provide decent security for myself and my parents. Composition and playing remained secondary matters, since I lacked all encouragement and help, and especially the latter (playing) with the demands now made upon virtuosos, could not possibly be cultivated to the degree which is now so kindly expected from my abilities.

And now shall I—although I have not performed before the vast, knowledgeable Viennese public for 14 years—appear again, suddenly, without any preparation, having hardly 2 days' practice time, to produce one of your greatest, most thoroughly thought-out compositions,[3] and even more so in the most dangerous place that exists for pianists! The Grosser Redoutensaal is the most ungrateful[4] location for this instrument, and *all* piano players who have played there up to now have regretted it.

Otherwise my consideration is not for myself, rather for the well-founded fear that it is impossible for me to perform your elevated work in an accomplished manner in this short, overly hurried period of hardly two full days, as well as my unbounded respect pledged to you — the reason for which I most necessarily forgo this honor.

In order to appear as a virtuoso, I need at least 3 months' time to get my technique fully back into practice — the greatest pianists of our time devote their health and their entire existence to this purpose, and feel happy when they merely satisfy the critics to some extent. While I am convinced that I am not promoting your friendship by anything more worthy, nor by this frankness, rather I feel it to the benefit of Art and the good cause. . . .

1. Carl Czerny (1791–1857), Viennese-born pianist, composer and teacher, met Beethoven at age ten and began studying with him shortly thereafter. Of frail health, Czerny began to withdraw from the public stage after he himself started to teach, in about 1806. On February 12, 1812, he gave the first Viennese performance of Beethoven's Piano Concerto No. 5, Op. 73, at a benefit concert and thereafter seems to have restricted his activities to weekly salon recitals. Czerny was among the thirty signers of the petition asking Beethoven to give a concert that the composer received on February 26 (No. 344 above).

In a letter to the pianist and composer Johann Peter Pixis (1788–1874), who had moved from Vienna to Paris in 1823, Czerny wrote on June 24, 1824: "There is surely no more significant musical news that I can write you about from our dear old Vienna than that Beethoven finally gave repeated performances of his long-awaited concert, and in the most striking manner astonished everyone who feared that after ten years of deafness he could now produce only dry, abstract works, bereft of imagination. *To the greatest extent,* his new Symphony breathes such a fresh, lively, indeed youthful spirit; so much power, innovation and beauty as ever [came] from the head of this ingenious man, although several times he certainly gave the old wigs something to shake their heads about" (Thayer-Deiters-Riemann, V, 97; Thayer obtained this letter from one Schebek, Prague).

2. The draft letter is undated, but references within it to a request from Beethoven and a potential performance in the Grosser Redoutensaal, combined with the approximate dates that may be deduced from Czerny's chronological statements, place this letter just before Beethoven's concert of May 23, 1824, on which the

Symphony No. 9 had its second performance. The premiere had taken place on May 7, in a concert that had also included the *Consecration of the House* Overture, Op. 124, as well as the Kyrie, Credo and Agnus Dei from the *Missa solemnis,* Op. 123 (called "Three Grand Hymns" on the censored program).

Beethoven's conversation book for around Thursday, May 20, provides a vivid portrait of the last-minute preparations for the Sunday, May 23, repeat concert, at which several of the complementary compositions were to be changed. His nephew Karl writes, "Czerny ought to play the Concerto," in expectation of a rehearsal on the next day, Friday. Secretary Anton Schindler chimes in: "Just write a few lines to Czerny, and I will tell him the rest personally. Which Concerto should he play? He has already played the one in E♭ often, so it would cause him little trouble." A few moments later in the same conversation, which notes that one hymn (the Kyrie) will also appear on the concert, the secretary writes: "Czerny will probably only be able to play the first movement, for the whole concerto will make the concert last too long." Schindler also notes that Czerny's presence on the program would attract his large following among the nobility.

Beethoven then wrote Czerny: "Do me the favor to play in the Grosser Redouten-saal the day after tomorrow [*sic*] the Adagio and Rondo of my Concerto in E♭. If you do, you will add lustre to the whole concert. As the choruses have not been sufficiently rehearsed, it is not possible to perform more than one of the Hymns."

At the end of the conversation, Karl tells Beethoven: "I am going with Schindler to see Czerny."

Later, probably still the same day, they returned to report to Beethoven. Schindler writes: "Czerny made a thousand excuses that since he is absolutely unprepared as a [public] player, he will therefore have to excuse himself." The present letter, then, is Czerny's drafted reply to Beethoven's invitation, written after Schindler and Karl's visit on around May 20. It must have been finalized and sent to Beethoven within the next day or so and (possibly even before the May 23 concert) elicited a warm reply from the composer: "My dear and beloved Czerny! I have learned . . . that you are in a situation such as I really never suspected. . . . just tell me how some things might perhaps be improved for you (this is no vulgar desire on my part to patronize you). As soon as I can breathe freely again I must see you. . . ."

Ultimately, the May 23 concert included the *Consecration of the House* Overture; the trio *Tremate, empi, tremate,* Op. 116; one hymn (the Kyrie from the *Missa solemnis*); "Di tanti palpiti" from Rossini's *Tancredi* (a bow to current Viennese tastes, seemingly imposed by theatrical manager Duport); and the crucial Ninth Symphony. It was not the financial success for which Beethoven had hoped.

See Köhler et al., *Konversationshefte,* VI, 208–210; Schindler-MacArdle, pp. 281–282; Thayer-Forbes, p. 912; Anderson Nos. 909 and 910. On the basis of Czerny's own statements, Anderson dates these letters from 1818. Various reports in the

Allgemeine musikalische Zeitung indicate performances of Beethoven's works in 1818 (the Seventh Symphony, Beethoven conducting, to benefit the university law faculty on January 17, the *Egmont* Overture and *Wellington's Victory* at the Grosser Redoutensaal at Christmastime to benefit the Bürgerspital Fund etc.), but the circumstances described in Beethoven's letters more closely correspond to the events of around May 20–23, 1824.

3. Piano Concerto No. 5 in E♭, Op. 73.

4. Czerny originally wrote "dangerous" again, but changed it to "ungrateful."

Incipit: Ihr Wunsch, der mich so hoch ehrt als ich nicht auszudrücken vermag. . . .

Sources: Unpublished draft in the Archiv of the Gesellschaft der Musikfreunde, Vienna, Autographe Czerny ad 65, Nr. 1.

367. Beethoven to an Unnamed Creditor (Sigmund Anton Steiner?) (Draft)

[Vienna; probably May 21, 1824]

The 70 florins will be paid immediately after the second *Akademie*,[1] since I am really down on my luck because of the many expenses; concerning the other items, Bach[2] is arranging everything, either with works or with money.

1. The dating of the conversation books places this draft probably on May 21, two days before Beethoven's repeat concert (featuring the Symphony No. 9) on May 23. Sieghard Brandenburg, Beethoven Archiv, Bonn, believes that the intended addressee was publisher Sigmund Anton Steiner.

2. Dr. Johann Baptist Bach, Beethoven's attorney.

Incipit: Die 70 fl. werden gleich nach. . . .

Sources: Köhler et al., *Konversationshefte*, VI, 189 (© Deutscher Verlag für Musik, Leipzig). Autograph in the Staatsbibliothek zu Berlin–Preussischer Kulturbesitz.

368. Sigmund Anton Steiner to Tobias Haslinger, Vienna

Leipzig; May 24, 1824[1]

Likewise, I also pity our unique Beethoven, and no one here will believe that so great a man is treated so absolutely without cooperation[2] [as in Vienna].

1. The Viennese publisher, here writing to his business associate, was probably in Leipzig for the trade fair, as he had been in the spring of 1822 (see Schlesinger to Beethoven, July 2, 1822, No. 292 above, and associated correspondence among him, Beethoven, Peters and Steiner, Nos. 294–296 above).

2. The German reads "gar so sehr ohne Theilnahme," probably a reference to the logistic difficulties Beethoven encountered in arranging his concerts of May 7 and 23, 1824.

Incipit (this excerpt): Ebenso bedaure ich auch. . . .

Sources: Thayer-Deiters-Riemann, V, 98. This excerpt was in Thayer's papers and served Riemann as a note to Beethoven's letter to Haslinger, May 1824 (ultimately Anderson No. 1294).

369. Beethoven to Anton Schindler (?) (Draft)

[Vienna; ca. May 26 or 27, 1824]

I ask you not to come to me at all, under any pretext, either alone or with anyone. I am saddened, in any case, that it happened the third time. . . .[1]

1. This is probably a draft for a letter to Beethoven's secretary and factotum Anton Schindler. The composer had been intermittently vexed with Schindler during preparations for the May 7 *Akademie* on which the Ninth Symphony was premiered. He became angry with Schindler again over the poor receipts from the repeat *Akademie* of May 23, 1824, and seemingly banished the secretary from his circle of friends. No entries by Schindler appear in the surviving conversation books from this point until around July 11, 1824; thereafter, he remained only an infrequent visitor to Beethoven until the final reconciliation early in December 1826.

Incipit: Ich ersuche Sie unter gar keinem Vorwand. . . .

Sources: Köhler et al., *Konversationshefte*, VI, 237 (© Deutscher Verlag für Musik, Leipzig). Autograph in the Staatsbibliothek zu Berlin–Preussischer Kulturbesitz.

370. Prince Nicolas Galitzin to Beethoven

St. Petersburg; June 16, 1824[1]

I have just received, Monsieur, your letter of May 26, which has given me inexpressible pleasure, such as I feel every time I receive one of your letters.

I hasten to reply to it by the first post. It is with very real impatience that I await the shipment of the quartet[2] that you promised me, and if I have a request to make of you it would be that its shipment be hastened. If you had not offered them to me, I would have promptly asked that you send me your latest compositions such as the Symphony,[3] the overture[4] and the trio.[5] These are masterworks that I am really anxious to know; I implore you to have them copied very quickly upon my account, and my gratitude will be great: I impatiently await everything that comes from you.

I thank you for the verses that you sent me; they are dedicated to me because I am your most sincere friend.[6] I have already read in the journals that the King of France has conferred a medal upon you.[7] May all sovereigns imitate this King of France in doing justice to your merit. I confess that the court here does not concern itself much with music, and furthermore, the contemptible Rossinian charlatanism has overrun everything.[8] The sacred fire of fine music is maintained by only a small number of the elect, and you know that to be right it must have the majority. People of genius like you are rewarded by posterity, whose judgment always ends up being just; but it is a sad consolation for the genius who cannot earn a living from it. According to an order issued a little while ago, and which has been published in all the journals, all foreign artists who want to dedicate any work to His Majesty[9] must address themselves to the minister of foreign affairs, Count de Nesselrode.[10] If you intend to dedicate your Mass[11] to His Majesty, I advise you very simply to write to Count Nesselrode: your name at the bottom of a letter is the finest recommendation, and the Count prides himself on being a musician. If you have your Mass printed, I shall try to distribute as many copies of it as I can; only I shall point out to you that a work of this nature will not sell as easily as another whose performance is, so to speak, a daily occurrence and easy. — Because to perform a Mass requires an orchestra, choruses and solo voices. — For those who are not able to assemble all these people (and it is a very great number), the score becomes, also so to speak, unusable, for, unfortunately, there are few people who will purchase a [full] score for study, and meditate upon it as this Mass deserves. I wish to say that although works such as the sonatas [and] quartets can be sold a great deal more easily, I hope, however, also to sell several copies [of them] for you. In your next letter, I would like you to tell me with which works you are occupied at the moment, and what we have to expect from your genius.

I hope to travel next year, and I shall head in the direction of Vienna for I want to become acquainted more intimately with him who has provided me the most beautiful joys of my life. Prince Radziwill has made a stay of some months here,[12] and we have played nothing but your Quartets, and especially the five latest ones.[13]

Accept, please, the assurance of my very sincere friendship and my boundless devotion.

N[icolas] Galitzin

[P.S.] If ever you find yourself in the least kind of difficulty, apply quickly to me; I shall be only too happy to be able to be useful to you.

1. Answers Beethoven's letter of May 26, 1824 (Anderson No. 1292).

2. String Quartet, Op. 127, commissioned by Galitzin.

3. Op. 125.

4. *Consecration of the House*, Op. 124.

5. *Tremate, empi, tremate*, Op. 116.

6. At the end of his letter of May 26, Beethoven said that he was sending Galitzin "Italian verses about me." The paper of that letter was so badly damaged that Emily Anderson had to reconstruct his meaning, but she noted that, at the second performance of the Ninth Symphony on May 23, an Italian ode to Beethoven by one Calisto Bassi was distributed in the hall. Galitzin's statement that the copy was dedicated (*dédiés*) to himself is unclear, unless Beethoven added an inscription on the copy designating it a gift to the prince.

7. With his letter of May 26, Beethoven had sent Galitzin "an impression" (doubtless a pencil rubbing) of the medal from Louis XVIII.

8. In his letter to Beethoven of November 29, 1823 (No. 338 above), Galitzin had already decried "Italian charlatanry," without naming Rossini specifically. His term here is "le charlatanisme pittoyable Rossininien [*sic*]," if Thayer's transcription is accurate.

9. Czar Alexander I (1777–1825).

10. Count Carl Robert Nesselrode (1780–1862), of German ancestry, was Russian minister of foreign affairs from 1822 to 1856.

11. Op. 123.

12. Anton Heinrich Radziwill had arrived in St. Petersburg a few days before the performance there of the *Missa solemnis* on April 7.

13. Op. 59, Nos. 1–3, Op. 74, and Op. 95.

Incipit: Je viens de recevoir, Monsieur, votre lettre. . . .

Sources: Thayer-Deiters-Riemann, V, 560–561; summarized in Thayer-Forbes, p. 927. When Thayer copied it, the autograph was in the possession of Beethoven's nephew Karl's widow, Caroline, Vienna. It has since disappeared.

371. Ludewig Krause,[1] Private Secretary of Prince Anton Heinrich Radziwill, to Beethoven

Berlin; June 28, 1824

Highly born Sir!
Highly honored Herr *Kapellmeister!*

On April 6, in the name of His Highness, Prince Anton Radziwill, I forwarded to you an assignment of 50 ducats, and requested a receipt for it, in order to have a copy of your Mass reserved for and sent to His Highness, but as of now I have neither of them. His Highness has now returned from Russia to Posen, and inquired of me whether I had not yet received the Mass, since he wished to have it.[2]

Therefore, I request you most urgently and most devotedly to give me a report about the receipt of the 50 ducats as soon as it pleases you, and also to have the Mass sent to me, so that I can forward it to the Prince.

Krause

1. The details of this man's signature are virtually illegible. Kalischer read his name as Krause or Krauts, while Bartlitz provides "Krauss [?]." On examining his August 3, 1824, letter (No. 375 below), Astrid-Herma Smart read "Kranig." Sieghard Brandenburg, Beethoven-Archiv, Bonn, has confirmed that the secretary's name was, in fact, Ludewig Krause.

2. Radziwill's subscription to the *Missa solemnis* was made in response to Beethoven's "form letter" invitations to subscribe, sent out in the first months of 1823 (see Anderson No. 134 and, e.g., No. 303 above). As Prince Galitzin reported to Beethoven in his letter of April 8 (No. 355 above), Radziwill was present for the St. Petersburg premiere of the *Missa* on April 7 and was enthusiastic about the work—thus the urgency of tone in the present letter. Schindler annotated this letter as follows: "Bad copies were responsible for the delay in shipment to the subscribers. Many sheets had to be rewritten in each copy."

Incipit: Euer Hochwohlgeboren habe ich am 6. April. . . .

Sources: Thayer-Deiters-Riemann, IV, 358–359. Autograph in the Staatsbibliothek zu Berlin–Preussischer Kulturbesitz, Mus. ms. autogr. Beethoven 35, 48; listed in Kalischer, "Beethoven-Autographe," p. 50, and Bartlitz, p. 133.

372. B. Schotts Söhne to Beethoven

Mainz; July 19, 1824[1]

Herr Lud[wig] v[an] Beethoven
Vienna

Herr *Kapellmeister!*

We do not want to neglect any longer in replying to your honored letter of the 3d of this month, since we have made arrangements with the business house of Herr Fries & Co. there[2] to render the payments according to the time schedule designated by you, upon the bill of exchange that we presented, and that they, in turn, will show you, and against which you will have the kindness to transfer to Herr Fries & Co. both manuscripts, namely the grand Mass and the new grand Symphony.[3]

Please provide both works with your seal and tie up each one with twine.

We shall undertake the publication of the two works without delay and shall issue to the public the piano arrangement and the individual parts all at the same time.

We hope to receive clear and correct copies of the scores, to which you will kindly add all the annotations that the engraver might possibly need to know.

We shall apply the utmost care in the proofreading, and if you perhaps wish to undertake the final corrections yourself, please let us know.

Since, according to your promise, we can surely count on the String Quartet[4] as our property, it gladdens us all the more that we shall receive it in six weeks' time, and you may rest assured that, according to the time schedule of payments that you designated, this shall be accomplished through Herr Fries & Co. just as punctually.

We would wish that in your next letter you tell us all the news that your overwhelming affairs did not allow you to say in your last letter, and look forward with true joy to this report.

With regards for your goodwill and friendship for us, we sign with esteem and devotion,

B. Schotts Söhne

1. Replies to Beethoven's letter of July 3, 1824 (Anderson No. 1299).
2. The banking house of Count Moritz Fries (1777–1826), which had also served as a medium for payment by George Thomson in the previous decade.
3. The *Missa solemnis,* Op. 123, and the Symphony No. 9, Op. 125, respectively.
4. Op. 127.
Incipit: Dero verehrte Zuschrift vom 3. dies. . . .
Sources: Thayer-Deiters-Riemann, V, 110–111; Staehelin and Brandenburg, *Briefwechsel,* pp. 13–15. Briefly quoted in Nohl, *Beethoven's Leben* (1877), III, 519–520; Schindler, 3d ed. (1860), pt. 2, p. 102; Schindler-MacArdle, p. 299. Autograph in the Staatsbibliothek zu Berlin–Preussischer Kulturbesitz, Mus. ms. autogr. Beethoven 35, 72e; listed in Kalischer, "Beethoven-Autographe," p. 52, and Bartlitz, p. 142.

373. *Beethoven to Heinrich Albert Probst, Leipzig*

Baden, near Vienna; July 26, 1824[1]

Dear Sir!

Just as I was about to journey here, I wrote to you in haste on the 23d of this month [to say] that all the works that you wanted are ready and have been correctly copied. As far as I remember, I have never received your letters through the post [office], and so there could perhaps be some delay. I therefore ask you to send your letters directly by post, [addressed] simply to Ludwig van Beethoven, Vienna, where I myself am most sure to receive them.

You can now publish the Overture[2] immediately, as well as all the other works;[3] indeed it matters a great deal to me that they appear soon. To prove to you my interest, I have likewise written these Bagatelles completely anew,[4] and they will surely take their place among the best of mine that have already been published.[5] As soon as this matter is settled, I shall notify you of new works, since you will remember that I would like to have dealings with only one publisher, or at most with only a few.

In expectation of a letter soon and a conclusion to this matter, I sign myself with pleasure,

Your most devoted,

Beethoven

[Exterior:]
[From] Vienna
To Herr A. Probst
Famous Art and Music Publisher
Leipzig

1. Follows Beethoven's letter of July 3, 1824 (Anderson No. 1298), Probst's letter of July 10 (lost), and Beethoven's letter of July 23 (also lost). Probst's annotation on the present letter indicates: "Received August 2d; replied August 9." On August 9, Beethoven (lost) and Probst (No. 378 below) both wrote letters, which crossed in the mails. Tyson, pp. 28–29, provides a fine summary of the entire Beethoven-Probst correspondence.

Baden had been one of Beethoven's favorite resorts for two decades; he had arrived there for the first time that summer on July 17 and was staying in the Hermitage of Schloss Gutenbrunn, which belonged to Johann and Barbara Schimmer.

2. *Consecration of the House* Overture, Op. 124.

3. The songs *Opferlied,* Op. 121b, *Bundeslied,* Op. 122, and *Der Kuss,* Op. 128, as well as the Bagatelles, Op. 126.

4. Whether or not Beethoven had written them *completely* anew, he had in fact altered and added to the Bagatelles since offering them to Peters two years earlier. A sketch for Op. 126, No. 5, appears in a conversation book entry of May 9, 1824.

5. The passage reads: "[Bagatellen,] welche wohl zu den Besten von meinen schon herausgegebenen gehören werden." Beethoven carefully avoids the word *Werke* here; possibly he *implies* it, but what he actually says is that Op. 126 will belong among the best of his *bagatelles* that have already been published, a reasonable assessment of their merits.

Incipit: Eben im Begriff hierher zu reisen. . . .

Sources: Tyson, "New Beethoven Letters and Documents," pp. 26–29. The autograph (of which a careful copy had been made) was at one time in private hands in the United States; subsequently its location became unknown, but most recently it has been reported again in a private collection in the United States (see Tyson's "Addenda," in *Beethoven Studies 3,* ed. Alan Tyson [Cambridge: Cambridge University Press, 1982], p. 299).

374. Prince Nicolas Galitzin to Beethoven

St. Petersburg; July 28, 1824

In the last letter that I wrote you,[1] Monsieur, I asked you kindly to send me your new overture and your new symphony.[2] I now repeat my request, asking you to send them to me as soon as possible, and for payment kindly to draw upon agreement with Messrs. Stieglitz & Co. for the amount you wish, and I shall honor it. I have read in the journals the account of the brilliant concert that you gave in Vienna.[3] This made me desire even more ardently to become acquainted with these sublime masterworks. What I would not have given to be in Vienna at that moment. The ingratitude that that capital has shown you disgusts me, and I think that you would be rather more admired if you had not established it as your residence. Even now, I am convinced that if you wanted to travel through Europe without any resources other than your compositions and without any recommendations other than your immortal masterworks, you would have the universe at your feet. Just your presence in Paris or London would make all the others [i.e., other composers] forgotten, and the concerts that you would give there would not resemble those in Vienna. You have enthusiasts everywhere, and how many others who have scarcely heard your compositions will join their number when they attend the concerts that you will give! I tell you this because I desire it as much for your benefit as for your glory and the glory of science [i.e., the science of music]. Your genius is revered everywhere, and everywhere you will find friends and admirers! . . . Do not be angry with me for the wish that I make to see you leave Vienna: I would desire that all the world might appreciate you and admire you as I do.

They say that you are working on an opera, *Melusina,* by Grillparzer,[4] and on a cantata by Bernard:[5] O, that I might soon know all your masterworks! As for my Quartets,[6] my impatience requests them out of your friendship for me,

Your very devoted,

P[rince] N[icolas] Galitzin

1. Galitzin's most recent letter was that of June 16, 1824 (No. 370 above). Beethoven had not had time to respond before the prince penned this epistle.

2. *Consecration of the House,* Op. 124, and Symphony No. 9, Op. 125.

3. Beethoven's *Akademie* of May 7, 1824.

4. Beethoven and the poet (1791–1872) had been discussing *Melusine* since about May 1823, but after three years nothing came of it.

5. *Der Sieg des Kreuzes;* see Beethoven's letter to the Gesellschaft der Musikfreunde, January 23, 1824 (Anderson No. 1260).

6. Opp. 127, 130 and 132.

Incipit: Dans la dernière lettre que je. . . .

Sources: Thayer-Deiters-Riemann, V, 561–562; summarized and quoted briefly in Thayer-Forbes, p. 927. When Thayer copied it, the autograph was in the possession of Beethoven's nephew Karl's widow, Caroline, Vienna. It has since disappeared.

375. Ludewig Krause, Private Secretary of Prince Anton Heinrich Radziwill, to Beethoven

Berlin; August 3, 1824

Highly born Sir!

Highly honored Herr *Kapellmeister!*

Has it still not pleased you to answer me for my two devoted letters of April 6 and June 28?[1] As of this late date I have not been sent a report telling whether or not you have received the fifty ducats that I had the honor of forwarding to you in the name of His Highness, Prince Anton Radziwill. His Highness arrived here yesterday and, when I waited upon him today, asked at once about your Mass.[2]

Therefore, I request you most urgently and most devotedly to advise me, even with only a few words, concerning the receipt of the money and, if you can, to send me the Mass, or at least report to me when the Prince may count upon receiving it.

Please accept the assurance of the greatest esteem with which I have the honor to be

Your entirely most devoted,

Krause[3]

1. For the letter of June 28, see No. 371 above.

2. Radziwill had subscribed for one of the manuscript copies of the *Missa solemnis*.

3. On examining this signature, Astrid-Herma Smart read it as "Kranig." The reverse of the autograph also bears the annotation "Kranig" in an unknown hand. Sieghard Brandenburg, Beethoven-Archiv, Bonn, however, has confirmed the secretary's identity as Ludewig Krause.

Incipit: Ew. Hochwohlgeboren ist es immer. . . .

Sources: Alfred Christlieb Kalischer, "Beethoven und der Preussische Königshof unter Friedrich Wilhelm III," *Nord und Süd* 49 (May–June 1889), 203; reprinted in his *Beethoven und seine Zeitgenossen,* vol. 1, *Beethoven und Berlin* (Berlin: Schuster & Loeffler, 1909), p. 337. Autograph in the Staatsbibliothek zu Berlin–Preussischer Kulturbesitz, Mus. ms. autogr. Beethoven 35, 49; listed in Kalischer, "Beethoven-Autographe," p. 50, and Bartlitz, p. 133.

376. Hans Georg Nägeli to Beethoven

Zürich; August 3, 1824[1]

Honored Friend!

Finally I can write to you again with something worth reading. In six South German cities (Frankfurt, Darmstadt, Mainz, Karlsruhe, Stuttgart and Tübingen), I have given Lectures on Music, in which you are historically and critically portrayed as the artistic hero of the new century. For a long time you have had many admirers there, as well as in all of culturally educated Europe. Nevertheless, I may claim to have raised the appreciation for your unique high art to a *more conscious level of recognition.* My *Lectures* will be published by Cotta around the first of the year.[2] What you may have read about them in the daily papers is, for the most part, gossip, with much misunderstanding and little of their true content.

If you have only half as much feeling for my *words* as I do for your *music,* you will make every endeavor, as I now ask you to do, to promote subscriptions to my poems[3] among your acquaintances, and thus also to help me gain recognition—as I did for you—*si licet parva componere magnis.* In this connection, I would very much like to obtain, through your kind intercession, H[is] I[mperial] H[ighness] and E[minence], the Archduke Rudolph, for my subscription list. As a trial piece for the musical poems, I have had an offprint made of the one addressed to *you;* and I thought, although it must trouble you, to apply to you personally for a subscription. It is enclosed here.[4]

Gladden me soon with a compliant reply, and be assured of my unbounded esteem and friendship!

H[an]s Georg Nägeli

[Address:]
> Herr Ludwig van Beethoven
> Famous Musician
> Vienna

["Vienna" crossed out;
forwarding address in another hand:]
> Baron Wetzlar's Houses
> Gutenbrunn, Baden

1. Beethoven replied on September 9, 1824 (Anderson No. 1306); see also, e.g., Streicher to the Gesang-Verein in Zürich, September 17, 1824, and Nägeli to Beethoven, February 21, 1825 (Nos. 382 and 395 below).

2. *Vorlesungen über Musik* (Stuttgart and Tübingen: J. G. Cotta, 1826), dedicated to Archduke Rudolph.

3. *Liederkränze* (Zürich, 1825).

4. The laudatory poem "Ludwig van Beethoven," seven stanzas laden with Romantic imagery, is included in the sources cited below.

Incipit: Endlich kann ich Ihnen wieder. . . .

Sources: Theodor Frimmel, "Ein unveröffentlichter Brief Hans Georg Nägelis an Beethoven," in his *Beethoven-Studien* II (Munich: Georg Müller, 1906), pp. 127–130; Geiser, *Beethoven und die Schweiz*, pp. 74–77; and Martin Staehelin, *Hans Georg Nägeli und Ludwig van Beethoven* (Zürich: Hug, 1982), pp. 43–45 (with extensive commentary). Autograph in the Stadtbibliothek, Vienna.

377. Anton Diabelli to Beethoven, Baden

Vienna; August 7, 1824[1]

Herr Ludwig van Beethoven

Since I have not received a letter from you, much less seen anything of you yourself, I take the liberty herewith to inquire whether I can definitely count on receiving a *grand 4-hand Sonata in F* from your hand.[2] Since I must arrange my business affairs according to the works that are received, and since a grand Sonata *a 4* concerns me very much, I request you to let me know as soon as possible whether I can still count on receiving it *this year*. At the same time, I also wish to know the price of it. In expectation of a speedy reply,[3] I remain with greatest regards,

Your most obliging servant,

Ant[on] Diabelli

[Exterior:]
   To Herr Ludwig van Beethoven
   Famous Composer
   living in Guttenbrunn in the Schloss
   Baden

1. Beethoven was staying in Baden when this letter was written and made occasional trips back into the city for business or social affairs. Thayer, Kalischer (letters collection) and Kastner read the date as August 7. The number is unclear in the autograph, and Kalischer ("Autographe") read it as "4," as does Bartlitz. Examining the autograph of this letter, and comparing it with Diabelli's handwriting in other documents, Astrid-Herma Smart decided on "4," while I continue to read "7."

2. This sonata was never composed; for other references, see Beethoven to Diabelli, late 1822 or early 1823 (No. 302 above), and Diabelli to Beethoven, on or after August 24, 1824 (No. 380 below).

3. Beethoven wrote in the margin of the letter: "answered on Aug. 24" (Anderson No. 1304).

Incipit: Da ich weder ein Schreiben. . . .

Sources: Thayer-Deiters-Riemann, V, 141; Kalischer (German), V, 39–40; Kalischer-Shedlock, II, 326; Kastner (1910), pp. 822–823. Autograph in the Staatsbibliothek zu Berlin–Preussischer Kulturbesitz, Mus. ms. autogr. Beethoven 35, 44b; listed in Kalischer, "Beethoven-Autographe," p. 49, and Bartlitz, p. 131.

378. Heinrich Albert Probst to Beethoven

Leipzig; August 9, 1824[1]

Herr Ludwig van Beethoven
Baden, near Vienna

Already on the 10th of last month, I sent off the 100 ducats along with an enclosure for you by post to Herr Joseph Loydl and Co. in Vienna.[2] Therefore, if you still have received no report about it from this firm, since the departure of your honored letter of July 26, I ask that you be so kind as to inform them of this, for it is quite possible that your absence from Vienna could have prevented my friends from settling our business until now.

Otherwise I refer to the contents of my last letter of July 10,[3] and await the results of your kindness.

With truly highest regards,

H. A. Probst

1. Answers Beethoven's letter of July 26 (No. 373 above), with additional references to the composer's letter of July 3 (Anderson No. 1298).

2. Joseph Loydl and Co. was a leatherwares merchant at Bischofgasse No. 769. In his July 3 letter, Beethoven spells the agent's name "Loidl."

3. This letter seems not to have survived.

Incipit: Bereits am 10. vorigen Mts. sandte ich. . . .

Sources: Thayer-Deiters-Riemann, V, 104. Autograph in the Staatsbibliothek zu Berlin–Preussischer Kulturbesitz, Mus. ms. autogr. Beethoven 35, 71b; listed in Kalischer, "Beethoven-Autographe," p. 52, and Bartlitz, p. 141.

379. Heinrich Albert Probst to Beethoven

Leipzig; August 16, 1824

Herr Ludwig van Beethoven
Vienna

Your letter of the 9th of this month[1] crossed with mine of the same day. If, following the last one, our business is not fully settled to your satisfaction, just deliver the enclosure to Herr Loydl and Co., and receive the 100 # [ducats] for the manuscripts.

I am placing my hope in the great veneration that I have for your talent and gladly rely upon your word that you have designated only something substantial for me. Therefore I am breaking the rule by buying manuscripts unseen. But you are fully correct if you seek the reason for my policy not in me myself. A lot of gossip about a disagreement that a publishing house here had in a similar undertaking with you[2] is, to speak candidly, the reason why I would wish to see the manuscripts first.

Here you frankly have my confession, which I assume, however, to be said only to you.

Certainly, honored sir and friend, the more we are acquainted with each other, the more you shall find in me a reliable and honest publisher since, as often as I can, I prefer the honor and the pleasure to be of service rather diligently for Art. I would gladly have published your Ninth Symphony, but I hope in the future to remain securely in your confidence and friendship. Unfortunately, the pirate reprinting taking place everywhere, and especially in Austria, often prevents the German publisher from paying for a work appropriately.[3] Already I see the highway robbers[4] in Vienna waiting in ambush for new works to be supplied by you, in order to steal from me under the protection of the law. In order to escape from them, one could not publish anything that was any good; and I would truly prefer to publish no music at all, rather than enrich the world with something bad. Your works ought to appear as soon as possible and in fine printings — on this you can rely.

Accept the enduring esteem of

Your most obedient servant,

H. A. Probst

[Beethoven's pencil annotation on the exterior:]
"Answered on Wednesday, September 1, and wrote concerning the Symphony."[5]

1. Beethoven's letter of August 9 seems not to have survived.
2. A reference to Beethoven's aborted deal with C. F. Peters, Leipzig, in 1822–1823. Beethoven annotated the letter: "Do not believe the gossip; I have no time now

to explain about it, but have all the evidence in my hands. More later." Beethoven addresses this subject in his reply of August 28, 1824 (Anderson No. 1305).

3. Publisher Gottfried Christoph Härtel, Leipzig, had complained often about this widespread practice in his letters to Beethoven of two decades before.

4. Probst's word, *Raubschützen,* requires a more picturesque translation than simply "thieves" or "robbers." Indeed, its nearness to the word *Rabe* (raven, magpie; i.e., a stealing bird) also invoked the image of "birds of prey on the watch" for Lady Wallace, translating Nohl in the 1860s.

5. Beethoven's reply (Anderson No. 1305), dated August 28, was probably finished and sent on September 1.

Incipit: Ihr Brief vom 9. dieses begegnete. . . .

Sources: Thayer-Deiters-Riemann, V, 105. Excerpted in Schindler, 3d ed. (1860), pt. 2, p. 101; Schindler-MacArdle, p. 299; Nohl, *Briefe* (1865), p. 264; Nohl-Wallace, p. 154. Autograph in the Staatsbibliothek zu Berlin–Preussischer Kulturbesitz, Mus. ms. autogr. 35, 71c; listed in Kalischer, "Beethoven-Autographe," p. 52, and Bartlitz, p. 141.

380. Anton Diabelli to Beethoven, Baden

Vienna[; on or shortly after August 24, 1824][1]

With pleasure I see from your worthy letter that you intend to fulfill my wish. I therefore request you most courteously for a grand 4-hand sonata, the sooner the better.[2] As for the fee, I consent to your wish and pay you 80 ducats in gold for it, since I am convinced that your works are created not for the moment but for eternity. At the same time it is doubly valuable to me since you have not yet written any grand 4-hand sonatas, and you can also work here much more freely and more spontaneously since the whole keyboard is at your disposal and, so to speak, a whole army of tones is under your command. In complete confidence in the promise that you made, I remain with greatest esteem,

Your most obliging servant,

A. Diabelli
from Vienna

[Address:]

Herr Lud[wig] van Beethoven

Famous Composer
Guttenbrunn in the Schloss
Baden
Deliver in person

1. Answers Beethoven's letter of August 24, 1824 (Anderson No. 1304).

2. In his letter of August 7 (No. 377 above), Diabelli had requested such a sonata from Beethoven, who had promised it to the publisher already in late 1822 or early 1823 (No. 302 above). The discussion seems to have continued into the next year: see Beethoven to Diabelli, possibly after January 27, 1825 (No. 392 below).

Incipit: Mit Vergnügen ersehe ich. . . .

Sources: Thayer-Deiters-Riemann, V, 142–143; Kalischer (German), V, 41; Kalischer-Shedlock, II, 326. Autograph in the Staatsbibliothek zu Berlin–Preussischer Kulturbesitz, Mus. ms. autogr. Beethoven 35, 44c; listed in Kalischer, "Beethoven-Autographe," p. 49, and Bartlitz, p. 131.

381. *Johann Andreas Streicher*[1] *to Beethoven, Vienna*

Baden; September 5, 1824[2]

Most worthy Beethoven!

I have already thought very often about your situation, and especially about how and in what manner you could earn greater profit from your extraordinary talents. I take the liberty of placing this idea before you now, and ask you, out of truly affectionate feeling, to subject what you read here to serious consideration.

The first proposal is to give six subscription concerts this winter, on which not only your newest works but also older ones would be given, only with the greatest possible perfection. The arrangements for them, as with everything that concerns logistics, should be made by your friends, of which you have very many. Only these [friends] should not be sought among those who want to derive profit from you. For these six concerts one needs only the hall of the *Landstände*[3] or the University.[4] If there are 600 subscribers and each pays 2 florins *Conv. Geld* for a concert, then this makes 1,200 florins for each program,[5] and 7,200 *Conv.* florins for all six. If we suppose that the expenses for each concert should amount to 400 florins (which, however, is impossible), thus totaling 2,400 florins, then this still leaves 4,800 *Conv.*

florins or 12,000 florins *W.W.* remaining.[6] These 12,000 florins *W.W.* can be completely pure profit, and it only depends upon finding as many pieces as can fill up these six concerts. Surely they need not be only symphonies and vocal works?[7] One can also choose instrumental pieces now and then.[8]

If you want to agree to this proposal, the complete plan for it will be submitted to you at the end of October; one of the main points of this plan is that you will have to do *nothing at all* in connection with the entire matter except:

1. deliver the pieces of music, and determine when and in which order they should be done;
2. appear at the general rehearsal and also
3. [appear] at each performance.

The second proposal—which depends entirely upon you in its execution, and which, if you carry it out, must bring in at least 10,000 *Conv.* florins or 25,000 florins *W.W.*—is the publication of your collected works, as has been organized in the cases of Mozart, Haydn and Clementi.[9] This publication would be announced *a half year in advance* throughout Europe for prepayment or subscription, and a contract, according to the number of subscribers, would be concluded with the publisher who makes the most advantageous terms. If you state in the announcement that you will here and there alter all the keyboard pieces that were written before the introduction of the 5½ or 6 octave piano and adapt them for the present instruments; and (2) if you also supplement the piano works with a few new unpublished pieces, then this publication is to be regarded as a completely fresh, newly composed work and also must be purchased by those who already possess your earlier works. It is impossible that this matter could cause you so much trouble that you could not undertake it. You owe this to yourself, your nephew (for whom you can then do things more easily), and to posterity.

Both proposals lie within the bounds of possibility and have to be profitable. The latter appears to me the easiest and most useful, and is well worth your consideration.[10]

Take what I have said as the opinion of a friend who has known you for fully 36 years and to whom nothing could give greater joy than to see you free from care.

I am

                Your most sincerely devoted,

                Andreas Streicher

1. Streicher (1761–1833), piano manufacturer and composer; married to Nannette Stein (1769–1833), daughter of a famous Augsburg keyboard maker. Beethoven had met Nanette in Augsburg in 1787 and probably made the acquaintance of Andreas there as well. The couple set up business in Vienna in 1794. Several days after this letter, Streicher must have penned another note to Beethoven, which was answered on September 16 (Anderson No. 1307).

2. Follows a conversation that Streicher had with Beethoven in Baden on September 3 or 4 since he told the composer in a conversation book: "I shall write everything down for you [concerning the proposal] by tomorrow or the day after tomorrow" (Köhler et al., *Konversationshefte,* VI, 322). Shortly thereafter, Beethoven and his nephew Karl went to Vienna for a few days of apartment hunting and returned to Baden by September 9. Thus, Streicher, still in Baden on September 5, was writing to Beethoven in Vienna.

3. Known today as the Landhaus, this seat of the Lower Austrian provincial government had most recently been used by Beethoven for one of the rehearsals for his May 7 concert and was a location seriously considered for the May 23 repeat.

4. The University Hall is often depicted in conjunction with a performance of Haydn's *Creation* there on March 27, 1808, with Beethoven in attendance.

5. Streicher uses the term *Musik* here, just as Beethoven's brother Carl had done on April 22, 1802 (No. 38 above), to designate a concert.

6. The remaining 4,800 *Conv.* florins would more closely equal 10,000 florins W.W.

7. Such an expensive combination had essentially constituted Beethoven's recent concerts of May 7 and 23.

8. Instrumental works using more modest forces would, of course, be less expensive to produce.

9. These were not *Gesamtausgaben* in the modern musicological sense but essentially collections of piano music and/or chamber music that involved the piano.

10. Well-meaning friends are always long on such advice as this, minimizing the amount of work and worry that will ultimately have to be expended. Indeed, despite Streicher's lucrative projections, both these projects represented a potentially great deal of time, energy and stress on Beethoven's part.

Incipit: Ich habe schon sehr oft über Ihre Lage nachgedacht. . . .

Sources: Thayer-Deiters-Riemann, V, 118–119. Autograph in the Staatsbibliothek zu Berlin–Preussischer Kulturbesitz, Mus. ms. autogr. Beethoven 35, 46a; listed in Kalischer, "Beethoven-Autographe," p. 49, and Bartlitz, p. 132.

382. Johann Andreas Streicher to the Gesang-Verein, Zürich[1]

Vienna; September 17, 1824

To the Honorable Board of Directors of the
Singing Society, Zürich

The grand Mass of Herr Ludwig van Beethoven, which was heard in public here for the first time on May 7,[2] is, according to the unanimous declaration of all connoisseurs, the most remarkable religious composition that has appeared since Handel's *Messiah,* indeed as much for the novelty of its setting, its harmonic and melodic originality, as for (indeed most importantly) its pious sense of devotion to God, which every note expresses. Entirely in accordance with the spirit that should prevail in church music, arias and duets that direct the [listener's] attention to only a few people singing are completely avoided, and for this reason a *quartet* of soloists was selected, which alternates with the chorus or performs simultaneously with them.

Since it will take a very long time for the public to become acquainted with this work,[3] the undersigned has requested Herr van Beethoven to make it available to various singing societies, but in a version for voices and a reduction for piano or organ, especially because a few societies have already made inquiries about it. Herr van Beethoven is completely willing, and thus it happens with his approval (as the enclosure[4] shows) that the undersigned takes the liberty to offer such an arrangement to your honored Singing Society under the following conditions:

1. The Singing Society obligates itself to retain this work solely for its own use, and to pass it on to no one, either for publication or for any other purpose.
2. This Mass will be supplied in a piano reduction, over which all the vocal parts will be placed in score, and yet each part will still be copied separately in a clean and correct manner, and will be checked and confirmed by Herr van Beethoven himself that this work has been composed by him and copied error free.
3. For the above Herr van Beethoven would receive, through exchange

or draft on a local bank, Fifty Ducats in specie, in which price the expenses of copying are included.

4. [Upon receipt of] your reply, as well as the remittance of the amount, made out to *Herr Ludwig van Beethoven, Vienna,* the work itself will be dispatched to the venerable Society 14 days afterward.

The undersigned has taken this proposition upon himself with great pleasure, all the more so because it has been proven that very many benefits have already been derived from public performances by large singing societies,[5] and that, especially at church festivals, religious edification has been heightened.

With great esteem and devotion,

Andreas Streicher

1. The intended addressee was probably the Zürich Singinstitut, whose conductor was publisher-composer Hans Georg Nägeli. Beethoven himself had written to Nägeli on September 9 (Anderson No. 1306). The present letter, along with Beethoven's letter to Streicher of September 16 (Anderson No. 1307), was earlier in the possession of Nägeli's son, Zürich, and by 1865 in the possession of the wife of Major Charras, Basel. While Nägeli had been away on a lecture tour (see his August 3, 1824, letter, No. 376 above), the choral society had collapsed.

2. Only three movements of the *Missa solemnis* (the Kyrie, Credo and Agnus Dei) appeared on the May 7, 1824, program. The entire *Missa* had been performed in St. Petersburg on April 7 of that year.

3. Streicher means here the *Missa solemnis* in its original form, with orchestral accompaniment.

4. Beethoven's form attestation to Streicher, copied in another hand and signed by the composer, September 16, 1824 (Anderson No. 1307). As Anderson implies, Streicher must have sent copies of the present letter as well as copies of Beethoven's endorsement to several singing societies.

5. Beginning early in the second decade of the nineteenth century, secular singing societies, often with social and patriotic overtones, patterned after Zelter's Berlin *Liedertafel* (1809), proliferated in Germany and German-speaking regions.

Incipit: Die grosse Messe des Herrn. . . .

Sources: Nohl, *Briefe* (1865), pp. 271–272; briefly quoted in his *Beethoven's Leben* (1877), III, 522. Nohl made his copy from the autograph, then in the possession of Hans Georg Nägeli's son, living in Zürich. The endorsement, signed by Beethoven, was sold by the younger Nägeli to the music dealers Fries und Holzmann (Zürich), who in turn sold it to the wife of Colonel Charras in Basel. At the time Emily Anderson made her collection, the autograph could not be traced.

383. *Johann Andreas Streicher to Beethoven, Baden*

Vienna; September 29, 1824[1]

Most honored Beethoven!

Today my wife brought me your charming, very pleasant letter that you were so kind as to send me yet in Baden.[2] Your excuse that you are seldom at home is very valid, and you would be wrong if you did not strengthen yourself as long as possible for the coming winter.

The bearer of this is Herr Stumpff,[3] a fine German man who has already lived for 34 years in London, and who is traveling a short time in his Fatherland for his recreation. The reason why he is coming to Baden is to see you — most worthy Beethoven — the man of whom Germany is proud. Receive him in a kind and friendly manner, as a saint would receive a devout pilgrim who had made a journey from afar.

I have spoken with Czerny today. He will gladly undertake the arrangement of the Symphony for [piano] 2- and 4-hands, and asks only that he be sent the score.[4] Herr Lachner will do the same, with true devotion, in the case of the Mass.[5]

God keep you well, so that you may soon again see

your,

A. Streicher

1. As given in Thayer-Deiters-Riemann, V, 121, 132, both the present letter and Beethoven's letter to Stumpff (now Anderson No. 1311) are dated September 29. Kalischer and Bartlitz both agree that the present letter reads September 29, although Nohl interpreted the date as September 24. Beethoven's open and friendly tone in Anderson No. 1311 indicates that he and Stumpff were already on cordial terms. Stumpff's reminiscences indicate that Beethoven took to him quickly on his arrival in Baden; indeed the composer probably remembered him from the summer of

1818, when he came from London to tune and regulate his Broadwood piano (see Broadwood to Beethoven, July 17, 1818, No. 252 above.

2. As can be seen from Streicher's letter of September 5, he, like Beethoven, had spent some time at Baden. Streicher's wife was Nannette Stein Streicher (1769–1833), who often counseled Beethoven in household matters.

3. Johann Andreas Stumpff (1769–1846), born in Thuringia and active as a harp manufacturer in England, played a significant role from afar during Beethoven's physical decline and final illness. See n.1 concerning their earlier acquaintance.

4. Ultimately Carl Czerny made an arrangement for piano four-hands, published by Schott (Mainz) and Probst (Leipzig) in 1829.

5. Franz Lachner (1803–1890), organist at the Luthern church in Vienna, seems not to have made the proposed arrangement.

Incipit: Meine Frau überbrachte mir heute. . . .

Sources: Thayer-Deiters-Riemann, V, 121. Excerpted in Nohl, *Briefe* (1865), p. 335, and Nohl-Wallace, p. 236. Autograph in the Staatsbibliothek zu Berlin–Preussischer Kulturbesitz, Mus. ms. autogr. Beethoven 35, 46b; listed in Kalischer, "Beethoven-Autographe," p. 49, and Bartlitz, p. 132.

384. Beethoven to B. Schotts Söhne, Mainz

Vienna; November 16, 1824

Dear Sirs!

My answer to your last [letter] has waited a long time[1] because I became ill in the country; however, I have now fairly well recovered. I therefore report to you only that by the day after tomorrow both works[2] will be delivered to Fries and Company. By the end of this month, the Quartet[3] will also follow; I would be pleased if, by then, I could receive the fee designated for it directly upon delivery of the Quartet.

For today it is not possible for me to tell you anything else further, except that I shall write to you again in a few days,[4] when I shall make you a proposition that will perhaps please you.

With esteem and friendship,

Your most devoted,

Beethoven

[Exterior:]
   Herren B. Schotts Söhne
   Grand Ducal Court Music Publisher and Dealer
   Mainz
   Weyergarten Lit. F. No. 382

1. It is not clear to which letter from Schott Beethoven refers.
2. Symphony No. 9, Op. 125, and *Missa solemnis,* Op. 123.
3. String Quartet, Op. 127.
4. Beethoven's letter (Anderson No. 1321); Staehelin and Brandenburg date it ca. November 23, 1824.
Incipit: Meine Antwort auf ihr letztes. . . .
Sources: Joseph Kerman, "Comment and Chronicle," *19th Century Music* 8, no. 2 (Fall 1984), 183–184 (with facsimile); fuller transcription in Staehelin and Brandenburg, *Briefwechsel,* pp. 17–18. Autograph in the Ira F. Brilliant Center for Beethoven Studies, San Jose State University, San Jose, California.

385. Prince Nicolas Galitzin to Beethoven

St. Petersburg; December 5, 1824

My dear and worthy Monsieur de Beethoven!

I received your last letter upon my return from a long journey that I made into the interior of the country, and since my return I have been witness to a flood that very nearly submerged all of St. Petersburg.[1] All of this means that I have been a long time in replying to you, and I am all the more sorry since my reply should bring you assistance, which I am delighted to be able to send you, but the delay in forwarding it was beyond my control. I am delivering to Count von Lebzeltern,[2] the Austrian minister, the sum of 50 ducats to be delivered to you, and I hope you will have it soon.

I am truly very sorry that your health suffers so much, but suffering is the indispensable lot of the human condition, and it seems that geniuses such as you ought to impose themselves upon nature and force it to respect those who, like you, distinguish themselves from the rest of humanity.[3]

I cannot express with what impatience I await the first of the Quartets.[4] I have also asked you for a copy of your latest symphony and overture,[5] for which I will pay the expenses with much pleasure. I am planning to have your beautiful Mass[6] performed one more time for the benefit of the flood victims of St. Petersburg, and I will want the Symphony and the overture to arrive also in time that they can be performed.

Do not forget me in all that I have requested of you.

You ask me if the number of subscribers to your Mass in St. Petersburg will be considerable. I think that one could assemble about forty of them, especially if there is a *Klavierauszug*[7] added to the score.

Accept the expression of my very sincere affection,

P[rince] N[icolas] Galitzin

[P.S.] I never received the two pieces of music for piano that you sent to me last year.

[On the outside of the letter is designated Beethoven's residence in Baden and then a remark in the composer's hand:] "From the address it must be supposed that the letter was delivered to Stieglitz & Co."[8]

1. Late in August 1824, Czar Alexander I set out from St. Petersburg on a journey that took him southeast to Perm, Svertlovsk, Orenburg and the Kirghiz Steppes, returning on November 5. Since no letter from Galitzin seems to have survived from between July 28 and December 5, it is possible that Galitzin may have been in the czar's entourage for all or part of that tour.

Shortly after November 5, torrential rains broke out across the face of Europe and continued for two weeks. In St. Petersburg, the waters of the Neva reached eighteen feet above ordinary level on November 18–19, with the result that between twelve and fifteen hundred people in the city alone lost their lives.

2. Ludwig von Lebzeltern had been Austrian envoy to St. Petersburg since 1811.

3. Beethoven answered this patronizing remark sarcastically in late July 1825 (Anderson No. 1405).

4. String Quartet, Op. 127.

5. Symphony No. 9 and *Consecration of the House* Overture, requested first in Galitzin's letter of June 16 and then again on July 28, 1824 (Nos. 370 and 374 above).

6. *Missa solemnis*, Op. 123.

7. Galitzin uses the German word for piano reduction in this French-language letter.

8. Galitzin's financial agent, mentioned in previous letters, most recently July 28,

1824. Beethoven had spent the summer in Baden and seems to have returned to Vienna around mid-October.

Incipit: J'ai reçu votre dernière lettre à mon retour. . . .

Sources: Thayer-Deiters-Riemann, V, 562–563; summarized in Thayer-Forbes, p. 927. Details on Alexander's journey and the St. Petersburg flood may be found in Alan Palmer, *Alexander I: Tsar of War and Peace* (London: Weidenfeld & Nicolson, 1974), pp. 394–396. When Thayer copied it, the autograph was in the possession of Beethoven's nephew Karl's widow, Caroline, Vienna. It has since disappeared.

386. Johann Reinhold Schultz[1] to Tobias Haslinger

London; December 10, 1824

Herr Haslinger, *Kapellmeister*
c/o Herr Steiner & Comp., Vienna

Best, most loyal and excellent old Friend!

[The letter begins with greetings to Frau Haslinger.[2] Schultz wants to interest Haslinger in becoming a sort of Viennese agent and correspondent for the *Harmonicon,* in order to obtain music and books from Vienna. He wants to begin "speculating" with Conradin Kreutzer's opera *Libussa*[3] and also wants to acquire other opera scores.]

Further, I would like to know if you could not obtain for me the beautiful Overture by Beethoven for the opening of the Josephstadt Theater,[4] in case it is not sold to [a publisher in?] London or elsewhere.

[Beyond this, Schultz inquires about what is happening in the lives of Mayseder and Carl Czerny, in order to report on them in the *Harmonicon.*[5] Then he urgently presses Haslinger once more concerning *Libussa* and closes the letter.]

J. R. Schultz[6]

[Postscript in the left margin:]

After I had so much misfortune with Beethoven's Trio,[7] I do not want to risk printing the agreed-upon Sonatas that you sent with me.[8] I am therefore keeping them for you.

I have a few little things for your wife, which are, however, more worthy of acceptance than those for which you have thanked me, in an entirely unmerited manner, through Stumpff[9] — also something for Beethoven[10] — and I only await a secure opportunity.

1. Johann Reinhold Schultz (previously misidentified as "Edward" Schultz) was a London businessman of German origin, closely associated with William Ayrton's music journal, the *Harmonicon*. He had met Beethoven briefly in 1816 and (in the company of Tobias Haslinger) spent September 28, 1823, visiting Beethoven in Baden; his account subsequently appeared in the *Harmonicon* 2 (January 1824), 10–11, was included in Sonneck, *Impressions,* pp. 149–154, and summarized in Thayer-Forbes, pp. 870–871. Schultz also translated and edited several letters from Vienna, recounting Beethoven's final illness and death, for that journal. See Alan Tyson, "J. R. Schultz and His Visit to Beethoven," *Musical Times* 113 (May 1972), 450–451.

2. Early in 1826, Tobias Haslinger took over proprietorship of the publishing business from his partner Sigmund Anton Steiner. On Haslinger's death in 1842, his wife, Caroline (died 1848), and son Carl (1816–1868) assumed ownership of the firm.

3. Kreutzer's *Libussa* was successfully premiered in Vienna in 1822, and a vocal score (published in Vienna by Pennauer) had appeared by May 1823. Extensive excerpts (possibly pirate reprintings) were published in Braunschweig by May 1824 and in Hamburg by May 1825.

4. *Consecration of the House* Overture, Op. 124, published by Schott (Mainz) in piano arrangements by Carl Czerny (April and July 1825) and in full score (December 1825). Haslinger would not have approached Beethoven for materials to send to Schultz because at this time the composer was greatly upset over Trautwein's Berlin publication of the unauthorized arrangement by C. W. Henning in December 1824. See Beethoven to Henning, January 1, 1825 (Anderson No. 1343), and related correspondence.

5. Joseph Mayseder (1789–1863), prominent Viennese violinist (previously a member of the Rasumovsky Quartet) and composer; Carl Czerny (1791–1857), Viennese pianist, pedagogue and former student of Beethoven's.

6. Prompted by Thayer's misidentification of the author's first name as "Edward," Frimmel read the unclear initials as "J. E."

7. Variations on Wenzel Müller's song "Ich bin der Schneider Kakadu," Op. 121a. See Alan Tyson, "Beethoven's 'Kakadu' Variations and Their English History," *Musical Times* 104 (February 1963), 108–110; (May 1963), 343.

8. Probably the Piano Sonatas, Opp. 109, 110 and 111, published virtually simultaneously in 1821–1822 by the Schlesingers (Berlin and Paris), Steiner (Vienna) and London publishers as well. Haslinger's letters to Hummel (November 10, 1825, No. 419 below) and Peters (October 18, 1826, No. 440 below) indicate that Haslinger (and his partner Steiner) bore little love for the Schlesingers and may have been promoting the piracy of their mutual publications in Schlesinger's marketing territory by giving

copies to Schultz. At any rate, as Schultz probably learned, these works had been available in London for over a year.

9. Johann Andreas Stumpff had returned to London on December 6, 1824, having visited Beethoven in Baden in late September. During Stumpff's visit, Beethoven expressed his admiration for Handel and lamented that he had been able to examine only such works as *Messiah* and *Alexander's Feast*. "At that moment," wrote Stumpff in his memoirs, "I made a secret vow: Beethoven, you shall have the works of Handel for which your heart is longing if they are anywhere to be found" (Thayer-Deiters-Riemann, V, 122–127; summarized in Thayer-Krehbiel, III, 181–182, and Thayer-Forbes, pp. 918–920). Stumpff had obviously brought thanks (possibly even gifts) from Haslinger home for Schultz.

10. Probably an early reference to Stumpff's gift of Handel's collected *Works*, mentioned (in his letter to Beethoven, July 29, 1825, No. 414 below) as having been obtained shortly after his arrival back from Vienna. Ultimately, Stumpff sent the set on August 24, 1826 (No. 435 below).

Incipit: Unknown.

Sources: Excerpts (above) in Frimmel, "Beethovenstellen aus zeitgenössischen Briefen," pp. 49–51; partially reprinted in his *Beethoven-Handbuch*, II, 160. In 1925, the autograph was in the possession of Dr. Gustav Riehl, professor at the University of Vienna. Riehl, in turn, had obtained it, sometime earlier, from Haslinger's decendants in Windischgarten.

387. Beethoven to Loydl und Co.,[1] through Johann van Beethoven (Draft)

[Vienna; ca. December 13–14, 1824]

My brother [Johann] is writing to Loydl, so that he sends this letter to Probst:[2]

Report that the amount [offered by] Herr Probst really displeases me; my brother [Ludwig] is too kind, and because of his high standing, is contemptuous of all the little vexations of life, but I do not think [so]. Immediately after the letter from Herr Probst, I inquired around and other publishers offered themselves; since my brother had given me these works[3] in payment of a debt, I had the right to see where I [could get] more, and all the more so, because I am certain that I would not have received this

[sum] from Herr Probst, all the more since he already sought to press my brother to a terrible degree, since it now publicly shows that my brother is not in a position to deal [in business affairs], so I have handled this work myself; the great number of my own business affairs was the reason that I did not do so earlier.

This letter to the baker,[4] to be closed with his seal, and sent on from there.

1. Leatherwares merchant Joseph Loydl and Co. was the Viennese business partner of the Leipzig publisher Heinrich Albert Probst. See the Probst-Beethoven correspondence earlier in 1824 (Nos. 345, 349, 378 and 379 above and also in Anderson) for further details. In the conversation book, Beethoven spells Loydl's name "Sodel."

2. Thus Beethoven hoped to place the following words into Johann's mouth, or rather his pen.

3. The works included the *Consecration of the House* Overture, Op. 124, the Bagatelles, Op. 126, the *Opferlied,* Op. 121b, the *Bundeslied,* Op. 122, and *Der Kuss,* Op. 128. On August 16, 1824 (No. 379 above), Probst had offered Beethoven 100 ducats for them; on ca. November 23 (Anderson No. 1321), Beethoven offered them to Schott for 130 ducats; and on December 29, 1824 (No. 389 below), Johann did likewise.

4. The baker is probably Johann's brother-in-law, Leopold Obermayer.

Incipit: Der Bruder schreibt. . . .

Sources: Köhler et al., *Konversationshefte,* VII, 46–47, 360 (© Deutscher Verlag für Musik, Leipzig). Autograph in the Staatsbibliothek zu Berlin–Preussischer Kulturbesitz.

388. *Charles Neate to Beethoven*

London; December 20, 1824[1]

My dear Beethoven!

For a long time I have wished to see you in this country, where I believe that your talent will be appreciated more than in any other. I have just now received the pleasant charge from the Philharmonic Society to invite you to come to England, and doubtless to stay a long time. You will be in the position here to acquire a significant sum of money, and thereby more than sufficiently compensate yourself for the fatigue and difficulties of the journey.

The Philharmonic Society is disposed to give you 300 Guineas for your visit, and expects in return that you will take charge of the direction of your own works, at least one of which will be performed at each concert. Also it expects that you will write a symphony and a concerto that will be presented during your stay; afterward, however, you can regard these compositions as your property.

I hope, dear Beethoven, that you will accept this proposal, for the Society will not be persuaded to offer a more lucrative one; and I think, in truth, that you will fare all the better when you visit this country, since you will find nothing but friends.

You can also give a concert during your stay, at which you might bring in at least £500; also there are many opportunities to win honor and money from your great talent and widespread fame.

If you bring along the Quartets of which I wrote you, that is as good as £100 more,[2] so that you can be assured of taking a large sum of money home with you; and I see no reason why you should not take enough with you to make all the rest of your life pleasant and free from cares.

I hope that you will write immediately and accept the proposal; then I will have the opportunity better to convince you that I am your true friend. Here you will find yourself surrounded by many who will gladly express to you their esteem and veneration for the great Beethoven, whose fame is greater than anyone's has ever been before in this country.[3]

Our concerts begin in the middle of February and finish at the end of June. Your new Symphony has arrived and will be rehearsed for the first time on January 17; I hope, however, that you will be here to conduct it yourself on our first concert.[4]

By the way, they say that there is a copy of it in Paris; I believe, however, that this report is unfounded.

Please do not fail to write to me quite soon, and be assured that I remain

Your very sincere friend,

Charles Neate

My address is
Foley Place
London

[P.S.] Be so kind as to write me either in French or in German using French letters.[5]

1. Answered by Beethoven's letter of January 15, 1825 (Anderson No. 1344).

2. Beethoven had offered Neate three quartets for 100 guineas on February 25, 1823 (Anderson No. 1144). Neate mentioned a payment scheme for them in his letter to Beethoven on September 2, 1823 (No. 334 above). By July 16, 1823, however, Beethoven mentioned only one quartet to Ries (Anderson No. 1209), as he did to Neate on January 15, 1825 (Anderson No. 1344).

3. Probably an allusion to Haydn's visits to England in the 1790s.

4. The Symphony No. 9 received its London premiere by the Philharmonic Society on March 21, 1825.

5. Neate would thus avoid having to decipher cursive Gothic German.

Incipit (as translated): Es war lange Zeit mein Wunsch. . . . / Lange schon habe ich gewünscht. . . .

Sources: The French original may not have survived, but there are two German translations: Thayer-Deiters-Riemann, V, 159–160, and Nohl, *Neue Briefe* (1867), pp. 257–258. The version in Thayer-Deiters-Riemann may have been made by Beethoven's nephew Karl or Schindler; it is partially quoted in Schindler (1860), pt. 2, p. 90, and Schindler-MacArdle, p. 292. The manuscript of this translation is in Schindler's *Nachlass*, Staatsbibliothek zu Berlin–Preussischer Kulturbesitz, Mus. ms. autogr. Beethoven 35, 43b; listed in Kalischer, "Beethoven-Autographe," p. 49, and Bartlitz, p. 130. A close comparison of the texts indicates that Nohl's salutation and body (translator unknown) may be slightly closer to Neate's original, while Thayer-Deiters-Riemann provides the postscript material omitted in Nohl. The version printed in Nohl was taken from the Fischhof Manuscript (Staatsbibliothek zu Berlin–Preussischer Kulturbesitz); see Brenneis, "Fischhof-Manuskript," pp. 72–74. The whereabouts of the autograph are unknown.

389. Johann van Beethoven to B. Schotts Söhne, Mainz

Vienna; December 29, 1824[1]

Dear Sir!

Since my dear brother has now transferred to you, for 130 Viennese ducats, the works that he had earlier transferred to me,[2] I now notify you that I agree to everything that my brother does, although I had very good offers for these works from two parties;[3] nevertheless, out of respect for my brother and your firm, I transfer these works at the agreed-upon price of 130 ducats, with the condition that you send me three copies of each.

These works are now already cleanly copied, and I am ready to deliver these works to the firm of Fries and Co. as soon as I receive from you the bill of exchange at three months, and it is accepted by Fries.

Accept the assurance of my esteem, with which I am

Your most devoted,

Johann van Beethoven
Landowner

1. Follows as a result of four letters written by Beethoven: to Schott in November 1824 (Anderson No. 1321) and on December 5 (Anderson No. 1322), to his brother Johann on December 10 (Anderson No. 1323), and to Schott on December 17 (Anderson No. 1325). This letter accompanied a letter from Beethoven to Schott ("Ich sage Ihnen nur . . ."), which Anderson (No. 1357) had placed in March 1825, but which Staehelin and Brandenburg date as December 29, 1824. To these must be added Beethoven to Johann (Anderson No. 1089), which Sieghard Brandenburg, Beethoven-Archiv, Bonn, has recently redated as "shortly before or on December 29, 1824."

2. *Consecration of the House* Overture, Op. 124; six Bagatelles, Op. 126; three songs (*Opferlied*, Op. 121b; *Bundeslied*, Op. 122; and *Der Kuss*, Op. 128) — offered by Beethoven as a single lot for 130 ducats on ca. November 23, 1824 (Anderson No. 1321).

3. Johann may have been bluffing, although Beethoven's letter of December 10 indicates that he had been negotiating with Probst for them. The bagatelles and songs had been part of a package offer made to Peters some years before, with negative results.

Incipit: Da mein lieber Bruder die Werke. . . .

Sources: Nohl, *Neue Briefe* (1867), p. 257; Thayer-Deiters-Riemann, V, 115–116; Kalischer (German), V, 85; Kalischer-Shedlock, II, 347–348; Staehelin and Brandenburg, *Briefwechsel*, p. 24. Autograph in the Stadtbibliothek, Mainz.

390. Beethoven to Tobias Haslinger

[Baden?; ca. 1824?][1]

Paternoster Gässel,

Be so kind as to send the enclosure to Karl prestissimo, since I do not know whether the letter carrier takes letters there.

Vale

Beethoven

[Reverse/exterior:]
To Herr von To*bia*s Hasslinger[2]
in Vienna.
Deliver to the Paternoster Gässel
at the Graben.

1. The Beethoven-Haus previously determined this letter (one sheet, two sides) to have originated in about 1824. Given the destination Vienna in the address, it may have been written from some nearby resort (e.g., Baden), which the composer frequented in the summers. More recently, however, Sieghard Brandenburg, Beethoven-Archiv, Bonn, has hypothesized that this note may have been written after nephew Karl's suicide attempt on August 6, 1826, therefore while the young man was recuperating in the Allgemeines Krankenhaus.

2. Beethoven plays with Haslinger's name in several ways: adding a misplaced *von;* underlining the central syllable of his first name; doubling the *s* in his surname (a common practice) for the potential humorous effect on *Hass* (hate).

Incipit: Seyd so gut zum Karl zu schicken. . . .

Sources: Helms and Staehelin, "Bewegungen . . . 1973–1979," p. 353. Autograph in the Stadtarchiv, Bonn (Ii 98/529) since 1975. Acquired from O. Kiraly, Hayward, California.

1825

391. Carl Wilhelm Henning[1] to Beethoven

Berlin; January 13, 1825[2]

The astonishment that you express to me in your letter of January 1 is, I can assure you, surpassed by that which I felt upon reading its contents, and I am convinced that you will deem it well founded if I herewith recall to your memory the following facts that pertain to the settlement of the business matter in question between you and the Direction of the Königstädtisches Theater. This business matter, to be sure, has been concluded so that the above Direction, for the purchase price of 56 *Louis d'ors,* has come into possession of your composition to the *Ruins of Athens,*[3] along with the Overture[4] under discussion, whose score you handed to me personally; and that they exclusively could do with it as they like; and according to your wish the assurance was given to you through me that the *Overture* would not be published earlier than one year after receiving of it.

With the best desire to comply with your wish, however, the edition for 4-hands that has appeared through Herr T. Trautwein[5] absolutely cannot be recalled, since this honorable firm came into possession of this piece by legal means, and has already published it. Concerning other *arrangements,* however, that likewise were to appear, I shall now, out of respect for your person and your wishes, gladly give up my intention and lay aside the material that is already completed in manuscript. Since this matter is based upon legal principles, and since nothing further about it can be changed on my part, I only wish that it will cause you no further unpleasantness. With the assurance that I shall never cease to honor in you the esteemed master, I ask you to retain your affection for me, and I have the honor to remain

Your most devoted,

C. W. Henning

1. Henning (1784–1867), music director of the Königstädtisches Theater in Berlin, 1824–1826. In October 1823, he and Heinrich E. Bethmann, general director of the theater, had come to Vienna, where they purchased a score of *The Ruins of Athens,*

Op. 114, from Beethoven. Evidently with it, but not part of the deal, as the composer intended its terms, was a score of the *Consecration of the House* Overture, Op. 124. For the opening of the remodeled Josephstadt Theater in 1822, Beethoven had revised his Op. 114 score, adding new music and replacing the original overture (not considered integral to the incidental music itself) with Op. 124.

2. Answers Beethoven's letter to Henning of January 1, 1825 (Anderson No. 1343); Beethoven's declaration as a result of this exchange appeared in the *Wiener Zeitschrift*, March 5, 1825 (Anderson, III, 1442–1443).

3. Op. 114.

4. Op. 124.

5. Traugott Trautwein, Berlin publisher.

Incipit: Das Erstaunen, welches mir Ew. Wohlgeboren in Ihrer Zuschrift. . . .

Sources: Kalischer (German), V, 136–137; Kalischer-Shedlock, II, 376. Autograph (copy) in the Staatsbibliothek zu Berlin–Preussischer Kulturbesitz, Mus. ms. autogr. Beethoven 48, 1; listed in Kalischer, "Beethoven-Autographe," pp. 36–37, and Bartlitz, p. 195.

392. *Beethoven to Anton Diabelli*

[Vienna; possibly after ca. January 27, 1825][1]

My good fellow!

Why, then, do you still want a sonata from me?![2] You have a whole army of composers who can do it much better than I can. Give each of them a measure—what marvelous work may be expected from it? Hurrah for this, your Austrian *Verein*, which knows how to turn a cobbler's patch into a masterwork![3]

Now, my good fellow, I have a request for you: do me the *kindness* of not reprinting this bungled, corrupt and—in spite of all assurances of proprietary rights—illegally printed piano version of the overture.[4] Therefore, be so kind, I ask you—in the name of *our old friendship* (for the *new* [friendship] is not worth much to you).

Farewell—grant my request.

Your old *Amicus,*

Beethoven

1. In the midst of selling the *Consecration of the House* Overture, Op. 124, to Schott and dissolving his publication agreement with Probst in Leipzig, Beethoven spent January and February 1825 in saving face following Trautwein's Berlin publication of Henning's arrangement of the overture in December 1824 (see No. 391 above). When he wrote to Henning on January 1, 1825 (Anderson No. 1343), Beethoven had heard news of the Berlin edition but presumably had not yet seen it. He seems to have seen the arrangement by the time he discussed it with Schott on February 5, 1825 (Anderson No. 1349), but surely had done so by the time he printed his admonitory declaration in the *Wiener Zeitschrift*, March 5, 1825 (Anderson, III, 1442–1443). Moreover, from the wording in the second paragraph, Beethoven had probably already received Henning's defensive letter of January 13, 1825 (No. 391 above).

Diabelli's collection of fifty variations by as many composers had appeared in June 1824, but Beethoven still noted the title in his conversation book on January 27, 1825, or a day or so afterward (Köhler et al., *Konversationshefte*, VII, 118); thus the allusion in the first paragraph may have been fresh on his mind. On the basis of the above, this letter possibly dates from the period ca. January 28–ca. February 5, 1825, although it could have originated as much as three weeks on either side of this time frame. Sieghard Brandenburg, however, dates this letter "Summer 1825."

2. On August 7, 1824 (No. 377 above), the publisher Diabelli had repeated his request—seemingly made almost two years earlier—for a sonata in F for piano four hands. Beethoven set the fee at 80 ducats on August 24, 1824 (Anderson No. 1304), and Diabelli consented shortly thereafter (No. 380 above). The present undated letter seems to derive from a later period, when Diabelli may have approached Beethoven yet again for a work in this style. In any case, Beethoven never composed a four-hand sonata for Diabelli.

3. Beethoven humorously alludes to Diabelli's 1819 scheme to submit a waltz of his own to prominent native composers, with a request to compose a variation on it. In June 1824, Diabelli published the work of fifty musicians under the collective title *Vaterländischer Künstlerverein* (Patriotic Society of Artists, made up of "Composers and Virtuosi of Vienna and the I.R. Austrian States"). The collection was popular, but of mediocre artistic worth. Even though Beethoven himself had responded with his own set of Thirty-Three Variations, Op. 120, Diabelli's other collection still inspired his tongue-in-cheek commentary here.

4. Beethoven had urgent reason for not wanting Diabelli to reprint the Overture, Op. 124: not only had he and his brother Johann sold the rights to Schott (see No. 389 above), but, according to the title page of the fifty *Veränderungen* by members of the *Vaterländischer Künstlerverein*, its publisher Diabelli had a cooperative business agreement with Probst in Leipzig, from whom Beethoven was withdrawing his offer to publish the selfsame overture.

Incipit: Wozu wolltet ihr denn noch eine Sonate. . . .

Sources: Sotheby & Co., *Catalogue of Valuable Printed Books, Music, Autograph Letters and Historical Documents,* auction catalog (London, June 13, 1966), item 147, p. 34. Autograph in the Beethoven-Archiv, Bonn, NE 68, since 1966; listed in Schmidt, "Beethovenhandschriften," p. 78. Text transcription kindly furnished by Sieghard Brandenburg, Beethoven-Archiv, Bonn.

393. *Charles Neate to Beethoven*

London; February 1, 1825[1]

My dear Beethoven!

After communicating the contents of your letter to the directors of the Philharmonic Society, I must inform you with great sorrow that it is not possible to modify the first proposal that they made to you with the offer of 300 guineas.

If it depended upon me alone, I would very gladly offer you the sum that you wish, but the directors, *as a body,*[2] must comply with the statutes that rule the Society; therefore they are not in all cases masters of their own affairs. I flatter myself with the hope that these reasons will move you to accept our proposition, and that you will set out on your journey as soon as possible, since I am convinced that you will certainly gain a profit from it and be completely satisfied with your stay in England.

Now it will surely no longer be possible for you to arrive in time for the *first* concert,[3] but the directors will expect you with impatience at the *second,* which will take place at the beginning of March. I advise you to lodge at the Hotel *de la Sablonnière* in Leicester Square; it is a French house, which is often frequented by foreigners.

In any case, write to me, please, by the *next post,* and let me know when you believe that you will arrive here, so that I can have the pleasure of going to meet you. The Symphony is error free, and is to be rehearsed again this evening.[4] God be with you, my friend! In the hope of seeing you soon, I ask you to consider me your most ardent admirer, as well as your eternally sincere friend,

C[harles] Neate

[P.S.] If you unfortunately resolve not to come, I hope that you will not fail to write me occasionally, and that you will always turn to me as long as you maintain any contact with our country, with the assurance that there is no one in the world in whom you could better place your confidence and sincere friendship.

1. Answers Beethoven's letter of January 15, 1825 (Anderson No. 1344), which in turn replied to Neate's letter of December 20, 1824 (No. 388 above).
2. The phrase is "en masse" in the original.
3. In mid-February.
4. If the projection in Neate's December 20 letter was correct, the first rehearsal of the Ninth Symphony was held on January 17. The performance took place on March 21.
Incipit: Nachdem ich den Directoren der Philharmonischen Gesellschaft den Inhalt. . . .
Sources: Thayer-Deiters-Riemann, V, 161–162; summarized in Thayer-Krehbiel, III, 187; Thayer-Forbes, pp. 930–931; Brenneis, "Fischhof-Manuskript," pp. 74–75. Riemann notes that the letter was in Thayer's materials; probably Thayer himself possessed only a German translation, presumably copied from the Fischhof Manuscript (Staatsbibliothek zu Berlin–Preussischer Kulturbesitz). The whereabouts of the French original are unknown.

394. Johann van Beethoven to B. Schotts Söhne, Mainz

Vienna; February 4, 1825[1]

Herr B. Schott[s] Söhne in Mainz!

Enclosed you are receiving the seven works by my brother,[2] cleanly copied, and just now inspected and corrected by him, so that they can be engraved immediately. In doing so I shall mention that you not send all the works that you have in hand (namely the grand Mass,[3] the Symphony,[4] and the works that you receive now) back to my brother for proofreading of the engraving; rather transmit them to the well-known, skillful Herr Gottfried Weber,[5] in order not to delay their publication too much. I do not doubt that this man will undertake the proofreading with pleasure, out of love for the author and the works.

Furthermore, I indicate herewith in my and my brother's names that you can regard the above seven works as your legal property, which my brother will confirm in his next letter to you.

I sign myself with high esteem,

> Your most devoted,
>
> Johann van Beethoven
> Landowner

[On receiving this letter, Johann Joseph Schott apparently underlined Weber's name in red and sent it to him, writing in the blank space below brother Johann's signature: "They are placing a great demand upon you."

Weber jotted in reply to Schott: "I cannot possibly undertake the proofreading and have no desire to become Herr Beethoven's proofreader. Damned impudence of the tomfool!"][6]

1. This letter was enclosed with Beethoven's letter of February 5 (Anderson No. 1349). See also his brother Johann's similar letter to Stumpff, February 24, 1825 (No. 396 below).

2. The *Consecration of the House* Overture, Op. 124, in full score as well as for piano two hands and four hands (counting as three works in this reckoning); the Bagatelles, Op. 126; the *Opferlied*, Op. 121b; the *Bundeslied*, Op. 122; and *Der Kuss*, Op. 128. Johann's letter to Stumpff of February 24 spells out the list of works and opus numbers even more explicitly.

3. Op. 123.

4. Op. 125.

5. Gottfried Weber (1779–1839), trained as a jurist, active as a theorist, composer, critic and, since 1824, editor of Schott's journal, the *Cäcilia*.

6. Possibly as a result of this perceived affront, Weber published an article, "Über Tonmalerei," in the *Cäcilia* (August 1825), 155–172, incorporating his review, "Wellington's Sieg," which had appeared in the *Jenaischer Allgemeine Literatur-Zeitung* 13, pt. 3 (August 1816), cols. 217–227.

On reading Weber's negative opinion of *Wellington's Victory* in the *Cäcilia*, Beethoven angrily scrawled on p. 166: "Ach du erbärmlicher Schuft, was ich scheisse ist besser, als was du je gedacht" (Oh you miserable scoundrel, what I shit is better than anything you ever thought). This page, with Beethoven's annotation, is reproduced in *High Fidelity* 21 (January 1971), 59; and Kross, *Beethoven: Mensch seiner Zeit*, p. 85.

Incipit: Beyliegend erhalten Sie die sieben Werke meines Bruders. . . .

Sources: Nohl, *Neue Briefe*, pp. 266–267; Kalischer (German), V, 105; Kalischer-Shedlock, II, 359–360; Staehelin and Brandenburg, *Briefwechsel*, pp. 32, 34. The autographs of this letter and Ludwig's letter of February 5 are in the Stadtbibliothek, Mainz.

395. Hans Georg Nägeli to Beethoven

Zürich; February 21, 1825[1]

Herr L[udwig] van Beethoven
Famous Composer
Vienna

Honored Friend!

My poems were already printed two months ago.[2] In vain I hoped for an opportunity to enclose them [before this time].

In the next few days, I am now sending them to the highly commendable General Post Office in Vienna, with a note on the package that it contains a shipment of books to which H[is] I[mperial] H[ighness] and E[minence] the Archduke Rudolph has been pleased to subscribe. I am enclosing the 6 copies designated for H.I.H. & E., the 2 for Herr Bihler,[3] and the one for you, not doubting that, through your close relationship with H.I.H. & E., you will conveniently be able to obtain these 3 remaining copies. Accept *your* copy as a gift from a friend — you will, I hope, not refuse me.

Among the poetic greetings I would also gladly have added one to H.I.H. & E.; but since I am a Protestant and republican poet, I really did not want to dare it, although I am convinced that H.I.H. & E., as an enlightened clergyman and secular prince, will take no offense at those poems that recall something foreign to him by way of politics or creed. Otherwise I have not yet written my last poems, and who knows what will happen in the future.

Herr Cotta wants to postpone the publication of my Lectures until this coming winter, and I must give in to this.[4]

With high esteem and friendship,

H[an]s Georg Nägeli

P.S. I shall also notify the Post Office that perhaps *you* will come to get the package!

1. Answers Beethoven's letters to Nägeli of September 9 and November 17, 1824 (Anderson Nos. 1306 and 1319).

2. Nägeli's *Liederkränze* (see his letter of August 3, 1824, No. 376 above).

3. Dr. Johann Bihler (or Biehler), trained as a physician, was tutor to the family of Archduke Karl (see Anderson No. 1319). In August 1817, Beethoven had written letters of introduction on Bihler's behalf to both Nägeli and his fellow Swiss Xaver Schnyder von Wartensee (Anderson Nos. 803 and 804), so it is possible that Bihler was personally known to Nägeli.

4. *Vorlesungen über Musik* (Stuttgart: Cotta, 1826), dedicated to Archduke Rudolph; also discussed in Nägeli's letter of August 3, 1824.

Incipit: Schon seit 2 Monaten. . . .

Sources: Thayer-Deiters-Riemann, V, 139; Geiser, *Beethoven und die Schweiz*, pp. 89–90; Staehelin, *Hans Georg Nägeli und Ludwig van Beethoven*, pp. 49–51 (facsimile, p. 50). Autograph in the Staatsbibliothek zu Berlin–Preussischer Kulturbesitz, Mus. ms. autogr. Beethoven 35, 50; listed in Kalischer, "Beethoven-Autographe," p. 50, and Bartlitz, p. 133.

396. Johann van Beethoven to Johann Andreas Stumpff, London[1]

Vienna; February 24, 1825

Dear Sir!

I have the honor of sending you herewith seven of my brother's newest works, which I have received from *him,* with the request that they be sold immediately to an art dealer in London. N.B. these works are to be sold to only *one* art dealer for London, Scotland, Ireland, America and India, since these works are also to be sold on the Continent, because in any case [publishing rights] for the Continent would be of no use to you in London, since everything will be pirate-reprinted immediately. But an art dealer in Germany would not get these works before an art dealer in London has bought these works; *it then has the entirely exclusive proprietary rights for the entire of England.*[2] The Philharmonic Society in London has only the Overture, but they may not publish it.

The works are as follows:

1. Newest grand Overture,[3] 56 pages;[4]
2. Same, for piano 2-hands by Karl Czerny, 32 pages;
3. Same, for piano 4-hands by Karl Czerny, 28 pages;
4. Bagatelles, brand new, for piano,[5] 36 pages;
5. Song with chorus, with piano or wind instruments,[6] 32 pages;
6. Song with chorus, with piano or full orchestra,[7] 24 pages;
7. Song, completely through-composed, with piano alone,[8] 16 pages.

These seven works together cost *forty pounds*, with the condition that they must be engraved within six months.

Finally, I request you to notify me of the result of this transaction in the shortest possible time, through the art dealership of Herr von Leidesdorf, and I remain,

With greatest respect,

Johann van Beethoven

[Opposite page:]
The works have the following *opus numbers:*[9]

Overture, Op. 124;
Same, for piano 2-hands, Op. 125;
Same, for piano 4-hands, Op. 126;
Bagatelles for piano, Op. 127;
Song with chorus, for piano, Op. 128;
Song with piano or full orchestra, Op. 129;
Song, through-composed, with piano alone, Op. 130.

1. The addressee is unnamed, but Tyson reasoned that Stumpff (1769–1846) had visited Vienna in the fall of 1824 and had struck up an acquaintance with Johann as well as with Beethoven himself. The conjectural identification of the recipient is virtually confirmed by the fact that the seven works mentioned below were listed among Stumpff's estate sale in 1847.

2. The foregoing two sentences are just as long, repetitive and awkward in the original.

3. *Consecration of the House* Overture, Op. 124.

4. The pagination of these items was originally expressed in *Bogen*, folded sheets of four pages each. Thus the Overture consisted of fourteen *Bogen*.

5. Bagatelles, Op. 126.

6. *Bundeslied,* Op. 122.

7. *Opferlied,* Op. 121b.

8. *Der Kuss,* Op. 128.

9. Of Johann's opus numbers, only 124 and 128 remain valid today. The piano arrangements of the overture justifiably received no separate opus numbers at all. Thus Ludwig was probably a more realistic (and possibly even more honest) calculator of opus numbers than was his brother.

Incipit: Ich habe die Ehre Ihnen hier. . . .

Sources: Tyson, "New Beethoven Letters and Documents," pp. 29–32, with extensive commentary; also his "Addenda," in *Beethoven Studies 3,* ed. Alan Tyson (Cambridge: Cambridge University Press, 1982), p. 299. Autograph in the Royal College of Music, London.

397. *Lower Austrian Landesregierung to Beethoven*

Vienna; March 5, 1825

Third Reminder

Official Notice[1]

Notification No. 12078

Ludwig v. Beethoven is in arrears for the year 182 4 for:

Graduated Income Tax, amounting to . . . . 21 fl. __ kr. M.M.

Penalty for the above . . . . __ fl. __ kr. M.M.

I.R. Lower Austrian Provincial Accounting Office
Vienna, March 31, 182 5

Franz Xaver Stress
State Accountant

Wenzel Melaun
Accounting Councillor

The tax arrears noted here by the Provincial State Accounting Office are to be settled without fail and without delay, for otherwise the Lower Austrian Government would find the unpleasant necessity, according to its duty, to take all measures prescribed by the highest authority in the collection of this outstanding tax sum.

Everyone is warned not to give the sum owed either to the agent delivering the payment notice or to the guard sometimes sent upon serving the papers, but rather to pay directly at the I.R. Tax Cashier's Office, which is at Minoritenplatz No. 40, in the I.R. Lower Austrian Government Building, on the ground floor.

I.R. Lower Austrian Regional Government
Vienna, March 5, 1825

Augustin Reichmann, Freiherr v. Hochkirchen
Government President

Joseph von Perger
Government Councillor

[Exterior:]

City: 969
Suburb:
No.:

To: Ludwig von Beethoven

     Composer

     Urgent

     12078

1. This notification bears two dates, March 5 and March 31, 1825. It concerns taxes for 1824, and, if the tax notice for 1825 (dated March 30, No. 400 below) is similar, then Beethoven's tax payments for 1824 would originally have been due at the end of April and the end of July of that year. In April 1824 Beethoven was busily engaged in preparations for his May 7 *Akademie,* and by the end of July he had departed for Baden after the financial failure of the second *Akademie* on May 23. He was assessed the same amount of income tax in both 1824 and 1825, with no penalty for not having paid the 1824 tax on time.

Incipit: Aemtliche Anzeige (Dritte Erinnerung). . . .

Sources: Autograph in the Staatsbibliothek zu Berlin–Preussischer Kulturbesitz, Mus. ms. autogr. Beethoven 35, 23; listed in Kalischer, "Beethoven-Autographe," p. 46, and Bartlitz, p. 124. This document is a printed form; hand-entered information has been transcribed above as *underlined.*

398. *Traugott Trautwein to the* Wiener Zeitschrift für Kunst, Literatur, Theater und Mode, *with an endorsement from Carl Wilhelm Henning*

Berlin; March 15, 1825[1]

To supplement and discuss this notice, which in many regards has severely injured me and is incomplete [in the information it provides], is the purpose of the following declaration:

The concertmaster C. W. Henning, in October of last year, offered me for publication the arrangement in question of the overture by Herr v[an] Beethoven. Since he openly wanted to verify his right to do so by adding his name on the title page (and this was actually done later), there would have been no reason for me, as publisher, to doubt Concertmaster Henning's authority to publish this overture if the disclosure to the contrary had not made it completely beyond question, and the simple assurance of Herr v[an] Beethoven that the advertised arrangements by Herr Czerny were the only legitimate editions is not sufficient to take legitimacy away from the publication that I have issued.

No less doubt surrounds the protestations of Herr v[an] Beethoven that the publication that I have issued is full of mistakes and unfaithful to the original score, since Herr Henning has strictly adhered to the original score and has avoided everything that could have caused any deviation from it.

T. Trautwein
Book and Music Dealer

* * * *

I hereby attest that the above declaration is in accordance with the truth, and that I am prepared to answer for the legitimacy of the arrangement under discussion at any time.

C. W. Henning
Concertmaster

1. Answers Beethoven's complaint in the *Wiener Zeitschrift,* March 5, 1825 (Anderson, III, 1442–1443), claiming that Trautwein had published an unauthorized arrangement of the *Consecration of the House* Overture, Op. 124.

See also Beethoven's letter to Henning, January 1, 1825 (Anderson No. 1343); Henning's letter to Beethoven, January 13, 1825 (No. 391 above); and Schott's notices in the *Cäcilia,* April 20 and July 30, 1825 (Nos. 404A and 415 below).

Incipit: Diese mich in mehrfacher Hinsicht. . . .

Sources: Thayer-Deiters-Riemann, IV, 308 (giving Trautwein's initial as P., doubtless a misprint or misreading).

399. Ferdinand Wolanek[1] to Beethoven

[Vienna; ca. March 24, 1825][2]

Herr Herr Ludwig v. Beethoven!

Since I can finish entering the Finale[3] in score only at Easter,[4] and [since] you will no longer need it at that time, I am sending all of the parts, including those only begun, for your favorable disposition.

I remain gratefully obliged for the honor you have done me by employing me; as far as the other disagreeable behavior toward me is concerned, I can regard it smilingly as just a fit of temper to be accepted:[5] in the ideal world of tones there exist so many dissonances, so should they not also exist in the real world?

I am comforted only by the firm conviction that the same fate as mine would have been allotted to Mozart and Haydn, those celebrated artists, if they had been employed as your copyists.

I only request that you not confuse me with those common copyists who consider themselves fortunate to be able to maintain their existence by being treated like slaves.

Otherwise, be assured that I never have the slightest cause to blush before you on account of my behavior.

With high esteem,

Yours truly,

Ferd. Wolanek

[Beethoven crossed through Wolanek's letter in two bold strokes and wrote in large letters:]

Stupid, conceited, asinine Churl.[6]

[In the margin below, he wrote in a more composed manner:]
So I must yet compliment such a scoundrel, who steals money from people! Instead of that, I'll pull him by his ass's ears.

[On the blank reverse, Beethoven wrote horizontally in large letters:]
Lousy scribbler![7] Stupid Churl! Correct your mistakes made through ignorance, arrogance, conceit and stupidity. This is more fitting than to want to teach me, which is exactly as though the *sow* wanted to teach Minerva.[8]

Beethoven[9]

[In the right margin, Beethoven wrote vertically in a smaller hand:]
You show Mozart and Haydn the *honor* by *not referring* to *them*.

[And in the left margin in a similar manner:]
It was decided already yesterday, and even earlier,
not to have *you* copy for me any *more*.[10]

1. Born in Prague, Ferdinand Wolanek (1789–?) was the son of composer-conductor Anton Joseph Wolanek (1761–1817). Weber mentioned him as a copyist in the Ständetheater, Prague, between 1813 and 1816.

2. Wolanek's final entry in Beethoven's conversation books was made on March 23, 1825, and reflects what may have been an unpleasant encounter. On March 26, Beethoven's nephew Karl entered the word *Schreibsudler* (scribbler), a term for Wolanek that Beethoven angrily scrawled on the copyist's letter. Beethoven's reference to a decision "yesterday" not to reengage Wolanek may refer to the episode on March 23.

3. Probably the finale of the Ninth Symphony, promised to Ferdinand Ries in Beethoven's letter of March 19, 1825 (Anderson No. 1353), with further discussion of various sets of parts for the several movements.

4. Easter fell on April 3 in 1825.

5. From the conversation books it becomes apparent that Beethoven and Wolanek may have had words as early as December 18–19, 1824, when the copyist evidently compared Beethoven's manuscripts unfavorably to Rossini's. By January 26, 1825, Beethoven complained about Wolanek in denigrating terms, in a letter to Schott (Anderson No. 1346).

6. Beethoven probably originally wrote "Dummer Kerl" and then added "Einge-bildeter" and "Eselhafter" in between. I have translated *Kerl* as "churl" rather than "fellow" because the former, a near cognate, also has a more negative meaning in English.

7. "Schreib-Sudler" in German. Emily Anderson translated it "Slovenly copyist," technically correct, but missing the rhythm and venom of the version given here.

8. Beethoven also used this metaphor in his letter to Joseph Carl Bernard, June 10, 1825 (Anderson No. 1387). For an explanation, see Anderson, III, 1207, n. 1.

9. This angry retort was probably never sent, but it appears as Anderson No. 1463, an otherwise undated item in 1825.

10. See n. 2, this letter, for the relevance of this remark to dating Wolanek's letter and Beethoven's retort.

Incipit: Da ich mit dem Einsetzen des Finale. . . .

Sources: Thayer-Deiters-Riemann, V, 175–176; Thayer-Forbes, p. 937; Kalischer (German), V, 101–102; Kalischer-Shedlock, II, 357–358; Kastner (1910), pp. 834–835; Kastner-Kapp, pp. 747–748. Autograph in the Beethoven-Haus, Bonn; facsimile in *Musical Times* (December 15, 1892); Bory, p. 185; and Schmidt and Schmidt-Görg, *Beethoven,* p. 250. Nohl, *Neue Briefe* (1867), pp. 265–266, indicated that the letter was then in the possession of the artist Friedrich von Amerling (1803–1887), Vienna. See also Köhler et al., *Konversationshefte,* VII, 51–53, 103, 119, 178, 189–191, 199; and Anderson No. 1463.

400. Lower Austrian Landesregierung to Beethoven

Vienna; March 30, 1825[1]

Graduated Income Tax for the Military Year 1825

Tax Assignment No. <u>10509</u>

Obligation / Discharge

Annually	Installments	
	at latest by the end of April	at latest by the end of July 1825
<u>21</u> fl. __ kr.	<u>10</u> fl. <u>30</u> kr.	<u>10</u> fl. <u>30</u> kr.

The present notice is to be produced every time an installment payment is made to the I.R. Income Tax Liquidator, to be found at Minoritenplatz No. 40, in the I.R. Lower Austrian Government Building on the ground floor, and will serve as confirmation of the assessed sum when presented at the window to the side of the Cashier's Office, instead of a receipt. Whereby, however, everyone is warned not to give the sum owed either to the agent delivering the payment notice or to any executor, but rather to pay directly at the Income Tax Cashier's Office, since only a confirmation of payment written by the Cashier frees the individual from further liability, and the personnel serving the notices are strictly prohibited from taking any payment of either tax or penalty.

I.R. Lower Austrian Regional Government
Vienna, March 30, 1825

Augustin Reichmann, Freiherr von Hochkirchen
Government President

Joseph von Perger
Government Councillor

[Exterior:]

City No. 969
Suburb:
No:

To: Ludwig v. Beethoven
    Composer
    10509

1. This tax notice for 1825 must have reached Beethoven almost simultaneously with the third reminder for 1824, initiated on March 5, 1825 (No. 397 above), but seemingly sent only on March 31.

Incipit: Assignations-Nr. 10509. Schuldigkeit. . . .

Sources: Autograph in the Staatsbibliothek zu Berlin–Preussischer Kulturbesitz, Mus. ms. autogr. Beethoven 35, 22; listed in Kalischer, "Beethoven-Autographe," p. 46, and Bartlitz, p. 123. This document is a printed form; two columns on the right-hand side, concerning monthly payments etc. and seemingly not applicable to Beethoven, are not reproduced here. The hand-entered information has been transcribed above as *underlined*.

401. Beethoven to S. (Anton Schindler?)[1]

[Vienna; ca. end of March or April 1825?][2]

Room and board for students, sharing accommodations or especially alone, under responsible supervision, etc. Inquire at the porter of the stock exchange, Weihburggasse No. 939.

    1. Drouot Rive Gauche believed that this one-page note to "S." was directed to Anton Schindler; indeed, Beethoven's estranged secretary still visited him occasionally during the period from May 1824 to September 1826. Violinist Ignaz Schuppanzigh could also have run errands for the composer at this time. Helms and Staehelin and, more recently, Sieghard Brandenburg believe this note to be a leaf from a conversation book. If so, when it was removed and for what purpose are not clear; Beethoven himself could have done so, to use the leaf as a reminder to himself or as a note to another. If it were written after around April 3, 1825, "S." could also be Karl's landlord, Schlemmer (see n. 2, this letter).

    2. The note is undated; Brandenburg believes that it might refer to an advertisement in the *Wiener Zeitung* in April 1825. Beethoven probably sought lodgings for his nephew Karl at the end of March 1825, just before Karl entered the Polytechnic Institute at Easter. Easter Sunday fell on April 3 in 1825. At that time, Karl began living with the family of Matthias Schlemmer, auf der Wieden, Alleegasse No. 72, near the institute. Karl essentially remained there until his suicide attempt, probably on August 6, 1826.

    The present note may be related to an undated note to Karl but addressed to him "Near the Karlskirche, Alleegasse No. 72, 1st Floor, c/o Herr M. Schlemmer," and therefore dated after Easter 1825. Its text reads: "Do as you think [right] with this letter to S., to give it [to him] or not depends entirely upon your intention." In this case, "S" could be Schlemmer. A facsimile of the address appears in Musikantiquariat Hans Schneider, *Musikerautographen*, Katalog No. 225 (Tutzing, 1978), p. 8, item 15. (French text in Anderson No. 1486, dated end of May 1826, and identifying "S." as Schlesinger.)

    3. Building No. 939 (owned by Count Colloredo) in the Weihburggasse housed the Börse (stock exchange) from 1812 to 1841. The building also housed the banking

offices of Arnstein and Eskeles, with whom Beethoven occasionally did business, more consistently so after the failure of Count Fries's firm in April 1826.

4. As described by the auction house, the note bears a further annotation: "1829 12 fl. 4 cr." Possibly it was sold for 12 florins, 4 kreuzer (or 4 groschen) in 1829.

Incipit: Kost u[nd] wohnung für Studierende. . . .

Sources: Drouot Rive Gauche, *Autographes Musicaux,* auction catalog (Paris, June 20, 1977), item 12 (with facsimile); quoted briefly in Helms and Staehelin, "Bewegungen . . . 1973–1979," p. 356. In 1983, the autograph was in a private collection in France. Sieghard Brandenburg, Beethoven-Archiv, Bonn, kindly supplied a transcription of the text.

402. Johann Andreas Streicher to Carl Friedrich Peters, Leipzig

Vienna; April 6, 1825[1]

What you tell me about Beethoven is absolutely not unexpected,[2] although it bothers me very much that he does not behave properly toward you, toward the best publisher and best of men; that he harms himself and that he absolutely will not be counseled or helped. I very much fear that he could still find himself in a very deplorable situation, where he might very much regret that he did not follow reasonable advice earlier and better.[3]

1. This letter (one sheet, two written pages) answers a letter from Peters to Streicher, March 15, 1825. Its first paragraph begins, "Your letter of March 15 was very painful for me," and concerns illnesses of Peters and of his seven-year-old daughter, before moving on to the present excerpt. A subsequent paragraph discusses two exchange drafts, and another discusses the pianist Wilhelm Würfel, whose compositions Streicher had recommended to the publisher.

Wenzel Wilhelm Würfel (1790–1832), a Bohemian pianist, had studied with Johann Wenzel Tomaschek in Prague, lived in Warsaw, 1815–1824, and encouraged the young Chopin. After performances of his opera *Rübezahl* in Prague on October 7, 1824, and in Vienna on March 10, 1825, Würfel became vice-*Kapellmeister* at the Kärntnertor Theater, remaining there until 1826. Between May 1824 and May 1825, Peters published Würfel's *Rondeau brillant,* Op. 25, and Polonaises, Opp. 26 and 27.

2. By this time, Beethoven had been on poor terms with Peters for at least two years.

3. See Streicher's letter to Beethoven, September 5, 1824 (above), for an example of such well-intentioned but possibly impractical advice.

Incipit: Ihr Brief vom 15. Mart war mir sehr schmerzlich . . . (letter); Was Sie mir von Beethoven sagen . . . (this excerpt).

Sources: Kastner (1910), p. 841. Autograph in a private collection in the United States. Sieghard Brandenburg, Beethoven-Archiv, Bonn, kindly supplied the incipit, two brief additions to Kastner's text and a summary of the material not in Kastner.

403. Wilhelm Härtel[1] to Traugott Trautwein,[2] Berlin

Leipzig; April 10, 1825[3]

Herr Trautwein, Berlin

Kindly excuse me if my reply to your inquiry concerning the Fest-Ouvertüre for four hands by Beethoven is later than you might have expected it. Although my individual opinion on this occasion cannot count as any criterion for others, I still express it to you gladly because you wish me to do so.

I do not find the least injury to Herr Beethoven in your having printed the Overture in Herr Henning's arrangement, at least none that gives him the right to come out with a public, injustice-laden accusation against you. Had he sold his work to Herr Henning with provisions against any copy or any arrangement being made from it, then Herr Henning would indeed be in the wrong and Herr Beethoven in no way rightly to be blamed that he enters the field against Herr Henning as the one who injured him, and publicly censures his actions. He may not do this to you, however, especially [since] you had stated on the title page that you obtained it from Herr Henning, who indeed must have called your attention to Herr Beethoven as seller[4] of the manuscript.

I find it completely in order that you reply to his notice [in the *Wiener Zeitschrift*] in a fitting manner, and if I were in your place, I would have done likewise and in the same way, as the sheet that you most obligingly sent me expresses it. As much esteem as I have for Herr Beethoven's genius, I would be just as little induced to tolerate a compromise with him in public; in such cases, I must be true to myself, and my honor means just as much to me as that of the great man.

Nonetheless, both sides usually suffer from the great publicity surrounding such disputes. Therefore, if Beethoven has referred to the incident only in a Viennese newspaper or some other south German journal, I would have the reply placed only in these, and thereby satisfy myself that I had presented the true circumstances in the matter to the public. The topic is really of no importance, and the profit that this edition might earn for you will likewise not be very significant, for, I must admit candidly, the Overture does not especially please me, even though I have heard it well played several times in your arrangement. Otherwise, you would do very badly if you considered the matter from the viewpoint of a book dealer and gave in to your concern that people could regard your edition to a certain extent as a [pirate] reprint; in the music business people are unfortunately not so particular about this, and a small encroachment upon the rights of another seldom attracts attention. I am holding your announcement pending instructions.

With respectful devotion,

Your,

Wilhelm Härtel

[P.S.] My obliging thanks for the prompt cashing of my draft.

1. Wilhelm Härtel opened a Leipzig music dealership under his own name in 1824 and by May 1825 had negotiated northern distribution rights for the publications of Mathias Artaria and A. Pennauer (both of Vienna). He was also a distributor for B. Schotts Söhne, Mainz, the legitimate publisher of the *Consecration of the House* Overture, Op. 124.

2. Traugott Trautwein opened a book and music dealership in Berlin in 1820.

3. Follows as a result of Beethoven's notice in the *Wiener Zeitschrift*, March 5, 1825 (Anderson, III, 1442–1443), protesting Trautwein's publication of C. W. Henning's piano arrangement of the *Consecration of the House* Overture under the title *Festival Overture*. Angered, Trautwein drafted a reply to Beethoven's notice and sent it to Härtel to examine, possibly for publication in the *Allgemeine musikalische Zeitung*. In prose loaded with circumlocutions and gratuitous adverbs, Härtel essentially dissuades Trautwein from escalating the argument further in print. See also Henning's letter to Beethoven, January 13, 1825 (No. 391 above).

4. Härtel writes, "Herr B. als Käufer" (buyer), but probably he means *Verkäufer* (seller), unless he was somehow referring to Berlin theater director Heinrich Bethmann, who had accompanied Henning to Vienna.

Incipit: Entschuldigen Sie gefälligst. . . .

Sources: Autograph in the Staatsbibliothek zu Berlin–Preussischer Kulturbesitz, Mus. ms. autogr. Beethoven 48, 2; listed in Bartlitz, p. 195.

404. B. Schotts Söhne, Advertisement
in the Intelligenzblatt of the Cäcilia

Mainz; April 20, 1825[1]

Invitation for Subscriptions
to the
Three Newest Great Works
of
L. van Beethoven,
namely

1. *Missa solennis* [*sic*], D major, Opus 123
2. Grand Overture, C major, Op. 124 and
3. Symphony with Choruses, Op. 125

The Spirit of Music has been particularly favorable to our times. Hardly has one shining star gone out in the musical heavens, hardly have the tones of a gifted composer become silent, when there shines another spirit to replace the lamented loss. Mozart and Haydn vanished, then Providence gave us a Beethoven, who has followed their immortal works with his own, fully worthy of sharing admiration alongside them. The originality of his harmony, charm and appeal of his modulations are unsurpassable and flow unalloyed from the fullness of a fertile genius.

The undersigned music dealership is overjoyed to be able to offer to the friends of art the long-desired pleasure of the most excellent of his compositions. These admired works are to appear in the following form:

1. The grand *Missa solemnis*
   a. in full score
   b. in individual orchestral and vocal parts, and
   c. in piano reduction with vocal parts;
2. The Overture for grand orchestra[2]
   d. in score
   e. in orchestral parts;

    3. The grand Symphony with choruses and solo voices
    (on Schiller's "Lied an die Freude")
       f. in score
       g. in orchestral and vocal parts;

All with appropriate ripieno or doubling parts.[3]

The whole will still be issued in the course of this year. The publisher will consider as one of its finest obligations to have such valuable works presented in the most correct [versions], in the finest musical engraving and on fine paper.

In order to make the acquisition of these harmonic treasures as easy as possible for the public, the way will be opened by means of subscriptions under the following conditions: one may, if he chooses, subscribe for all of the works together (thus for the entire edition), or for only one or several of them; for example, merely for the score of the Mass (without the performance parts) — or merely for one without the other — or merely for the piano reduction, etc.

Since, however, the number of folios[4] cannot yet be determined precisely, we shall adhere to the general principle that the printed folios will *not* cost *over ten Rhenish kreuzer.*

After the course of the subscription period, which remains open until the end of October of this year, a significantly higher sales price will take effect.

Subscriptions may be made in any respectable book or music dealership.

B. Schotts Söhne

1. The proximity of this advertisement to the first appearances in the *Cäcilia* of Beethoven's *Warnung* and Schott's complementary endorsement (No. 404A below) as well as its implications for performance practice warrant its inclusion here.

2. Although Czerny's (authorized) two- and four-hand piano versions of the *Consecration of the House* Overture are not mentioned here, they are listed elsewhere in this *Intelligenzblatt* (no. 7, p. 53), along with their actual or projected availability through the dealership of Wilhelm Härtel in Leipzig (p. 49). For further implications of this situation, see Nos. 403 above and 404A below.

3. Beethoven had employed an orchestra of 12 first violins, 12 second violins, 10 violas and a total of 12 violoncellos and contrabasses as well as doubled winds for the May 7, 1824, premiere of his Ninth Symphony, along with the *Consecration of the House* Overture and three movements from the *Missa solemnis* (see Shin Augustinus

Kojima, "Die Uraufführung der Neunten Symphonie Beethovens: Einige neue Tatsachen," in *Bericht über den Internationalen Musikwissenschaftlichen Kongress, Bayreuth, 1981,* ed. Christoph-Hellmut Mahling and Sigrid Wiesmann [Kassel: Bärenreiter, 1984], pp. 393–398). The anticipation that other performers of these works might likewise utilize enlarged forces (without the customary necessity of having extra parts copied by hand) surely motivated Schott to offer *Ripien- oder Verdoppelungs-Stimmen.*

    4. *Bogenzahl* in German, folded sheets of four pages each, probably indicating a generic page count here.

    Incipit: Der Genius der Harmonie. . . .

    Sources: Cäcilia 2 (1825), *Intelligenzblatt* no. 7, pp. 43–45.

404A. B. Schotts Söhne, Notice in *the* Intelligenzblatt *of the* Cäcilia

Mainz; April 20, 1825

    Herr van Beethoven has publicly warned against the illegal as well as incorrect edition of a four-hand piano reduction of his Festival Overture, made by Herr Henning [and] issued by Trautwein in Berlin.[1] Not to mention the obvious, that such an advance publication is even more disgraceful than a pirate reprint, we notify the honored public only that we already acquired the exclusive right to publish this work from the famous composer long ago, and that a reduction of it for four hands, made by the well-known piano virtuoso Herr Czerny under the eyes of the composer, is already being printed by us.[2] We are therefore in the position, as the legitimate publisher, to offer a more worthy version of this ingenious original work than the contraband by Herr Henning.

B. Schotts Söhne[3]

    1. Beethoven's notice in the *Wiener Zeitschrift für Kunst, Literatur, Theater und Mode,* warning against the Henning-Trautwein arrangement of the *Consecration of the House* Overture, was published on March 5, 1825 (Anderson, III, 1442–1443). The composer had already warned Schott of the Trautwein publication on February 5 (Anderson No. 1349); Trautwein and Henning replied to Beethoven's protest on March 15, 1825 (No. 398 above).

With slight modifications, Schott reproduced Beethoven's notice in the supplementary *Intelligenzblätter* of their journal *Cäcilia*. In *Intelligenzblatt* no. 7, pp. 45–46, Beethoven's notice (here headed *Warnung*) appears for the first time, undated, but followed by the present notice from Schott, endorsing Beethoven's position and dated April 20, 1825. Since it also contained an unrelated notice dated April 23, 1825, *Intelligenzblatt* no. 7 must have appeared several days after the aforementioned April 20.

A few weeks later, *Intelligenzblatt* no. 8, p. 58, included Beethoven's notice (now headed *Anzeige*), still undated, and a slightly altered version of Schott's endorsement, but still dated April 20, 1825. For the final version of Schott's endorsement, dated July 30, see No. 415 below.

2. Czerny's two-hand arrangement appeared in April 1825, the four-hand arrangement in July. The orchestral material was not published until December 1825.

3. A list of new music published by B. Schotts Söhne indicates that the firm's wares could also be obtained through the dealer Wilhelm Härtel in Leipzig (*Intelligenzblatt* no. 7, p. 49). See Härtel to Trautwein, April 10, 1825 (No. 403 above), and Schott's advertisement (No. 404 above).

Incipit: Herr van Beethoven hat öffentlich die eben so unrechtliche. . . .

Sources: Cäcilia 2 (1825), *Intelligenzblatt* no. 7, pp. 45–46; *Intelligenzblatt* no. 8, p. 58. See also Thayer-Deiters-Riemann, IV, 308.

405. Prince Nicolas Galitzin to Beethoven

St. Petersburg; April 29, 1825

I have many thanks to give you, worthy Monsieur de Beethoven, for the precious parcel with the sublime Quartet that I have just received.[1] I have already had it played several times, and I find in it all the genius of the master, and when the playing of it has become more perfect, the pleasure will be all the greater. I have also just received your two letters[2] and am delighted to hear that the two other quartets will soon be finished.[3] — Tell me the date by which you want me to have the money transferred to you, and because I myself am going to spend a few months in the country I might ask you to give me the consolation of having at least one of the two quartets by the time I depart, which will be in two months. — I ask you to tell me how much is subtracted from the 50 ducats that I send you; it is natural that I be the one who bears the costs of exchange. — I implore you also to send me your Symphony,[4] which I very much desire to have. I am writing to Messieurs Henikstein to ask that they pay you the costs. For a few days we shall play your new Quartet with Bernhard Romberg, who has been here for a month.[5] Do not delay, I ask you, in having it printed; such a beautiful masterpiece ought not to remain hidden for a single moment![6] May your health permit you soon to send the other quartets so that we may play them; I am impatient to receive them. — Write to me still at the same address. — Receive the assurance of my very sincere friendship!

Your very affectionate,

P[rince] Nicolas Galitzin

[P.S.] I am writing by the same post to Messieurs Henikstein.

1. Beethoven seemingly had delivered the Quartet, Op. 127, to Henikstein in Vienna on about January 26, 1825. The 50 ducats from Galitzin had arrived on about January 24; Beethoven, his brother Johann and their circle spoke at length about exchange rates on those days. See Köhler et al., *Konversationshefte*, VII, 111–115. Such exchange rates were also a subject of Beethoven's letter to Henikstein (Anderson No. 1384), which could not have been written before mid-May 1825, given the speed of the mails, and (judging from the draft in Köhler et al., *Konversationshefte*, VII, 315) was more likely written on July 6, 1825, or shortly thereafter.

2. These letters are not known and presumably have not survived.

3. Opp. 130 and 132.

4. Op. 125.

5. Prominent violoncellist, composer and conductor (1767–1841), a friend of Beethoven's since their youth together in Bonn.

6. Beethoven appears to have delivered Op. 127 to Schott's Viennese business correspondent, Fries and Co., on April 15, 1825. See Köhler et al., *Konversationshefte*, VII, 218, 401. Schott published the quartet in 1826 (the parts in March, the score in June).

Incipit: J'ai bien des remerciments à vous faire. . . .

Sources: Thayer-Deiters-Riemann, V, 564. When Thayer copied it, the autograph was in the possession of Beethoven's nephew Karl's widow, Caroline, Vienna. It has since disappeared.

406. Heinrich Friedrich Ludwig Rellstab[1] to Beethoven

[after May 4, 1825][2]

Enclosed, highly honored Sir, I am sending you a few *Lieder*[3] that I have had copied for you; several more in other tastes will follow soon. These perhaps are a novelty, in that they form a connected series in themselves, which creates a presentiment of happiness, union, parting, death and hope for the world to come, without describing specific incidents.

May these poems please you so much that you resolve to set them to music and in this manner open the collaboration with a business firm whose principle, as far as possible, is conducive to the true, highest art, and considers the inspiration of the composer as the first law according to which he shall write.

Day and night I am thinking about an opera for you, and I do not doubt that I shall chance upon the material that might satisfy *all* the demands of the composer, of the poet, and of the numerous public.

With deepest respect,

L. Rellstab[4]

1. Ludwig Rellstab (1799–1860), famous music critic and poet from Berlin, was still in his wandering student years when he came to Vienna in 1825 and met Beethoven.

2. The composer's three letters to Rellstab during April and through May 3, 1825 (Anderson Nos. 1366, 1366a and 1366b), provide background on Rellstab. The letter bears neither place nor date. Rellstab left Vienna on May 4, 1825, intending to return to his native Berlin.

3. These were later included in Rellstab's *Garten und Wald: Novellen und . . . Schriften* (Leipzig: Brockhaus, 1854).

4. The sources give the signature as "M. L. Rellstab."

Incipit: Innenliegend, hochverehrter Herr, übersende ich. . . .

Sources: Thayer-Deiters-Riemann, V, 201–202. Kreissle von Hellborn, *Schubert,* pp. 446–447 (English translation by Coleridge, II, 134), gives the letter, according to the original, and indicates that Thayer thought without doubt that it was addressed to Beethoven, to which Riemann, on the basis of its content, agrees.

407. Johann van Beethoven to Ferdinand Ries, Aachen[1]

Vienna; May 6, 1825

My noble, worthy Friend!

Enclosed here you are receiving the last remnant of the music that my brother gave me to send to you.[2] He will write to you as soon as he is better; unfortunately an *inflammation of the intestines* suddenly attacked him, from which he has now been saved, but he is still very weak and incapable of undertaking anything. Therefore, write to him very soon about the receipt of the works sent. At the same time, tell him when you will send him the agreed-upon 40 Carolines, which will certainly make him happy. *I must yet ask you* to encourage him to write the Oratorio. He has a fine libretto, namely *Der Sieg des Kreuzes*,[3] which he wants to compose; if you encourage him that the Rhenish Music Societies will take it, he will certainly compose it.

I am always

Your loyal friend,

Johann v[an] Beethoven
Landowner

1. Ries was in Aachen to conduct the Whitsun Festival. Partially answered in Ries's letter to Beethoven, June 9, 1825 (No. 409 below).

2. Another reference to these works is found in Beethoven's letter to Ries, April 9, 1825 (Anderson No. 1358). As noted in Ries's letter of June 9, however, they arrived too late for performance. The works included the Kyrie and Gloria from the *Missa solemnis*, "an Italian vocal duet" (possibly *Nei giorni tuoi felici*, WoO 93, or even the trio *Tremate*, Op. 116) and the march with chorus from *The Ruins of Athens*, Op. 114.

3. The libretto was by Joseph Carl Bernard. Over a year before, Beethoven had already been disinclined to set it; see his letter to the Gesellschaft der Musikfreunde, January 23, 1824 (Anderson No. 1260).

Incipit: Hier beiliegend erhalten Sie den letzten Rest. . . .

Sources: Thayer-Deiters-Riemann, V, 194; and Hill, *Ferdinand Ries*, pp. 227–228 (citing Thayer-Deiters-Riemann). Autograph in the Beethoven-Archiv, Bonn; listed in Schmidt-Görg, *Katalog der Handschriften* (1935), p. 48.

408. Beethoven to Karl van Beethoven (Draft)

[Probably Vienna; ca. June 5, 1825][1]

You received your florin,[2] and if you want something else, send word and give [me] a note with regard to lodging.[3]

1. This dating can be derived from the conversation books, whose editors, however, inexplicably failed to identify the addressee or the topics covered in the draft letter.

2. Beethoven's letter to Karl from Baden on Tuesday, May 31, 1825 (Anderson No. 1379), instructed the nephew (in Vienna), if he needed money, to borrow a gulden at the composer's home. Beethoven planned on coming into Vienna on Saturday, June 4; since he evidently knew that Karl had already gotten the money, he presumably penned the draft after his arrival from Baden.

3. The reference is unclear, but Beethoven was dissatisfied with his lodgings, may have had Karl looking for a new location on his behalf and (since the letter is in French) presumably did not wish German-reading eyes to pry into his business.

Incipit: Vous recevies votre florin. . . .

Sources: Köhler et al., *Konversationshefte*, VII, 295 (© Deutscher Verlag für Musik, Leipzig). Autograph in the Staatsbibliothek zu Berlin–Preussischer Kulturbesitz.

409. Ferdinand Ries to Beethoven

Godesberg; June 9, 1825[1]

Dearest Beethoven!

I have been back from Aachen a few days, and tell you with the greatest pleasure that your new Symphony was performed with extraordinary precision and was received with the greatest approbation.[2] It was a hard nut to crack and on the last day I rehearsed the Finale alone for three full hours—but I especially, and all the others, have been sufficiently rewarded by the performance. It is a work without equal, and if you had written nothing but this, you would have made yourself immortal. Where will you lead us from here??

Since it will interest you to hear a little more about the performance, I shall describe it to you briefly. The orchestra and chorus consisted of 422 persons,[3] among them many distinguished people. The first day was begun with a new Symphony of mine,[4] followed by Handel's *Alexander's Feast*. The second day began with your new Symphony, followed by *Davidde penitente*[5] by Mozart, the Overture to *Die Zauberflöte*, and *Christus am Ölberge*.[6] The applause from the public was almost terrifying. I had already been in Aachen since May 3 to conduct the rehearsals, and as evidence of the satisfaction and enthusiasm of the public, I was called out [on stage] after the performance, where a lady (she was pretty, too) presented me with a poem and a laurel crown. At the same time there followed a shower of flowers and [copies] of the poem from the upper loges.[7] Everyone was pleased and satisfied, and they avowed that it was the finest of the seven Whitsun Festivals they have had until now.

I am infinitely sorry that your other musical pieces arrived too late;[8] by then it was impossible to make use of them. I am sending you here, dear friend, a bill of exchange for 40 *Louis d'or* on Hippemayer and Co., in Vienna,[9] as promised, and ask that, as soon as possible, you confirm its receipt, with which I can have everything settled in Aachen.

We are glad that you have not accepted the engagement in England. If you want to go there, you must prepare yourself for it ahead of time, so that you can make a good profit from it. Rossini got 2,500 pounds sterling from the theater alone; if the Englishmen want something extraordinary, they must all get together so as to make it worth the trouble.[10] You will not lack applause or testimonials of honor there, but surely you have had enough of these during your life.

With all good wishes for your happiness, dear Beethoven,

Ever yours,

Ferdinand Ries

1. Answers Beethoven's letter of April 9 (Anderson No. 1358) and brother Johann's letter of May 6 (No. 407 above). Beethoven referred to this letter briefly in a note to his nephew Karl in early July (Anderson No. 1393).

2. The Symphony No. 9 was performed at the Niederrheinisches Musikfest (Lower Rhenish Music Festival) on May 23, 1825. Owing to the lack of rehearsal time, Ries

omitted the Scherzo and portions of the slow movement at the performance but, of course, neglected to tell Beethoven of this. Given the amount of music on this program, Ries had severely misjudged the Ninth Symphony's length, its difficulty or both.

3. Ries changed the number to 432 in a letter to Thomas D'Almaine on June 25 (Hill No. 144). The *Cäcilia* 4 (1826), 64, said 362, of which about 90 were chorus members; the *Allgemeine musikalische Zeitung* 27 (June 1825), col. 449, gave the number of participants as 400.

4. Ries's Op. 146.

5. Mozart's K. 469.

6. Beethoven's Op. 85.

7. The "Lobrede," dated May 21, was published in the *Stadt-Aachener Zeitung* on May 24 and in the *Allgemeine musikalische Zeitung* 27 (June 1825), col. 449. Before the concert, twelve hundred copies of the poem were printed so that they would fall from the balconies like snowflakes.

8. See Johann's letter dispatching these works, May 6, 1825 (No. 407 above), for identification.

9. Thayer gives the name as Hippemayer, the Fischhof Manuscript (and Nohl following it) as Hippenmayer.

10. Ries also alludes to organizational problems in England in his letter to D'Almaine (see n. 3, this letter).

Incipit: Seit einigen Tagen bin ich von Aachen zurück. . . .

Sources: Thayer-Deiters-Riemann, V, 168–169; Brenneis, "Fischhof-Manuskript," pp. 75–76; Nohl, *Briefe* (1865) (taken from the Fischhof Manuscript, now in the Staatsbibliothek zu Berlin–Preussischer Kulturbesitz), p. 299; Nohl-Wallace, pp. 194–195; Kalischer (German), V, 144–145; Kalischer-Shedlock, II, 380–381; Hill, *Ferdinand Ries*, pp. 229–230 (citing Thayer-Deiters-Riemann); summarized in Thayer-Krehbiel, III, 189, and Thayer-Forbes, pp. 933–934. The location of the autograph is unknown.

410. *Johann van Beethoven to Karl van Beethoven*

Gneixendorf; June 10, 1825[1]

Dear Karl!

Yesterday I came from Linz and found your letter, which gave me much joy, since I saw from it that you are diligent, and [that you] realize that a person who has not learned much is a wretched individual, for one can lose everything through misfortune, but not what he has learned. Therefore I advise you especially not to neglect your languages, for you would become only a common commercial clerk without having mastery of the English, Italian and French languages.[2] You will soon be 20 years old,[3] [and] thus do not have much time to bring your studies so far that you will not become a languishing servant, for this is a very cruel fate.

Enclosed here you are receiving a letter to your uncle [Ludwig].[4] I have lodged a complaint with him on your behalf, although I believe that you should often go out to him on Sundays.[5] It is true that he is somewhat difficult to be with; however, if you but consider what your uncle has already done for you: indeed he has already spent more than 10,000 florins on your behalf, and [yet] what pain and torment you have already caused him. In youth one does not understand this, but when you are older, you will then understand it better. For this reason I beg you to do what you can to lend him a helping hand, for you owe him a great deal, though you must arrange it so that your studies do not suffer. Concerning this winter, I myself believe that it would certainly be better if you remain there where you are: if you otherwise occupy your youthful years there as you are supposed to do, then you will not have to have the unpleasant feeling much longer that you are entirely a burden to your old uncle.[6]

And so farewell. Do not think about how you want to enjoy this life now; rather be diligent now so that you can enjoy life all the more later. This is the wish for you from

Your kindly disposed uncle

van Beethoven

P.S. The letter to your uncle [Ludwig] would be too long; therefore I have not enclosed it.

[Exterior:]
   Herr Carl van Beethoven
   living at
   Alleegasse No. 72
   1st floor[7]
   with Herr von Schlemmer
   Vienna

1. Beethoven's nephew Karl must have written Johann shortly after an entry made in Beethoven's conversation book on Sunday, May 29: "We must write soon to your Herr Brother." On around June 1, Beethoven made an entry in the book indicating that he wanted to advise Johann of an apothecary shop advertised for sale (Köhler et al., *Konversationshefte,* VII, 290, 292).

2. Johann's petition to the Viennese Magistrat, February 19, 1803 (No. 55 above), indicates that he himself was proficient in French and Latin.

3. Karl was born on September 4, 1806.

4. This letter seems not to have survived. Like Antonie Brentano, February 22, 1819 (No. 256 above), Johann also spells *uncle* as *Oncle.*

5. Beethoven spent much of the summer of 1825 living in Baden.

6. Both his nephew Karl and his brother Johann were experiencing great tension with Beethoven at this time, as evidenced in Beethoven's letters to Matthias Schlemmer (Anderson No. 1380), to Karl, June 9 (Anderson No. 1386), to Bernard, June 10 (Anderson No. 1387), to Karl (Anderson Nos. 1389–1394) etc.

7. American second floor.

Incipit: Gestern kamm ich von Linz. . . .

Sources: Vienna, Historisches Museum, *Führer* (1927), item 634, contains an excerpt, roughly one-sixth of the letter. Autograph in the Stadt- und Landesbibliothek, Vienna, HIN 36.448. Facsimile in Bory, p. 201.

411. *Prince Nicolas Galitzin to Beethoven*

St. Petersburg; June 21, 1825

This letter will be delivered to you, Monsieur, by Monsieur Thal, son of one of the foremost merchants of St. Petersburg, who resides at the moment in Vienna and who desires to have a letter from me for you so that he might make your acquaintance.[1] I would like very much to be in his place, because I aspire to have the good fortune to meet you personally. Please greet him as one of my countrymen. — Yesterday I received your last letter of June 4,[2] at the moment when we were playing your new Quartet,[3] indeed perfecting it, because Monsieur Lipinski was performing first violin.[4] Your letter could not have arrived at a more opportune time, but its contents gave us a great deal of sorrow; I hope, however, that your illness has passed with the return of fair weather. I await with impatience your reply to the letter that I wrote to you a week ago on the subject of a dispute among the musicians of the capital.[5]—I shall send to you immediately the 460 florins in silver that are due you, all too glad to be able to contribute in some way to the improvement of your situation.

Your very devoted,

N. Galitzin

[P.S.] I have subscribed to Schott in Mainz for the Mass,[6] the Symphony[7] and the Overture;[8] thus you will send me these last two pieces if they are copied and if you have occasion to do so; otherwise I shall wait until these works are printed.

1. For further mention of Thal, see Beethoven's letter to his nephew Karl, July 18, 1825 (Anderson No. 1402).

2. Beethoven's letter of June 4 seems not to have survived, nor has Galitzin's letter mentioned later here as having been written around June 14. It is probably Galitzin's June 14 letter to which Beethoven refers in his note to Karl of shortly after July 11 (Anderson No. 1396) because the composer addresses the musical dispute, which Galitzin related, in his (Beethoven's) letter to Galitzin of late July (Anderson No. 1405).

3. Op. 127.

4. Karol Józef Lipiński (1790–1861), Polish violinist, who spent the years 1819–1828 touring Poland, Russia and Germany. He was later the teacher of Joseph Joachim.

5. Beethoven's reply of late July (Anderson No. 1405) deals with the Andante con moto of the Quartet, Op. 127. Among the contestants who disputed certain notes in the text, Beethoven sided with Karl Traugott Zeuner (1775–1841) as being "perfectly right" in his interpretation.

6. Op. 123.

7. Op. 125.

8. Op. 124. Beethoven noted to Galitzin in late July (Anderson No. 1405) that he was giving agent Henikstein two overtures (Op. 124 and probably Op. 115) to be sent to Galitzin.

Incipit: Cette lettre vous sera remise. . . .

Sources: Thayer-Deiters-Riemann, V, 566. When Thayer copied it, the autograph was in the possession of Beethoven's nephew Karl's widow, Caroline, Vienna. It has since disappeared.

412. Hans Georg Nägeli to Beethoven

[Zürich; presumably June 1825][1]

My highly honored Friend!

Allow me to turn to you concerning a very unusual matter.

It has long been my life's ambition, when my sons were grown up,[2] to expand my music business, and for this purpose, to set up a [branch of my] business in Frankfurt, the principal city in south Germany, and then to proceed with new publishing activities, which would do the same thing for the present state of musical culture, as the *Works in Strict Composition*[3] and the *Répertoire des Clavecinistes*[4] did [two decades ago]. My plan has now matured to [the point of] being carried out. I have found a distinguished partner, whom I may not yet identify, a rich merchant [who] wants to back me up and is placing considerable capital at my disposal to establish myself in Frankfurt.

Now I have another difficulty. I ought to transfer my bookshop, with which a very extensive musical lending library is connected, to Frankfurt, and nevertheless retain the business in Switzerland. This expansion entails great expenses. For that purpose, in order to carry out the matter quickly rather than let it drag on for years, I am seeking to raise[5] a loan of ca. 6,000 florins on the basis of the stock and the accrued assets of the bookshop. Therefore, I am seeking a strong and impressive recommendation to Baron von Rothschild in Frankfurt,[6] with whom I am otherwise not acquainted. This man places great emphasis upon those from whom people are referred to him. Since he now stands in great credit with the *Viennese* court[7] as a sound-thinking and religious man,[8] would it be possible to obtain, through you, a recommendation from H[is] I[mperial] H[ighness] and E[minence], the Archduke Rudolph, if you told His Highness (to which purpose I hereby give you the authority) that this recommendation might also be indirectly advantageous *to you*, because, as a result, I would publish new works of yours for an adequate fee and continuously spread your fame.

The recommendation would be most effective for me if it were expressed that Herr von Rothschild would be favoring not just me alone as a worthy promoter of culture, but through me also the foremost composer of the new century, who stands in high favor with H.I.H. and E.: Beethoven.

Really I also have H.I.H. and E. in mind as a composer in my publishing undertakings, in the opinion that His Highness should also appear [in print] with a work in a continuation of the *Répertoire*.[9] I think, however, that it would be counterproductive to let anything about this leak out, because H.I.H. and E. might get the idea that someone wanted to win him over to [writing] the recommendation through such an offer.

Otherwise I ask you to keep the contents of this letter secret. The last thing I need is for some music dealer to get wind of it.

But be so kind as to send me your answer soon in any case; [for my part I would like] to be able [to report to you soon] on how the first well-calculated steps are little by little leading to a great goal.

1. This letter exists only in draft form. Evidence that Nägeli actually sent it may be found in a conversation book from June 30 or the beginning of July 1825, where Beethoven, among a shopping list for clothes and other personal items, also notes "Letter to the Archduke concerning Nägeli" (Köhler et al., *Konversationshefte*, VII, 312). Thus this letter dates at latest around June 24, 1825, given the speed of the mails.

2. Ultimately, Nägeli's son Hermann (1811–1872) took over the music business.

3. Nägeli here calls the series of compositions by Bach and Handel, begun in 1802, *Werke der strengen Schreibart*, although its proper name had been *Musikalische Kunstwerke in strengen Stile*.

4. In 1802, Nägeli had commissioned Beethoven for the Piano Sonatas, Op. 31, as part of this series. Op. 31, Nos. 1 and 2, appeared in 1803, while No. 3, combined with a pirate reprint of Op. 13, appeared in 1804. See the Nägeli-Beethoven correspondence of these years for further details.

5. Nägeli here uses the word *entheben* (to dismiss or be freed from), but he may mean *erheben* (to raise), unless he intended to use the stock and accrued assets as collateral to pay off an old loan.

6. Anselm Mayer Rothschild (1773–1855), son of Mayer Anselm Rothschild (1743–1812), who had founded the Frankfurt-based banking house. Anselm Mayer remained in Frankfurt, while other sons established branches elsewhere in Europe, including Solomon Rothschild (1774–1855), who settled in Vienna.

7. Nägeli uses the phrase *im grossen Kredit stehen* with double meaning: that the Viennese court was financially indebted to Rothschild (possibly through both father and brother) and that they also held him in high regard.

8. By contrast, in Nägeli's letter to Beethoven of February 21, 1825 (No. 395 above), the Swiss was worried that he, a Protestant, might be misinterpreted in writing

a dedication to Catholic Archduke Rudolph. Yet the Rothschild family had never abandoned their traditional Jewish faith.

9. Archduke Rudolph, as Beethoven's student, was also a moderately talented composer, generally for smaller combinations of performers. See Kagan, *Archduke Rudolph*.

Incipit: Erlauben Sie, dass ich mich in einer ganz besondern Angelegenheit. . . .

Sources: Rudolf Hunziger, "Hans Georg Nägeli: Einige Beiträge zu seiner Biographie," *Schweizerische Musikzeitung* 76, no. 22 (November 15, 1936), 633–634; Geiser, *Beethoven und die Schweiz*, pp. 86–88 (quoting Hunziger); Martin Staehelin, *Hans Georg Nägeli und Ludwig van Beethoven* (Zürich: Hug, 1982), pp. 55–56. Autograph in the Zentralbibliothek, Zürich, Ms. Car XV 195–196. The text above follows Staehelin, who logically filled in a brief gap near the end of the letter.

413. Karl van Beethoven to Carl Friedrich Peters, Leipzig

[Vienna;] July 19, 1825[1]

Dear Sir!

Since my uncle is presently in Baden to restore his severely impaired health, I am taking the liberty (according to written instructions on his part) to report to you in his name that he recently finished a new grand String Quartet,[2] and additionally to offer it to you for the [360] Conventions Gulden that you already sent him earlier.[3]

Should you not be inclined to do this, my uncle must therefore turn it over to another publisher, who has offered him the same amount for it.[4] In any case, however, I request that you send a speedy reply, so that the matter will not be delayed.

In closing, allow me to quote a passage from my uncle's note: "Remind Herr v[on] Peters that I am offering him the best that I *have* at present, *without mentioning the past.*"

I ask you to send your reply to my uncle himself at the following address: Baden near Vienna, at Schloss Gutenbrunn.

I sign myself respectfully

Yours,

Carl van Beethoven

1. Karl's letter partially responds to instructions from Beethoven in a letter of July 10, 1825 (Anderson No. 1394). Since all that Karl tells Peters is not in that letter, Beethoven must have given his nephew further oral or written instructions, now lost.

2. Op. 132. In his letter to Karl, Beethoven specifically instructed him to "call it a '*grand quartet.*'"

3. For further clarification, see Beethoven's letter to Peters, November 25, 1825 (Anderson No. 1451).

4. Beethoven was negotiating at this time with Adolf Martin Schlesinger in Berlin (see his letter, July 15–19, 1825, Anderson No. 1403) and shortly thereafter with Schlesinger's son, Moritz Schlesinger, the Paris publisher.

Incipit: Da mein Oheim sich gegenwärtig. . . .

Sources: Nohl, *Neue Briefe* (1867), p. 278. Autograph probably in the archives of C. F. Peters, Leipzig, presumably destroyed in World War II.

414. Johann Andreas Stumpff[1] to Beethoven

London; July 29, 1825

The person who will have the honor of delivering this letter to you is Sir George Smart,[2] my neighbor and friend, a musician and member of the Philharmonic Society in London, who is curious to become acquainted with the land that has generated, cultivated and perfected the creator of many immortal works of music.

First of all, I must right now beg your pardon for not having yet sent you the promised Handel *Works*,[3] because I immediately searched for them upon my return to London, and was so happy to obtain a set of them in good condition, since the plates of the better edition were long ago destroyed and have never been reengraved, and I am afraid that it is rather difficult to obtain a set in good condition.[4] I take the liberty here to confess to you that the main reason why it has not been sent to you is because I believed that I would have the indescribable pleasure of seeing the greatest musician in London, and then also because I lacked the specific opportunity and still lack one to send it to Vienna. Also, since you expressed to me the wish also to have a set for the I[mperial] R[oyal] Prince,[5] and should you still be determined to do this, I take the liberty to report to you that I also have found a set for this purpose. And so, both *Works* could be forwarded in one crate to Vienna in the least expensive manner, perhaps through the Austrian Embassy in London to the I.R. Prince's address. You would very much oblige me thereby, if you would be so kind as to let me know your wishes in a letter, and I then would be prepared to gratify them without delay.

Further, I take the liberty here to mention that I am very sorry that the seven compositions of yours, which your brother sent me to be sold in London,[6] remain in my possession unsold, despite all my efforts, and I begin to doubt a favorable outcome, because none of the many art dealerships want to concern themselves with them.

Concerning your *Battle of Vittoria* I have inquired in many places, indeed to those who are nearest the King, but I have learned nothing further than: they regret that they cannot serve me in this concern, and that the person who was head of the Musical Department at Court at that time was promoted to another position in a foreign country, and that perhaps a more favorable chance might come to pass to remind the King about it.[7]

Finally I also take the liberty to confess to you that my swelling heart thanks Providence most sincerely for leading me to dear Baden and allowing me to see the Beloved of the Muses and the creator of the most elevated tone paintings face to face, a person of whose kind reception I was deemed worthy, who has moved me deeply and has filled me with admiration and ardent gratitude.

In the expectation that you are enjoying a long period of health, I have the honor to be

Your most obedient servant,

J. A. Stumpff

44 Great Portland Street
Portland Place

P.S. The Handel *Works* mentioned above consists of 40 bound volumes, and I request the liberty once more to greet most heartily Herr Streicher and his family.[8]

[Exterior:]
  Herr Luis van Beethoven
  Vienna
  through the kindness [of the bearer].

1. Born in Thuringia, Stumpff (1769–1846) had lived for decades in London as a musician and harp manufacturer. Stumpff had first visited Vienna in the summer of 1818, and then again in the fall of 1824, arriving on September 25 and staying at least through early October, to judge by entries in the conversation books. His 1824 meeting with Beethoven took place in Baden. For Stumpff's earlier acquaintance with Beethoven in 1818 and 1824, see Nos. 252 and 383 above.

2. Smart (1776–1867) was prominent in London as a conductor, composer, violinist and teacher. Beethoven had written to him as early as March 16–19, 1815 (Anderson No. 534), so his name was probably not unfamiliar to the composer. Smart had conducted the first London performance of the Ninth Symphony on March 21, 1825. According to his own account (see Cox and Cox, *Leaves from . . . Smart,* pp. 104, 108–115, excerpted in Sonneck, *Impressions,* pp. 191–196), Smart delivered Stumpff's letter to Beethoven at a private performance of the String Quartet, Op. 132, held at the hotel Wilder Mann (where Paris publisher Moritz Schlesinger was lodging) on Friday, September 9, 1825. Thus this letter was delivered six weeks after it was written. Stumpff called the letter bearer "Herr Georg Schmart."

Delivered at the same time was a letter to Beethoven from Ferdinand Ries, whom Smart had visited in Godesberg (near Bonn) on August 7–9, 1825, on his way to Vienna (see Cox and Cox, pp. 69–70, 104). Ries's letter seems not to have survived.

3. *The Works of Handel,* [ed.] Dr. Arnold, 40 vols. (London, 1787–1797). The set is listed in Beethoven's *Nachlass* (Thayer-Forbes, p. 1070).

4. Chrysander commented in 1862–1863: "This edition is very often available for sale today in well-maintained sets, perhaps more frequently than then." Stumpff had arrived back in London on December 6, 1824. See Schultz to Haslinger, December 10, 1824 (No. 386 above), for a possible early reference to Stumpff's intention to send the Handel set.

5. Archduke Rudolph. This matter is discussed in Köhler et al., *Konversationshefte,* VI, 368.

6. See Beethoven's letter to Schott, November 1824 (Anderson No. 1321), brother Johann's letter to Schott, December 29, 1824 (No. 389 above), and Johann's letter to Stumpff, February 24, 1825 (No. 396 above), for identification of these works.

7. The contention over *Wellington's Victory* is discussed in Johann Baptist Häring's and Beethoven's letter of March 16–19, 1815 (Anderson No. 534). The dedication of Op. 91 was never acknowledged, and Beethoven remained bitter about the fact.

8. Johann Andreas Streicher, piano manufacturer, and his wife, Nannette (Stein).

Incipit: Der die Ehre haben wird. . . .

Sources: Friedrich Chrysander, "Beethoven's Verbindung mit Birchall und Stumpff in London," *Jahrbücher für musikalische Wissenschaft* 1 (1863), 447–448. The autograph (probably a copybook copy) was then in the possession of Robert Lonsdale, London. Chrysander corrected several inappropriate choices of words in the original.

415. B. Schotts Söhne, Notice in
the Intelligenzblatt *of the* Cäcilia

Mainz; July 30, 1825[1]

Herr van Beethoven has publicly warned against the illegal as well as incorrect edition of a four-hand piano reduction of his Festival Overture, made by Herr Henning [and] issued by Trautwein in Berlin. Not to mention the obvious, that such an advance publication is even more disgraceful than a pirate reprint, we notify the honored public only of the following: that we acquired the exclusive right to publish this work from the famous composer some time ago, and that a reduction of it for four hands, made by the well-known piano virtuoso Herr Czerny under the eyes of the composer himself, has just now appeared from us.[2] We are therefore in the position, as the legitimate publisher, to offer a more worthy version of this ingenious original work than the contraband by Herr Henning.

B. Schotts Söhne

1. For Schott's original version of this notice, which ran twice (with slight modifications the second time) under the date April 20, 1825, see No. 404A above.

2. Czerny's two-hand arrangement had appeared in April 1825. The phrase "bei uns so eben erschienen ist" confirms that his four-hand arrangement had been published in July. It is the most important of the modifications in this third printing of Schott's notice.

Incipit: Herr van Beethoven hat öffentlich die eben so unrechtliche. . . .

Sources: Cäcilia 3 (1825), *Intelligenzblatt* no. 11, pp. 30–31; Thayer-Deiters-Riemann, IV, 308. My gratitude to Dr. Calvin Elliker, music librarian, University of Michigan, for providing me with copies of the *Cäcilia* material used here and in Nos. 404 and 404A above.

416. Marie Leopoldine Pachler-Koschak[1] to Beethoven

Hallerschloss, near Graz; August 15, 1825[2]

Dear, honored H[err] v[an] Beethoven!

You will probably hardly remember me, much less the promise that you gave me two years ago to have a little look around our friendly Steiermark. Since then I have often wanted to remind you of it, but I lacked the courage to write this to you point-blank, and yet it is a matter in which I myself am so very much interested. The wish of the bearer of these lines to make your personal acquaintance now serves as the pretext for me to turn to you in writing. Herr Joh[ann] B[aptist] Jenger[3] is a friend of our family and a fervent admirer of your music. He is musical through and through, and although as a state official he is not allowed to make music his primary occupation, he nevertheless plays almost all instruments, and especially the piano very well. His transfer to Vienna robs the Musikverein here of one of its pillars, and robs everyone who has known him of a pleasant companion, full of sincerity and high spirits. In addition to possessing these qualities, he is just as ardent an advocate for my cause as I am for his; thus he will verbally assure you of that elevated manner of admiration that can only excuse my attempt to justify the claims that, aside from your words of promise, entitle me to nothing. Do not leave these words unfulfilled—Come! Autumn here with us is always the most pleasant season, and the month of September is the most beautiful in the entire year. Moreover, we are living this year on a very lovely country estate, in one of the most glorious areas surrounding our city. I have here more than 10 rooms at my disposal, and thus space enough to accommodate you and your nephew comfortably. With an express coach you would be here in 24 hours. Certainly such a trip would be conducive to your health and, at the same time, without leaving your genius idle, would grant it some beneficial rest. I could perhaps cite many points yet in favor of my wish, but I will have to consider not only all of my good reasons, but also something of your own free judgment, and therefore I will only add in writing my request that you tentatively let me know the day of your arrival, so that we can drive to meet you and immediately accompany you to our country place. Should you prefer to live in the city (which I doubt, however, in light of your predilection for country life), we can offer you the entire second story in our own house there, which now stands unoccupied anyhow, during our summer vacation.

My husband and my brother-in-law[4] send greetings, and hope, with me, that you will not refuse our offer.

In admiration, yours sincerely,

Marie L. Pachler-Koschak

My address is:
　Marie L. Pachler
　Koschak
　Herrengasse
　(Our own house)
　Graz

1. Marie Leopoldine Pachler, née Koschak (1794–1855), was born in Graz and played the piano solo in Beethoven's Choral Fantasy, Op. 80, there on December 22, 1811. In 1816, she married the lawyer Dr. Karl Pachler and, in the summer of 1817, traveled to Vienna, where she met Beethoven (although Sieghard Brandenburg, Beethoven-Archiv, Bonn, notes that Anderson No. 815, in which the composer admires her pianism, is a forgery). In the summer of 1823, she was in Vienna again, taking her leave on September 27 — thus her reference in the first sentence of this letter.

2. This letter did not get delivered to Beethoven until around December 19, 1826. See Frau Pachler's next letter to the composer, November 5, 1826 (No. 442 below), for details.

3. Jenger (1792–1856) was a military official and amateur musician. He is most closely associated with Schubert and in fact induced the Pachlers to invite Schubert to visit Graz, September 3–20, 1827, when the artist Joseph Teltscher portrayed Jenger with Anselm Hüttenbrenner and Schubert. Vivid descriptions of the visit as well as Pachler family life survive in the Schubert literature. From 1819 to 1825, Jenger was professionally active in Graz, where he became secretary of the Musikverein, thus influential in Beethoven's receiving the honorary membership from the society in 1822 (see the diploma of January 1, 1822, No. 282 above) and Schubert's similar honor in 1823.

4. Dr. Anton Pachler.

Incipit: Sie werden sich vielleicht kaum meiner. . . .

Sources: Thayer-Deiters-Riemann, V, 432–433. Autograph in the Staatsbibliothek zu Berlin–Preussischer Kulturbesitz, Mus. ms. autogr. Beethoven 35, 57a; listed in Kalischer, "Beethoven-Autographe," p. 51, and Bartlitz, pp. 135–136.

417. Moritz Schlesinger to Beethoven

[Vienna; probably September 22, 1825][1]

I the undersigned attest that I have acquired two Quartets as my property,[2] for one of which[3] I will immediately pay 80 ducats in gold here and now, and for the other,[4] H[err] Biedermann here in Vienna[5] will take over on my behalf, and likewise will pay out the fee of 80 ducats in gold upon delivery of the same.

M[ortiz] Schles[inger]

1. The Paris publisher Moritz (Maurice) Schlesinger visited Vienna from late August until around September 26, 1825, attending the coronation (of Empress Carolina Augusta as queen of Hungary) in Pressburg on September 25 before his departure. Conversation book no. 97, Bl. 38v–43v (Köhler et al., *Konversationshefte,* VIII, 161–164), seemingly covers a conversation on September 21, which probably occasioned the canon "Glaube und hoffe," WoO 174, mentioned on Bl. 42r. Although Beethoven was living in Baden, the conversation seems to have been held in Vienna. Beethoven's nephew Karl was to remain the next day to accompany Schlesinger to the banking house of Bernhard von Eskeles. Later in the conversation, future payment by Biedermann was also mentioned. Therefore this receipt was probably signed at noon on Thursday, September 22. According to Thayer, Beethoven had drafted it himself for Schlesinger to sign.

On the reverse, Beethoven later wrote a note to Karl (Anderson No. 1435).

2. That Schlesinger had possession of only one of them at this time is made clear by the wording that follows.

3. String Quartet, Op. 132.

4. Beethoven may have intended to sell Schlesinger the Quartet, Op. 130, which was still unfinished. Ultimately, however, Op. 130 went to Artaria, and Schlesinger received Op. 135 as his second quartet, when Beethoven sent it from Gneixendorf in October 1826.

5. Samuel Biedermann (born 1803) lived at the corner of Kärntnerstrasse and Walfischgasse. He was a partner in the wholesale firm H. Biedermanns Söhne.

Incipit: Ich Endes Unterschrieb. bezeuge. . . .

Sources: Thayer-Deiters-Riemann, V, 250–251, indicating that this material was in the Artaria Collection. Kalischer (German), V, 230–231, and Kalischer-Shedlock, II, 426, citing Otto Jahn's Beethoven papers in the Royal Library, Berlin (now the

Staatsbibliothek zu Berlin–Preussischer Kulturbesitz). Anderson (No. 1435) could not locate the autograph.

418. *Karl van Beethoven to Beethoven*

[Vienna; shortly after November 8, 1825][1]

My dear Father!

I would have willingly come to see you myself, but I am so busy at the moment that it is impossible for me to leave my studies.[2] My tutor, whose monthly term was finished on November 8, requested me, because of great expenditures that he has to make now, to ask you for his fee of 40 florins in paper.[3]

If you had come to see me yesterday, I would have told you this myself, but not knowing if you will give me the pleasure of coming today, I thought it necessary to let you know about this and ask you to bring the money to him when you come to visit me, or in case you cannot come, to have the sum delivered by one of your domestic servants, so that I can give it to him tomorrow morning.

I shall try not to need these lessons much longer; in short, I shall take every possible pain to gratify you in all respects. I embrace you with all my heart.

Your Charles

[P.S.] I ask that you give a big tip to the boy who brings this letter.

[Exterior:]
    To
    Herr Ludwig van Beethoven,
    Here [in the city].
    To be delivered at House No. 200 at the
    Schwarzspanier, on the 2d floor,[4]
    door to the left.

1. This letter, in French, is undated, as evidently Karl was wont to do, judging from Beethoven's complaint about this on October 12, 1825 (Anderson No. 1440).

This letter was sent to the Schwarzspanierhaus, where Beethoven had moved on October 15, 1825. Since both Beethoven and Karl were in Gneixendorf in November 1826, the reference to November 8 places this letter shortly thereafter in the year 1825.

    2. Karl was living with Matthias Schlemmer and attending the Polytechnic Institute at this time. He describes his regimen of study in a conversation book entry of November 6, 1825 (Köhler et al., *Konversationshefte,* VIII, 183; translated in Thayer-Forbes, p. 990).

    3. The tutor's sessions are mentioned in the above regimen (see n. 2, this letter). Beethoven had sent a previous fee of 40 gulden on September 14 (Anderson No. 1431) and probably did likewise at about the same time in October, possibly in person.

    4. American third floor.

Incipit: Je serais volontiers venu vous voir. . . .

Sources: Autograph in the Staatsbibliothek zu Berlin–Preussischer Kulturbesitz, Mus. ms. autogr. Beethoven 35, 60b; listed in Kalischer, "Beethoven-Autographe," p. 51, and Bartlitz, p. 137.

419. Tobias Haslinger to Johann Nepomuk Hummel,[1] Weimar

[Vienna;] November 10, [1825][2]

Herr Hummel,

    [Contents concern, first off, a kidney stone powder that is to reach Érard in Paris;[3] then a Rondo that Hummel has intended for Haslinger's publishing house. Haslinger's partner Steiner found the price of 200 florins, C.M., too high. Haslinger writes an aside: Steiner "is elderly and also somewhat strange."[4] There follows a peppery attack against the publishers Schlesinger, father Adolf Martin in Berlin and son Maurice in Paris.[5] In passing, Haslinger touches on the Löhlein-Müller *Klavierschule,* which at that time had been published by Peters (Leipzig) in a new edition by Carl Czerny.[6] Haslinger also turns to Hummel's piano concertos and asks how much a new one might cost.]

    We are still without opera, and musical [i.e., concert] life is in a miserable state. The nobility does absolutely nothing for it anymore. An endless *Lamento* could be wailed about it. Poor Worzischek has now been given up as hopeless by his doctors, and his end is expected with each passing day.[7] Beethoven is now well again, but he is aging very much.[8] Last Sunday, in his own benefit concert, Linke performed Beethoven's recently completed thirteenth Quartet in A minor, to great applause.[9]

[Two lines with hand kisses for Hummel's wife and other greetings constitute the letter's close.]

H.

1. Johann Nepomuk Hummel (1778–1837), pianist, composer and conductor. Trained in Vienna, he was employed by the Esterházy family and had been active as *Kapellmeister* in Weimar since 1818. From late March through late May 1825, he had visited Paris, the source of many allusions in this letter. For details, see Joel Sachs, *Kapellmeister Hummel in England and France* (Detroit: Information Coordinators, 1977), pp. 17–29.

2. This letter survives only as excerpted and paraphrased passages from the draft, which was dated merely November 10. The year can be determined by the letter's contents.

3. Hummel had given a series of concerts in the salon of the Parisian piano maker and publisher Érard. Possibly the powder was intended to cure an affliction suffered by Sébastian Érard (1752–1831) or more likely his brother and partner Jean-Baptiste (died 1826).

4. Probably Hummel's *Rondo brillant*, Op. 109, which was published by Steiner and Co. before May 1826. Steiner (1773–1838) retired from senior partnership early in 1826, and Haslinger pushed forward with several projects that Steiner's caution may have postponed, including the publication of several works by Beethoven. Nonetheless, Haslinger seems never to have published one of Hummel's piano concertos.

5. The Schlesingers (particularly Moritz in Paris) had pirated, and presumably continued to pirate, enough of Hummel's works to project a twenty-one-volume collection of them, with no remuneration to either the composer or his earlier publishers. Thus neither Hummel nor Haslinger could be counted on to speak kindly of Schlesinger.

6. G. S. Löhlein's *Clavierschule* (1765) reached a sixth edition, edited by August Eberhard Müller (1767–1817), as *Klavier- und Fortepiano-Schule* (Jena, 1804); its eighth edition (1825) was edited by Carl Czerny as *Grosse Pianoforteschule, oder Anweisung zur richtigen und geschmackvollen Spielart dieses Instruments*. Müller's wife Elisabeth Catharina had played the piano part in what was probably the first public performance of Beethoven's Triple Concerto, Op. 56, with the Gewandhaus Orchestra in Leipzig on February 18, 1808.

7. Composer and court organist Johann Hugo Worzischek (or Jan Václav Vořišek, 1791–1825), a former pupil of Hummel's, died on November 19.

8. Beethoven had suffered a severe illness in April–May 1825. On May 18, Beethoven wrote from Baden to his nephew Karl, "I am getting thinner and thinner, and feel more ailing than well" (Anderson No. 1375). Despite his recuperation during the summer, Beethoven's general health seems to have been in decline. On learning

of Beethoven's mortal condition early in 1827, Hummel (accompanied by his wife and his student, the young Ferdinand Hiller) came to Vienna for three final visits on March 8, 13 and 20, shortly before the composer's death. During the March 8 visit, Hummel solicited from Beethoven a petition to the Bundesversammlung in Frankfurt, requesting an abolition of "the positively disgraceful pirating of musical works in Germany" (Anderson, III, 1452). Hiller's account of these visits is printed in Sonneck, *Impressions*, pp. 214–219.

9. Opus 132 was premiered by Schuppanzigh's quartet, of which Joseph Linke (1783–1837) was the violoncellist, in the Gesellschaft der Musikfreunde's hall in the Rother Igel, on Sunday, November 6, 1825.

Incipit: Unknown.

Sources: Frimmel, "Beethovenstellen aus zeitgenössischen Briefen," pp. 49–51. In 1925, the autograph draft was in the possession of Dr. Gustav Riehl, professor at the University of Vienna. Riehl, in turn, had obtained it, sometime earlier, from Haslinger's descendants in Windischgarten.

420. Carl Friedrich Peters to Beethoven

Leipzig; November 30, 1825[1]

I hereby request Herr L[udwig] van Beethoven in Vienna to pay back now the three hundred and sixty gulden C.M., that you received from me in August 1822; since no business transaction took place between us, place the sum again at my disposal through Herr Steiner & Co., music dealer in Vienna, and accept this document in return as receipt from me.

C. F. Peters
Music Publisher

[On the same sheet:]

360 florins C.M.
The above amount received and
acknowledged,
S. A. Steiner & Co.
December 7, 1825

1. An immediate reply to Beethoven's letter of November 25, 1825 (Anderson No. 1451), signifying a long-delayed conclusion to an unfortunate episode.

Incipit: Herrn L. van Beethoven in Wien ersuche ich hiermit. . . .

Sources: Schindler (1860), pt. 2, p. 44; Schindler-MacArdle, p. 258; Thayer-Deiters-Riemann, V, 276–277. Autograph in the Staatsbibliothek zu Berlin–Preussischer Kulturbesitz, Mus. ms. autogr. Beethoven 35, 70; listed in Kalischer, "Beethoven-Autographe," p. 52, and Bartlitz, p. 140.

421. *Theodor Molt*[1] *to Beethoven*

Vienna; December 14, 1825

Highly honored Sir!

When I took the liberty to visit you the other day, I held back from you a wish, which I hereby submissively dare to put before you in this letter.[2] After my departure from here I will never again have the good fortune to be near you. Pardon me therefore, if I present to you a little page from my autograph book [*Stammbuch*] to be filled in: my return trip from here covers a distance of almost 3,000 hours, and when I am [home], this will always remain a precious document for me. I consider myself fortunate to have seen several of Europe's famous composers, whom I knew in America from their works, and will be proud to be able to say to my friends there, who are likewise your admirers:

"Look, Beethoven wrote this for me from his great soul!"[3]

I beg that you might give me your kind answer by tomorrow,

With great admiration,
Your most obedient servant,

Theodor Molt
Music Teacher in Quebec,
North America

1. Born in Gschwend, Baden-Württemberg, Molt (1795–1856) came to America in the early 1820s, settling in Quebec as a music teacher in 1823. He returned to Europe in 1825, for the purpose of travel and study. From 1826, he taught in Quebec and several places in New England.

2. Molt had met Beethoven on December 11 or very shortly thereafter. Judging from the single awestruck entry that he made in Beethoven's conversation book of the time, he must have been quite flustered in the composer's presence and gathered his courage to make this request only after the meeting (Köhler et al., *Konversationshefte,* VIII, 211).

3. In return for this request, Beethoven wrote the canon "Freu' dich des Lebens," WoO 195, dated Vienna, December 16, 1825, the autograph of which is in the Lawrence Lande Collection of Canadiana, Redpath Library, McGill University, Montreal. A facsimile of the canon is in Bekker, *Beethoven* (1911), plate supplement, p. 131.

Beethoven also gave Molt two other items. The first is a copy of the canon "Das Schöne zu dem Guten" (presumably WoO 203, to a line from Matthisson's *Opferlied* [set as Op. 121b]), dated December 16, 1825, but also included earlier in a letter to Ludwig Rellstab, May 3, 1825 (Anderson No. 1366b). See Helms and Staehelin, "Bewegungen . . . 1973–1979," p. 354.

The second was a copy of Höfel's engraved portrait, with the inscription: "Zum Andenk. für H. v. Molt von L. v. Beethoven." It was auctioned at Sotheby's, London, on November 21, 1990, for $33,000 (Ira F. Brilliant, "Music Auction Market," *Beethoven Newsletter* [San Jose] 6, no. 1 [Spring 1991], 22).

Incipit: Als ich letzthin so frey war. . . .

Sources: Thayer-Deiters-Riemann, V, 273. Thayer copied the letter when the autograph was still in the Artaria Collection. Later it was in the possession of Fritz Donebauer (Prague) and then offered for auction by J. A. Stargardt (Berlin) on April 6, 1908. See Kalischer (German), V, 318–319. Further information can be found in Helmut Kallmann, "Theodore Frederic Molt," *New Grove,* XII, 472–473; Köhler et al., *Konversationshefte,* VIII, 384; Hess, "Ein Beethoven-Autograph in Kanada," pp. 113–114.

422. Franz Gerhard Wegeler[1] to Beethoven

Koblenz; December 28, 1825[2]

My dear old Louis![3]

I cannot let one of the 10 Ries children[4] travel to Vienna without reawakening your memories of me. If you have not received a long letter every two months during the 28 years since I left Vienna, you may consider your silence in reaction to mine first to be the cause. It is in no way right and all the less so now, since we old people like to live so much in the past and especially take delight in scenes from our youth. To me, at least, my acquaintance and my close youthful friendship with you, blessed by your kind mother, remain a very bright point in my life, on which I look back with pleasure, and which especially preoccupies me while traveling. Now I view you as a hero, and am proud to be able to say: I was not without influence upon his development; he confided to me his wishes and dreams; and when later he was so frequently misunderstood, I knew well what he wanted. Thank God that I was able to speak about you with my wife and now later with my children, although my mother-in-law's house was more your residence than you own, especially after you lost your noble mother.[5] Tell us just once more: yes, I think of you in happier and darker moods! Even if he has such great stature as yours, a man is happy only one time in his life, namely in his youth; the stones of Bonn, Kreuzberg, Godesberg, the Baumschul, etc., etc. have served you as points from which you can happily refer many ideas.

Now I shall tell you something about me and about us, in order to give you an example of how you must reply to me.

After my return from Vienna in 1796, things went rather badly for me; for several years, I had to live from my practice alone, and I existed for some years in the most impoverished state until I was able to make a decent income. Then I became a *salaried* professor and married in 1802. The year after that I received a daughter,[6] who is still living and who has prospered very well. She has much true intelligence, the cheerfulness of her father, and likes best to play Beethoven sonatas. This is not so much due to hard work as it is to her innate talent. In 1807, a son was born to me, who is now studying medicine in Berlin.[7] After four years there, I shall send him to Vienna; will you receive him? Concerning the family of your friend, my father died, 70 years old, on January 1, 1800.[8] Concerning that of my wife, the schoolteacher [*Scholaster*] died four years ago, 72 years old;[9] and Aunt Stockhausen from the Ahr in this year, 73 years old.[10] Mama Breuning is 76;[11] the uncle in Kerpen, 85 years old.[12] The last is still enjoying life and speaks often of you. Mama, along with the Aunt, moved to Cologne again; they lived in the house of their parents, which they occupied again after 66 years, then had new additions made to it, etc.

I myself celebrated my 60th birthday in August in the company of some 60 friends and acquaintances, among whom were the most prominent people of the city. — I have been living here since 1807, have a fine house and a fine position. My superiors are satisfied with me, and the King gave me decorations and medals. Lore and I are also pretty healthy.

Now, all at once I have made you well acquainted with our situation; if you wish to continue the correspondence, simply reply. Among our acquaintances, Court Councillor Stupp died three years ago,[13] Fischenich is State Councillor in Berlin,[14] and Ries and Simrock are two fine old men, the latter, however, is far less healthy than the former.[15]

Two years ago, I was in Berlin for a month; there I made the acquaintance of the director of the *Singakademie,* Herr Zelter, a very gifted man and extremely frank; therefore people think him rude.[16] In Kassel, Hub[ert] Ries[17] introduced me to Spohr.[18] You see that I still remain in contact with artists.

Why have you not avenged the honor of your mother, when in the *Conversations-Lexikon* and in France, they make you out to be a love child?[19] The Englishman who wanted to vindicate you gave this crap a box on the ears, as they say in Bonn, and allowed that your mother would have been pregnant with you for 30 years, since the King of Prussia, your alleged father, had died already in 1740—an assertion that is thoroughly false, since Friedrich II came to the throne in 1740 and died in 1786.[20] Only your inherent aversion to having something of yours other than music printed is indeed to blame for this inexcusable indolence. *If you will inform the world about the facts in this matter, so will I.* That is surely one point at least to which you will reply.[21]

Will you never let the tower of St. Stephan's out of your sight?[22] Has traveling no attraction for you?[23] Don't you ever want to see the Rhein again? All heartfelt greetings from Frau Lore,[24] as well as from me,

Your ancient friend,

Wglr.

1. Wegeler (1765–1848) had known Beethoven since 1782 or 1783. He was a regular visitor to the cultured von Breuning household and married Eleonore von Breuning (1771–1841) in 1802. From September 1787 to October 1789, and again from October 1794 to mid-1796, Wegeler was in Vienna as a medical student. Although his own correspondence with Beethoven was sporadic, the two received news of each other through Stephan von Breuning, the Ries family and Nikolaus Simrock. With Ferdinand Ries, Wegeler coauthored the *Biographische Notizen über Ludwig van Beethoven* in 1838 and, by himself, a supplement in 1845.

2. This letter was accompanied by Eleonore Wegeler's letter of December 29 (No. 423 below). Beethoven did not reply for nearly a year, writing on December 7, 1826 (Anderson No. 1542).

3. Very few correspondents seemingly addressed Beethoven by his first name, and Wegeler called him by the French form here, as he may have when the two were young.

4. The family of violinist Franz Anton Ries (1755–1846).

5. Born in 1746, Maria Magdalena (Keverich) van Beethoven died on July 17, 1787. Wegeler means here that Beethoven spent more time at the von Breuning home than he did in the house occupied by his father and other family children.

6. Helene Wegeler, called Lenchen in Eleonore's accompanying letter.

7. Julius Wegeler, who ultimately did not come to Vienna until 1831.

8. Wegeler came from a family of modest means in Bonn.

9. Abraham von Kerich, canon and scholaster of the archdeanery of Bonn, died in Koblenz in 1821.

10. Sister of Frau Helene von Breuning.

11. Helene (von Kerich) von Breuning (1750–1838), widow of Court Councillor Christoph von Breuning, who died in a fire at the electoral palace in 1777.

12. Johann Philipp von Breuning, born in 1742 at Mergentheim, had been canon and priest at Kerpen, a town along the road from Cologne to Aachen; he died in 1832. Beethoven had made some summer journeys with the von Breuning family to Kerpen.

13. Forbes gives his name as Stupps, all others as Stup.

14. Bartolomäus Ludwig Fischenich (1768–1831), who on January 26, 1793, had written from Bonn to Charlotte von Schiller, enclosing Beethoven's song "Feuerfarbe," Op. 52, No. 2, and saying that he intended to compose Schiller's "An die Freude." Since 1819, he had been a councillor in the Ministry of Justice, Berlin.

15. Franz Anton Ries (see n. 4, this letter) and hornist-turned-publisher Nikolaus Simrock (1750–1832).

16. Karl Friedrich Zelter, a sometime correspondent of Beethoven's and teacher of Felix Mendelssohn's.

17. Hubert Ries (1802–1886), violinist and composer, youngest son of Franz Anton Ries, and a student of Louis Spohr's.

18. Louis Spohr (1784–1859), composer, violinist and conductor, active in Kassel from early 1822 until 1857.

19. This tale first appeared in Alexandre Choron and François Fayolle, *Dictionnaire historique des musiciens* (Paris: Valade, 1810), I, 40, giving Beethoven's supposed father as Friedrich Wilhelm II, king of Prussia. It was taken up in the Brockhaus, *Konversations-Lexikon,* 1st ed. (Leipzig, 1814), I, 559, with the father changed to Frederick the Great.

20. "Memoir of Ludwig van Beethoven," *Harmonicon* 1, no. 9 (November, 1823), 155–157. The author was probably editor William Ayrton. Wegeler continued this line of indignant thought in his portion of the *Biographische Notizen* (1838), p. 3

(Kalischer ed. [1906], pp. 7–9). In fact, Friedrich Wilhelm I of Prussia lived from 1688 to 1740, succeeded by his son, Friedrich II (1712–1786), called Frederick the Great. He, in turn, was succeeded by his cousin, Friedrich Wilhelm II (1744–1797).

21. In his reply of December 7, 1826 (Anderson No. 1542), Beethoven told Wegeler: "I have adopted the principle of neither writing anything about myself nor replying to anything written about me. Hence I gladly leave it to you to make known to the world the integrity of my parents, and especially of my mother." Ultimately the misinformation remained in the Brockhaus *Konversations-Lexikon* until it was dropped from the 8th edition (1833) at Schindler's instigation. The correct information on both Beethoven's parentage and his year of birth, however, had been published in John Sainsbury, *A Dictionary of Musicians* (London, 1824), I, 68, a work often criticized as being too reliant on Choron and Fayolle. Nonetheless, Beethoven may have spoken to Adolf Martin Schlesinger about publishing an article in the *Berliner Allgemeine musikalische Zeitung*, in order to "put an end to a great deal of untrue gossip" (see Beethoven to Schlesinger, October 13, 1826, No. 439 below).

22. At this time, St. Stephan's Cathedral was visible from virtually everywhere in Vienna and its environs.

23. A pun on *Reisen* (traveling) and *Reiz* (attraction).

24. It may have been Wegeler's original intention to send the letter without an enclosure from his wife Eleonore (with whom Beethoven once enjoyed a very close friendship and possibly even a romance), but the next item in this collection indicates that she prevailed.

Incipit: Einen der 10 Riesischen Kinder. . . .

Sources: Nohl, *Neue Briefe* (1867), pp. 295–296, omitting one phrase from the final paragraph; Thayer-Deiters-Riemann, V, 277–279; Thayer-Forbes, pp. 1018–1019; Schmidt, *Beethoven-Briefe*, pp. xxi–xxiv (citing Nohl). Schmidt erroneously gives the date as December 29; only the final paragraph is translated in Thayer-Krehbiel, III, 214; Thayer-Forbes dates the letter December 20 and omits three sentences from the final paragraph. When Thayer examined it, the autograph was in the possession of Beethoven's nephew Karl's widow, Caroline, Vienna.

423. Eleonore Wegeler (née von Breuning) to Beethoven

Koblenz; December 29, 1825[1]

For so long, dear Beethoven! it was my wish that Wegeler might write to you once again. Now that this wish is fulfilled, I believe that I must still add a few words — not only to bring myself somewhat closer in your memory, but to repeat the important question of whether you have no desire to see the Rhein and your birthplace again. You will be the most welcome guest with us at any time and at any hour, and will give Wegeler and me the greatest joy.

Our Lenchen is grateful to you for so many happy hours — listens so gladly to stories about you, and knows all the little details of our happy youth in Bonn — of the quarrels and reconciliations. How happy she would be to see you! Unfortunately the girl has no musical talent, but through great diligence and perseverance she has progressed so far that she can play your sonatas, variations, and the like,[2] and since music remains the greatest relaxation for Wegeler, she has given him many happy hours with them. Julius has musical talent, but has neglected it until now; just in the last half year he has been learning the violoncello with pleasure and joy. Since he has a good teacher in Berlin, I definitely believe that he will continue to learn. Both children are tall and like their father — also with the cheerful, happy disposition that, thank God, Wegeler has *not entirely* lost. He takes great pleasure in playing the themes of your variations; the old ones are his favorites, but many times he practices a new one with unbelievable patience. Your *Opferlied* is his absolute favorite.[3] He never comes into the living room without going to the piano.

From this, dear Beethoven, you can see how you still live among us in these lasting memories. Just tell us once that this means something to you, and that you haven't completely forgotten us either. If it were not often so difficult to satisfy our fondest wishes, we would already have visited my brother in Vienna,[4] and would certainly have considered it a pleasure to see you — but such a trip is not possible now, especially since our son is in Berlin.

Wegeler has told you how it is going with us; we would be wrong to complain — even the most difficult period was easier for us than for a hundred others. The greatest luck is that we are healthy and the children are good and honest, neither of them has ever given us any trouble, and we are happy and in good spirits. Lenchen has experienced only one great grief — that was when our poor little fellow died, a loss that all of us will never forget.[5] Farewell, dear Beethoven, and think of us in a kindly and friendly way.

Eln. Wegeler

1. Enclosed with Wegeler's letter of December 28 (No. 422 above); see that item

for clarification of many details in Eleonore's letter. It is obvious from the letter's contents that she has not forgotten her youthful affection for Beethoven.

2. Eleonore's description of their twenty-two-year-old daughter's aptitudes is almost the opposite of Wegeler's. Both confirm, however, that she can play Beethoven's piano sonatas.

3. "Die Flamme lodert" (text by Friedrich von Matthisson), WoO 126. Composed probably in 1796, it had been published by Simrock in Bonn in 1808. Sometime before Beethoven's letter to Wegeler of May 2, 1810 (Anderson No. 256), Wegeler had composed a new text ("Das Werk beginnet!") so the song could be used in Bonn's Masonic Lodge.

4. Stephan von Breuning, now Beethoven's neighbor near the Schwarzspanierhaus.

5. Wegeler did not mention this third child, a son. Several of the sentiments that Eleonore ascribes to young Helene in this letter may, in fact, be her own.

Incipit: Schon lange lieber Beethoven! war es mein Wunsch. . . .

Sources: Nohl, *Neue Briefe* (1867), pp. 296–297; Thayer-Deiters-Riemann, V, 279; Thayer-Forbes, pp. 1019–1020; Schmidt, *Beethoven-Briefe*, pp. xxiv–xxv (citing Nohl). Like the foregoing letter, when Thayer examined the autograph, it was in the possession of Beethoven's nephew Karl's widow, Caroline, Vienna.

423A. *Beethoven to Tobias Haslinger*[1]

[Vienna; probably December 31, 1825][2]

Best Little Adjutant!

Along with this I send you a New Year's greeting[3] — and further an invitational note; send it to all the real and pretend denizens of the little Paternostergasse. They are invited for beer.

We'll see each other this evening in your cellar.

Your

B——n

[Exterior:]
   Herr Tobias v[on] Hass-lin-ger
   P[ater]n[oster]g[asse]

1. Tobias Haslinger was first an employee, then junior partner in the publishing firm of S. A. Steiner & Co., Vienna. In 1826, he became sole proprietor. The firm was

located in a very short, narrow street, the Paternostergasse ("Our Father" Street) between the Graben and the Kohlmarkt in the heart of the city. Beethoven enjoyed puns and other wordplay; thus *Hass* ("hate," his customary play with Haslinger's name) and the diminutives *Adjutenterl* [*sic*] and implied *Gässel* or *Gässchen*.

2. Sieghard Brandenburg indicated two conversation book entries that clarify references made in this letter. Referring to Beethoven's nephew, Karl Holz writes on January 1, 1826: "Karl does not believe that beer was drunk at Steiner's yesterday"; a few days later, nephew Karl himself writes: "The whole town is already saying that the art shop in the Paternostergässchen has been turned into a beer house" (Köhler et al., *Konversationshefte*, VIII, 238, 251–252).

Thus, Beethoven may have had beer brought to the Steiner and Haslinger shop on December 31, 1825, for an impromptu New Year's Eve celebration.

Nephew Karl's subsequent remark may indicate repeated gatherings of a similar nature. On January 1, 1826, violinist and quartet leader Ignaz Schuppanzigh presented a subscription concert that included Beethoven's String Quintet in E♭, Op. 4, Mozart's Quartet in A, K. 464, and an unidentified Haydn quartet. After the concert, it is possible that Beethoven, Schuppanzigh and their colleagues repaired to Steiner's to finish off a keg that may have been tapped the evening before. (If, however, the beer had been brought *in buckets* from a nearby beer house on New Year's Eve, it would have been flat a day later, rendering the latter speculation much less tenable.)

Two undated and unaddressed Beethoven letters mention a beer house: Anderson No. 1069 (Kastner [1910], No. 999), supposedly from 1821; and Anderson No. 1250, possibly to Schindler in 1823. The former refers to a "musical beer house . . . established . . . for good and all" that cannot be identified further owing to the fragmentary nature of the letter. The latter refers to a "new beer house that was opened there [in the Graben] yesterday," therefore no direct allusion to gatherings at the shop in the nearby Paternostergasse.

3. Probably around December 27, 1825, nephew Karl noted in a conversation book: "On Saturday [December 31], we must buy a few New Year's cards; I must give [them] to the professors [at the Polytechnic Institute], etc. . . . On Saturday, I'll go early to Biedermann, and on Sunday, early to the professors" (Köhler et al., *Konversationshefte*, VIII, 228–229). Samuel Biedermann was a merchant to whom the String Quartet, Op. 132, was to be delivered (in exchange for payment) for shipment to the Parisian publisher Moritz (Maurice) Schlesinger. If, as projected, Beethoven and Karl shopped for commercial greeting cards on Saturday, December 31, 1825, one of those cards must have accompanied the present note to Haslinger.

Incipit: Beiliegend sende ich euch ein Neujahr. . . .

Sources: Photograph in postcard format without any designation of provenance; photocopy kindly supplied by Sieghard Brandenburg, Beethoven-Archiv, Bonn (letters, July 28, August 4 and August 16, 1995). Because of the note's unverified origins,

Brandenburg suspected that it might be a forgery and urged extreme caution. If a forgery, the note was created by someone familiar with both Beethoven's handwriting and his manner of expression as well as the recent Beethoven literature, including *Konversationshefte*, VIII, published in 1981. It would therefore be a much more skillful forgery than a bogus second letter to the "Immortal Beloved," described, depicted and debunked in Hans Schmidt, "Aus der Werkstatt eines Handschriftenfälschers: Ein Liebesbrief Beethovens," *Österreichische Musikzeitschrift* 29 (February 1974), 57–66.

424. Beethoven to an Unknown Recipient

[Vienna?; ca. 1825?][1]

It is impossible [for me] [to come] this evening, since I lay in bed the whole day and must remain lying [here].

Beethoven

1. This note (five lines, written in pencil) is undated; it bears neither place, address nor salutation; the paper shows no watermark. Beethoven was periodically ill for much of his life and especially during the period after 1820. The approximate year is given in Helms and Staehelin. Similarly, in the forthcoming Beethoven-Haus *Briefausgabe*, Sieghard Brandenburg designates the letter as "1825/26," while grouping it in 1826.

Incipit: Es ist [mir] unmöglich heute Abends. . . .

Sources: Helms and Staehelin, "Bewegungen . . . 1973–1979," p. 354, quoting an offering by Antiquariat Konrad Meuschel, Bonn, cited in *Gemeinschaftskatalog Deutscher Antiquare* (Bonn, Fall 1978), p. 94. In 1983, the autograph was in a private collection in Germany; it is presently in the Beethoven-Haus, Bonn, NE 136. Sieghard Brandenburg kindly supplied an edited transcription of the text.

Prince Anton Radziwill (1775–1833), subscriber to the
Missa solemnis, who attended its St. Petersburg premiere on
April 7, 1824. Lithograph by Faustino Anderloni. See
Nos. 371 and 375. Source: Kroll, *Weber*, p. 24.

Johann Andreas Stumpff (1769–1846), a Beethoven enthusiast in London, sent the composer a collection of Handel's works. Unsigned woodcut. See Nos. 396, 414, 435, 453 and more. Source: British Library; King, *Mozart*, p. 29.

Count Carl von Brühl (1772–1837),
Generalintendant of the Royal Theater, Berlin.
Lithograph, artist unknown. See No. 429.
Source: Kapp, *Weber* (suppl.), p. 14.

Ignaz Schuppanzigh (1776–1830), letter to
Beethoven, April 26, 1826. See No. 432. Source:
Staatsbibliothek zu Berlin-Preussischer
Kulturbesitz; Bekker (suppl.), p. 21.

Count Johann Peter von Goess (1774–1846), president,
Gesellschaft der Musikfreunde. Lithograph by Joseph Kriehuber
(1837). See No. 441. Source: Gesellschaft der Musikfreunde,
Vienna; Deutsch, *Schubert, Leben in Bildern*, p. 390.

Raphael Georg Kiesewetter (1773–1850), vice president,
Gesellschaft der Musikfreunde. Lithograph by
Anton Hänisch (1847). See No. 465. Source: Österreichische
Nationalbibliothek; Deutsch, *Schubert,
Leben in Bildern*, p. 401.

Conrad Graf (1782–1851), Viennese piano maker who loaned
Beethoven an instrument from January 1826 until his death. Miniature
on ivory by Joseph Kriehuber (1835). See No. 460 (postscript).
Source: Gesellschaft der Musikfreunde, Vienna; Deutsch,
Schubert, Leben in Bildern, p. 391.

Left: Ignaz Moscheles (1794–1870), pianist resident in London, who helped negotiate the Philharmonic Society's monetary gift to the dying composer. Engraving by L. Beyer after Friedrich Lieder. See Nos. 463, 467, 468 and more. Source: Österreichische National-bibliothek; Deutsch, *Schubert, Leben in Bildern*, p. 384.

Above: Karl van Beethoven (1806–1858), letter to Beethoven, from Iglau, March 4, 1827. See No. 464. Source: Staatsbibliothek zu Berlin–Preussischer Kulturbesitz; Bekker (suppl.), p. 133.

Friedrich Rochlitz (1769–1842), Leipzig author and editor of the
Allgemeine musikalische Zeitung, 1798–1818. Chalk drawing by
Johann Joseph Schmeller. See No. 488. Source: Stiftung Weimarer
Klassik; Deutsch, *Schubert, Leben in Bildern*, p. 513.

Karl van Beethoven (1806–1858),
Beethoven's nephew. Unsigned photograph
(probably mid-1850s). Source: Bekker
(suppl.), p. 132.

1826

425. Prince Nicolas Galitzin to Beethoven

St. Petersburg; January 14, 1826[1]

Dear and worthy Monsieur van Beethoven,

I have very much wronged you by not having yet acknowledged the receipt of the overtures[2] that you had the kindness to send me. I was waiting for the shipment of the quartet to combine all my thanks at the same time. Since then I have been very ill, and afterward I was obliged to make a journey to the heart of Russia. All these circumstances and unexpected changes here have prevented me from replying to you until now. I have just read in the *Musikalische Zeitung* of Leipzig that the new Quartet in A minor has been performed in Vienna,[3] and I am so impatient to become acquainted with this new masterpiece that I request you to send it to me without further delay, by post, like the preceding one. I am going to have sent to M[onsieur] Stieglitz the amount of 75 ducats for you, to be remitted by M[onsieur] Fries: 50 for the Quartet and 25 for the Overture, which is magnificent and which I thank you very much for having dedicated to me. The Leipzig journal expressed itself in such flattering terms about your new Quartet that I am extremely impatient to become acquainted with it. Would you forward it to me as soon as possible, for I shall soon depart for the coronation in Moscow,[4] and then I shall send you my address.

I wish you a good and happy New Year.

Your devoted friend,

Prince Nicolas Galitzin

1. Answers Beethoven's letter of late July 1825 (Anderson No. 1405) and a shipment of scores made at about the same time.

2. *Consecration of the House,* Op. 124, dedicated to Galitzin, and probably *Namensfeier,* Op. 115.

3. The Quartet, Op. 132, was finished in August 1825 and first performed by the Schuppanzigh Quartet on November 6; the report appeared in the *Allgemeine musikalische Zeitung* 27 (December 1825), cols. 840–841.

4. Czar Alexander I had died on December 1, 1825. After the Decembrist uprising, Nicholas I was crowned czar in Moscow on September 3, 1826. The attempts to induce Galitzin to make payment during these months are related in Thayer-Forbes, pp. 978–979.

Incipit: J'ai bien des torts envers vous. . . .

Sources: Thayer-Deiters-Riemann, V, 567; Thayer-Forbes, p. 978. When Thayer copied it, the autograph was in the possession of Beethoven's nephew Karl's widow, Caroline, Vienna. It has since disappeared.

426. Beethoven to Karl Holz (?)

[Vienna; late January or early February 1826][1]

She received 8 florins 20 kreuzer monthly.[2] Her month was up on January 5. For 20 days after that date, she was not paid, because she ran off on the last day. There must be punishment for *such people*. She left on Tuesday, January 24, and received the bread money for the entire week. Since she remained [in my employ] only a few days longer than 6 weeks, I had the right to deduct the New Year's gift and advance payment, which, however, was not done; also I laid out the money for the tax sheet. Why should she herself have gone to the Police Tribunal after having sneaked away? It is the first time that anything like this has happened to me, and I am called to give testimony about it. She is on a terrible path — it goes without saying that the entire first month was paid long ago.

That [is] all. At 1:30, the meal will be ready. I surely hope to see you. Now I must drive that fat lout away; that might be another fine mess.[3]

In haste,

Your

Beethoven

1. The letter includes neither date nor recipient but is consistent in tone and content with those that Beethoven sent to Karl Holz, his unofficial secretary from the summer of 1825 to September 1826. In 1826, January 24 fell on a Tuesday, as mentioned in this letter. The conversation books provide little direct assistance in dating the letter: *Heft* 102 covers January 16–ca. January 22, 1826; *Heft* 103 early February–February 12; and *Heft* 104 mid-February–ca. February 24, 1826 (Köhler et al., *Konversationshefte,* VIII,

265–321; IX, 21–50). This letter could easily have been written in the gap between *Hefte* 102 and 103. Another letter from Beethoven to Holz (Anderson No. 1467, oddly identified as possibly sent to Joseph Karl Bernard), evidently dated February 3, 1826, probably deals with the same domestic disagreement as the present letter.

2. Another letter from Beethoven, presumably to Holz (Anderson No. 1518, dating it summer 1826), indicates that a similar servant is also to receive 100 gulden (florins) per year, plus 36 kreuzer per week for bread. Thus the bread money mentioned later in the present letter was part of the servant's pay.

3. Beethoven seems to anticipate a disagreement with still another servant. *Incipit:* Sie hatte monathl. 8 fl: 20x.

Sources: Schwarz, "More Beethoveniana," pp. 143–145; facsimile on four plates between pp. 146 and 147; listed in Fishman, "Verzeichnis . . . Beethoven-Autographe . . . 1980," p. 136. Autograph formerly in the collection of Zinaida I. Yussupova; collection in the Institute of Russian Literature (Pushkin House), Academy of Sciences, St. Petersburg.

427. Beethoven to Dr. Anton Braunhofer[1]

[Vienna; probably ca. February 27–28, 1826][2]

Honored Master and Practitioner of the Art of Aesculapius!

I report to you only that my abdomen is better, that is, as far as my nature and the medicine up to now permit it. The powders are all used up; the diet the same. Now I wish to know what else you have decided about my body. My back is not yet entirely in its old condition; in the meantime I hope that it will not have to bow, *indeed Never.*[3] That is all I can tell you; you will now think about it, and this will be the last for

Your admirer and friend,

Beethoven

[Exterior:]
Herr Professor Dr. von Braunhofer

1. Born in 1773, Braunhofer was a physician and professor of natural history at the University of Vienna and practiced homeopathic medicine. He attended Beethoven from 1820 to 1826 but reportedly refused to come when called in early December

1826 during the composer's final illness. The present letter and the circumstances surrounding it may explain the doctor's later actions.

2. The following circumstances seem to date this letter as ca. February 27–28, 1826. As early as mid-July 1825, Beethoven's nephew Karl made some negative remarks in the conversation books concerning homeopathy—which combined strict diet with infinitesimal amounts of medication—and Dr. Braunhofer's connection with it. In early February 1826, violinist Ignaz Schuppanzigh seems to have assured Beethoven that Braunhofer was very skillful and that their mutual friend Zmeskall, a gout patient, was enthusiastic about homeopathy. Prior to ca. February 21, Beethoven summoned Braunhofer (Anderson No. 1471, undated), who probably came on about the 21st. He consulted with the composer and prescribed no coffee, no wine, a restricted diet and a small dose of medicine. They also discussed Beethoven's back and treatment for it. The doctor asked Beethoven to report to him "the day after tomorrow." In that letter, dated February 23 (Anderson No. 1469), Beethoven asked for another meeting, which must have taken place on February 25 or early on the 26th. During this second recorded consultation, Braunhofer asked him, "How much powder do you still have?" and told him, "In two days, let me know how you are; then I shall again send you some medicine." The present letter, therefore, seems to be that report, probably written on ca. February 27–28. Subsequent entries in the conversation books indicate that Beethoven soon strayed from the food and drink prescribed and proscribed by Braunhofer and probably earned the doctor's disinterest by doing so. (See Köhler et al., *Konversationshefte*, VIII, 21, 308; IX, 45–47, 58–59 and passim.)

3. This grumpily humorous tag reflects Beethoven's republican leanings.

Incipit: Ich melde Ihnen nur, dass. . . .

Sources: Anna Maria Russo, "Una lettera sconosciuta di Beethoven," *Nuova rivista musicale italiana* 25, no. 1 (January–March 1991), 74–82, containing facsimile, inaccurate transcription and Italian translation. Russo's transcription with (correspondingly inaccurate) English translation in "Miscellanea," *Beethoven Newsletter* (San Jose) 6, no. 3 (Winter 1991), 84–85; reply (with accurate transcription) by Hans-Werner Küthen, "Letters to the Editor," *Beethoven Newsletter* 7, no. 1 (Spring 1992), 30. Autograph in the Fondo Gonnelli, Biblioteca Nazionale Centrale, Florence.

428. Beethoven to S. A. Steiner and Co.

[Vienna; mid-March 1826][1]

Herr Steiner & Comp.

I request most courteously[2] that you send me the proof sheets,[3] and that you most obligingly write me as to when I shall receive them.[4]

Most devotedly,

Beethoven

[Exterior:]
Steiner and Company
Paternoster Gässel

1. The letter is undated but bears the annotation "Beethoven—1826" in Tobias Haslinger's hand. The present dating follows Bartlitz, who based hers on an examination of the conversation books.

2. At this time Sigmund Anton Steiner was in the process of publishing several works by Beethoven, some of which the firm had owned and held back from publication for a half-dozen years—thus Beethoven's thinly veiled irritation here. Moreover, the trio *Tremate,* issued the previous month, contained errors of which the composer disapproved. In time, Tobias Haslinger took over Steiner's stock and imprint.

3. The works included (with publication dates) the trio *Tremate, empi, tremate,* Op. 116 (Steiner, February 1826), the March and Chorus from *The Ruins of Athens/Consecration of the House,* Op. 114 (Steiner, April 1826), the *King Stephan* Overture, Op. 117 (Haslinger, July 1826), and the *Elegischer Gesang,* Op. 118 (Haslinger, July 1826).

4. At some point within the next two or three weeks after this letter was written, Beethoven complained to the censorship authorities, requesting that they not allow these works to appear with Steiner's and Haslinger's inaccuracies (Anderson No. 1479).

In a conversation book entry of April 5 or 6, 1826, secretary-factotum Karl Holz told Beethoven: "I was at your apartment at 5 o'clock; I brought the proof sheets from Tobias" (Köhler et al., *Konversationshefte,* IX, 158). The composer returned most of the proofreading to the publisher, still complaining of incorrect title pages, on April 9, 1826 (Anderson No. 1480).

Incipit: Ich ersuche höflichst, dass ich [*sic*]. . . .

Sources: Bartlitz, "Ein aufgefundener Beethoven-Brief," pp. 10–14, with facsimile in an appendix. Autograph in the Staatsbibliothek zu Berlin–Preussischer Kulturbesitz, Mus. ms. aut. 67. The letter was originally in the collection of Baroness Fanny von Richthofen, née Mendelssohn-Bartholdy (1851–1924), daughter of Paul Mendelssohn-Bartholdy (the brother of Felix). The Berlin library acquired the autograph in 1937.

429. Count Carl von Brühl[1] to Beethoven

Berlin; April 6, 1826[2]

The music dealer Schlesinger[3] has disclosed to me that you would not be averse to *writing a German opera for the Berlin Opera House,* and with the greatest eagerness I accept this proposal, since it can only prove the truest honor to the theater [that is] managed by me, [bestowed] by a man who stands as highly in the artistic world as you [do], to bring to this stage *a work composed especially for it.*

The libretto that Herr Schlesinger likewise passed on to me, *Die schöne Melusine* by Herr Grillparzer, appears to me by all means appropriate for offering plentiful material to an imaginative composer. The only hesitation that I have about it is that our theater already possesses an opera by Herren von Fouqué and Hoffmann, in which almost entirely the same material is treated, namely *Undine,* so very much beloved and highly celebrated in its time.[4] This is the only reason why I would have wished that you would have proposed yet another subject and that Herr Grillparzer would have been able to arrange it. I would therefore accept *Melusine* (otherwise a very successful and lovely poem) for performance only very reluctantly. I ask you most respectfully to give me, please, your views on this matter. In closing, I want to assure you of my sincerest esteem.

Brühl

1. Count Carl Friedrich Moritz Paul von Brühl (1772–1837) had succeeded August Wilhelm Iffland as *Generalintendant* of the Royal Theater, Berlin, on January 10, 1815.

2. According to an annotation, Beethoven did not answer this letter. Brühl wrote it on April 6 and sent a fair copy on April 7. The matters herein were discussed further, however, in Schlesinger's letter to Beethoven of April 15 (No. 430 below) and Beethoven's reply of May 31, 1826 (Anderson No. 1487).

3. Beethoven had written to Adolf Martin Schlesinger on February 27, sending with it *Die schöne Melusine,* a libretto that the poet Franz Grillparzer (1791–1872) had written for the composer in 1823. Beethoven never set the text.

4. The magic opera *Undine,* libretto by Friedrich de la Motte Fouqué, music by E. T. A. Hoffmann, had opened in the Berlin Theater on August 3, 1816, and ran for fourteen successful performances until July 27, 1817. After the opera house burned to the ground in 1817, Hoffmann's work was never revived.

Incipit: Der Musikhandler Schlesinger hat mir eröffnet. . . .

Sources: Wilhelm Altmann, "Zu Beethovens 'Fidelio' und 'Melusine,' " *Die Musik* 3, no. 2 (March 1904), 435–437; Unger, *Beethoven und seine Verleger* (1921), p. 32. Briefly summarized in Nohl, *Beethoven's Leben* (1877), III, 676, 943. In 1904, Brühl's draft was in the files of the Registratur, General-Intendantur, Königliche Schauspiele, Berlin.

430. Adolf Martin Schlesinger to Beethoven

Berlin; April 15, 1826[1]

L. Beethoven, Vienna

With your very honored letter of February 27, I received the text of Grillparzer's *Melusine,* which I immediately delivered in person to Count von Brühl. Afterward I reminded him several times concerning the reply, and it finally went off a week ago, and will be in your hands; as the Count told me, and as I do not doubt, [it is] entirely according to your wishes.[2] I have also spoken with Spontini on this account; he promised to do everything for it that was in his power.[3]

I am counting for certain that you will transfer this opera to me when it is finished, as well as the piano reduction and proprietary rights for all variety of arrangements, and request that you offer it to no one else.

The editor of the *Berliner Musikalische Zeitung* sends his best greetings. At the same time, he requests you (a request that I herewith endorse) to benefit us very soon with a [literary] contribution from your pen.[4]

Next summer I shall have the honor of paying my respects personally to you in Vienna, and to make your estimable acquaintance.[5] Carl Maria von

Weber's new opera *Oberon,* which he is presently performing in London, is appearing from my publishing house, and is already engraved in piano reduction.[6]

If you perhaps have something on hand that you could send me, I request your obliging news about it.[7]

With the greatest respect, I have the honor to be

A. M. S.

1. Beethoven's letter of February 27 seems not to have survived. Beethoven's next letter to Schlesinger was written on April 22 (Anderson No. 1481), replying to a letter the publisher had written on April 13 (lost?). Beethoven's specific reply to the present letter was penned on May 31 (Anderson No. 1487).

2. See Brühl's letter of April 6, 1826 (No. 429 above), concerning Grillparzer's libretto and the decision concerning it.

3. Gaspare Spontini (1774–1851) had been *Generalmusikdirektor* in Berlin since May 1820, when he had been championed by King Friedrich Wilhelm III over Count Brühl's candidate, Weber. Spontini's long tenure in Berlin was marked by continuous battles against the pro-German factions in opera. One of his severest critics was A. B. Marx.

4. Adolph Bernhard Marx (1795–1866), editor of the *Berliner Allgemeine musikalische Zeitung* from 1824 to 1830. From Beethoven's letter to Schlesinger of July 15–19, 1825 (Anderson No. 1403), it seems that the composer regarded his writings—what little he knew of them—highly. Nearly four decades later, however, in supporting the documentary methods of Jahn and Chrysander, Thayer decried Marx's lack of historical accuracy: "Of all [German] writers he is one of the worst in this respect—you cannot trust him a moment" (Alexander Wheelock Thayer, "Opera in the Family Hapsburg," *Dwight's Journal of Music* 23, no. 22 [January 23, 1864], 170, col. 3; reprinted as chapter 1 of Thayer's *Salieri, Rival of Mozart,* ed. Theodore Albrecht [Kansas City, Mo.: Philharmonia of Greater Kansas City, 1989], p. 18).

5. Schlesinger met Beethoven during the final week in September 1826. Shortly thereafter, Beethoven left for Gneixendorf.

6. *Oberon* opened at Covent Garden under Weber's direction on April 12, 1826. At the time he had less than two months to live.

7. On May 31, Beethoven offered Schlesinger the *Gratulations-Menuett,* WoO 3, and the entr'acte for Christoph Kuffner's *Tarpeja,* WoO 2b.

Incipit: Mit Ihrem sehr geehrten Schreiben vom 27./2. . . . .

Sources: Unger, *Beethoven und seine Verleger* (1921), pp. 96–97; taken from a copybook then in the possession of the Schlesinger Musikhandlung, Berlin.

431. Anton Halm[1] to Beethoven

Vienna; April 24, 1826

Herr v[an] Beethoven,

I have finished your Fugue, which I have the honor of sending along, with the greatest possible diligence and care! At every bar, I was amazed at your power of harmony and its flow, as well as the musical motives[2] that you used and their development to the point of exhaustion!

Concerning my arrangement, it was unfortunately not possible always to keep the *subjects* in their original shape; rather more frequently they had to be broken.[3] Otherwise it is so brilliant, so advantageously playable and, as I hope, still intelligible enough, that your most elevated masterwork will be acknowledged as that which it is. I shall take the liberty of *delivering your manuscript* at a quarter past three tomorrow afternoon, at the latest, to get your kind opinion of my arrangement.[4] Meanwhile, I am with highest esteem

Yours most sincerely,

Anton Halm

1. Halm (1789–1872), pianist, teacher, composer, commissioned by Mathias Artaria to make a piano four-hands arrangement of the *Grosse Fuge*, Op. 133.

2. The original reads "Kunstfiguren" (literally, "artistic figures").

3. On around April 16, 1826, Halm had visited Beethoven, discussing the setting of voices in the work (Köhler et al., *Konversationshefte*, IX, 193–194).

4. On May 12, Artaria paid Halm 40 gulden C.M. (100 florins W.W.) for the arrangement. Beethoven, however, did not like it, although he evidently was reluctant to tell Halm so: on or before June 9, Karl Holz noted in a conversation book, "Halm seems to notice that you are not satisfied; he dares not come to you" (*Konversationshefte*, IX, 282). By August 1826, Beethoven made his own arrangement, which was sold to Artaria for 12 ducats and published as Op. 134. For Halm's own account to Thayer, see Thayer-Deiters-Riemann, V, 298–299, and Thayer-Krehbiel, III, 223–224.

Incipit: Ich habe Ihre Fuge. . . .

Sources: Thayer-Deiters-Riemann, V, 298–299. Autograph in the Staatsbibliothek zu Berlin–Preussischer Kulturbesitz, Mus. ms. autogr. Beethoven 35, 63; listed in Kalischer, "Beethoven-Autographe," p. 52, and Bartlitz, p. 138.

432. *Ignaz Schuppanzigh*[1] *to Beethoven*

Vienna; April 26, 1826[2]

Mightiest Beethoven,

I thank you for the ruling yesterday concerning the Paternoster Gässchen.[3] Little Tobias[4] has only one copy of this March with Chorus.[5] If I can have from you, most noble Lord, duplicate copies of this chorus as well as of the Overture, namely in C major,[6] so I beseech you for them.

Your Primo Violino,

Schuppanzigh

1. Viennese violinist (1776–1830) and longtime friend of Beethoven's. Because of his obesity, he was known in Beethoven's humorous circle as "Mylord Falstaff." He, in turn, used a jocular tone with the composer, as this letter bears witness.

2. By mid-April 1826, Schuppanzigh had scheduled a morning concert at the Augarten on May 1. On April 22 or 23, Karl Holz wrote in a conversation book: "Mylord wishes to do the March and Chorus at the Augarten concert. He asked Haslinger for them. He [Haslinger] said, however, that he dares not give them to him without your prior knowledge, for it might not set well with you. Thus you would have to give written permission to Mylord which he can give to Haslinger, if you allow it to be performed" (Köhler et al., *Konversationshefte*, IX, 221). As can be seen in Beethoven's letter of April 9 (Anderson No. 1480), Haslinger was not just then in the composer's good graces. Ultimately, Schuppanzigh's concert was postponed to May 11, owing to inclement weather.

3. The Steiner-Haslinger publishing house was in the Paternostergasse, here given in diminutive.

4. Tobias Haslinger.

5. Originally part of *The Ruins of Athens*, Op. 113, this is the revised version for *Die Weihe des Hauses* (*Consecration of the House*), Op. 114, as distinct from the separately published overture.

6. The *Consecration of the House* Overture, Op. 124.

Incipit: Mächtigster Beethoven, Ich danke für den gestrigen Bescheid. . . .

Sources: Thayer-Deiters-Riemann, V, 306; facsimile in Bekker (1911), p. 21. Autograph in the Staatsbibliothek zu Berlin–Preussischer Kulturbesitz, Mus. ms. autogr. Beethoven 35, 62; listed in Kalischer, "Beethoven-Autographe," p. 51, and Bartlitz, p. 138.

433. *Beethoven to Karl Holz*[1]

[Vienna; late June 1826][2]

I only ask in great haste how you are — K[arl],[3] however, appears to do wrong; one would have to presume that he gave S[chlemmer] 10 florins less the first time.[4] Thus K[arl] would have to hope for an error, which it is impossible that he could either foresee or suspect. In great haste,

Your friend,

Beethoven

1. Karl Holz (1798–1858) was a minor government official, an accomplished amateur violinist and second violinist in Ignaz Schuppanzigh's quartet. From the summer of 1825 until his marriage in September 1826, Holz served as Beethoven's secretary and factotum. As described by Schneider, the autograph bears only a faded address.

2. This note is undated, but references to Karl van Beethoven's alleged misconduct seemingly place it in late June 1826 (see n. 4, this letter), when the relationship between uncle and nephew was close to a crisis point, shortly before the distraught young man attempted suicide, probably on August 6, 1826.

3. Despite Beethoven's abbreviations and rhetorical circumlocutions, "K" is surely a reference to his nephew Karl.

4. Seemingly on Sunday, June 25, 1826, Beethoven and his nephew Karl got into an argument (in the presence of Karl Holz) over receipts for Karl's laundry charges, and whether those charges were paid in advance or after the service was rendered, and how these figured in relationship to Karl's room rent at Matthias Schlemmer's, with 10 florins in hot contention. Therefore, the "S" here is probably Schlemmer, and the note itself probably dates from between June 26 and 28, 1826. See Köhler et al., *Konversationshefte*, IX, 322–323, 430 (n. 939).

Incipit: Ich frage nur eiligst, wie Sie. . . .
Sources: Musikantiquariat Hans Schneider, *Musikerautographen: Katalog No. 225*
(Tutzing: Schneider, 1978), p. 9; listed in Helms and Staehelin, "Bewegungen . . .
1973–1979," p. 355. Autograph in the Beethoven-Archiv, Bonn, NE 145.

434. Stieglitz and Co. to Beethoven

St. Petersburg; August 13, 1826

In reply to your honored letter of August 2,[1] we must notify you that Prince
Galitzin is not here at present, but, we are assured, is staying in the vicinity
of the town of Koslov in the Tambov District.[2]

As soon as he comes back, we shall remind him of the subject of your
letter and not fail to inform you of the result. With greatest esteem, we send
our warmest regards.

Stieglitz and Co.

1. Beethoven's letter of August 2, presumably lost, must have asked Stieglitz the
whereabouts of the 75 ducats that Galitzin had promised him on January 14 (No.
425 above). The prince was, at this time, involved in bankruptcy proceedings, and
his wife was mortally ill. For further developments, see Galitzin's letter of November
22, 1826 (No. 444 below).

2. About 250 miles southeast of Moscow.

Incipit: In Erwiderung Ihres geehrten Schreibens. . . .

Sources: Thayer-Deiters-Riemann, V, 569. When Thayer copied it, the autograph
was presumably in the possession of Beethoven's nephew Karl's widow, Caroline. It
has since disappeared.

435. Johann Andreas Stumpff to Beethoven (Dedication)

London[; on or shortly before August 24, 1826][1]

Herr Luis van Beethoven is requested to accept most kindly this well-
known and complete edition of Handel's *Works* in 40 volumes, as a token
of great esteem and deep veneration from

J. A. Stumpff

1. Taken from an entry in Stumpff's diary: "London, August 24, 1826. My nephew Heinrich Stumpff left me to return to his father, and travelled on a Hamburg ship named the *Thetis,* under Captain J. Rutherford. He took two chests with him: one contained his possessions and clothes, and the other the *Works* of Handel in 40 volumes, sent to the greatest living composer Luis van Beethoven as a gift designated for him, and to be delivered to him in Vienna through the piano maker Herr Streicher there. Heinrich will find an opportunity to send it to Vienna and pay all fees. I wrote the following words in the score of *Messiah:* [the dedication above]. The collection cost £45" (Chrysander, p. 449).

Chrysander noted that Stumpff, by no means a rich man, bought the copy from Christopher Lonsdale, paying for it partly in money and partly with a harp.

This shipment follows on Stumpff's letter to Beethoven, July 29, 1825 (No. 414 above), and was acknowledged by Beethoven's letters of December 14, 1826, to Johann Baptist Streicher, the son of Johann Andreas and Nannette (Stein) Streicher (Anderson, III, 1433), and to Stumpff himself (Thayer-Deiters-Riemann, V, 425; MacArdle & Misch No. 462).

Incipit: Herr Luis van Beethoven wird gebeten. . . .

Sources: Chrysander, "Beethoven's Verbindung" (1863), p. 449. Among its uncataloged materials, the Staatsbibliothek zu Berlin possesses a list of the contents of Beethoven's Handel edition made by Tobias Haslinger, who included a transcription of the present dedication (information courtesy of Sieghard Brandenburg, Beethoven-Archiv, Bonn).

436. Beethoven to Mathias Artaria, Artaria & Co.

[Vienna; August 1826][1]

1st. Penalty consisting of two copies of Clementi's *Klavierschule*[2] and three choice prints of the portrait of L. van Beethoven.[3]

2d. A fine for this, that and the other.

3d. The m[anuscript] of this piano arrangement will either be paid for or returned to the composer.[4]

1. Written on the draft of Beethoven's piano four-hands arrangement of the *Grosse Fuge,* Op. 133, published as Op. 134 by Artaria in May 1827.

Beethoven was dissatisfied with the arrangement of the *Grosse Fuge* made by Anton Halm the previous spring. Conversation book entries by Karl Holz in the final week of May and at the end of the first week in June indicate that Halm knew of

Beethoven's unhappiness (Köhler et al., *Konversationshefte*, IX, 254, 282). Beethoven then made his own arrangement during the summer and handed the manuscript to his secretary, Karl Holz, to take to the publisher Mathias Artaria, presumably sometime in August (Anderson No. 1500). Probably because Artaria had already paid Halm 40 gulden for his version of the fugue, Beethoven couched the above three wishes in diplomatically humorous terms.

2. Beethoven wanted at least one of the copies for young Gerhard von Breuning, who was then taking piano lessons with Anton Heller. In late September 1826, Gerhard finally received his copy of Muzio Clementi's *Vollständige Klavierschule* (Vienna: Tranquillo Mollo, [1807]) (see Anderson No. 1532).

3. A lithograph of Stieler's portrait of Beethoven (holding the score of the *Missa solemnis*), published by Mathias Artaria. Gerhard von Breuning recalled that Beethoven brought his family a copy of the portrait on August 28, 1826 (Breuning, *Schwarzspanierhaus*, pp. 69–72; Breuning-Solomon, pp. 75–78).

4. Beethoven received his payment of 12 ducats on September 5, 1826.

Incipit: 1. *Penale* bestehend aus 2 Clementi Klavierschulen. . . .

Sources: Kastner (1910), p. 893; Kastner-Kapp, p. 801; MacArdle & Misch No. 455. Full text in Schmidt, "Beethovenhandschriften," pp. 7, 253. Autograph in the Beethoven-Archiv, Bonn.

437. Baron Karl August von Klein[1] *to C. F. Peters, Leipzig*

Mainz; September 8, 1826[2]

Herr Peters
Music Publisher
Leipzig

Dear Sir!

Herr Heinrich Gugel of St. Petersburg, who recently stayed here, recommended you to me as a very active entrepreneur, and advised me to offer you a string quartet that I wrote and *dedicate* to our worthy Beethoven. How this great composer received the little work, you will see from the enclosed copy of his own letter. Should you be inclined to publish this quartet, I would send you the manuscript through the book dealer Kupferberg here when the opportunity presents itself. Concerning the fee, I would request only a number of copies and a few other musical items.

Looking forward to an obliging reply soon, I remain

Your most obedient servant,

Baron von Klein

1. Karl August, Freiherr von Klein (1794–1870), amateur pianist and composer, student of Gottfried Weber's and Georg Carl Zulehner's. Eventually he composed seven string quartets.

2. Sometime early in 1826, Beethoven received a letter (presumed lost) from Klein, sent through Ignaz von Mosel, asking Beethoven to accept a dedication. Beethoven replied to Klein on May 10 (Anderson No. 1484), a copy of which Klein enclosed with the present letter.

Incipit: Herr Heinrich Gugel aus Petersburg. . . .

Sources: Kalischer (German), V, 225–226; Kalischer-Shedlock, II, 423. Kalischer (or his later editor, Theodor Frimmel) learned of this letter through Dr. Erich Prieger, Bonn.

438. *Mathias Mann¹ to Beethoven*

[Vienna;] Michaelmas, [September 29,] 1826

Apartment No. 20

Herr Ludwig v[an] Beethoven has paid exactly 12 florins W.W. for house lighting from Michaelmas 1826 to Michaelmas 1827.

Mathias Mann
House Manager

1. Mathias Mann was *Hausmeister* (building superintendent) of the Schwarz-spanierhaus, where Beethoven lived, and cleaned up the building for the composer's funeral.

Incipit: Wohnung No. 20: Herr Ludwig v. Beethoven haben. . . .

Sources: Autograph in the Staatsbibliothek zu Berlin–Preussischer Kulturbesitz, Mus. ms. autogr. Beethoven 37, 22; listed in Kalischer, "Beethoven-Autographe," p. 65, and Bartlitz, p. 187.

439. *Beethoven to Adolf Martin Schlesinger, Berlin*

Gneixendorf; October 13, 1826[1]

Herr Schlesinger
Berlin

Finally I arrived here, to submit myself to a true rest in the country,[2] since I had to spend this summer in the city. From here I shall also send something for Herr Marx.[3]

The fatigue of the city has been cast off, and I feel in a good mood once again. The Quartet is finished, but not yet entirely copied out, but will be ready for delivery in a few days.[4] You must have some more patience with the marches;[5] I shall likewise send them to you soon.

Concerning the publication of my [collected] works, according to the opinion of my friends, the sum of 4,000 ducats [#] does not seem to be too sizable. Write me about this as soon as possible.

If I am not mistaken, you spoke to me about placing something about me in the *Zeitung*. This could not be in vain, in that it would put an end to a great deal of untrue gossip.[6]

Dr. Spicker[7] has taken the Symphony for the King with him, since the Legation found that it would go more quickly this way. I am eager [to know] whether H[is] M[ajesty] receives it as I wish.[8]

As for the opera, details soon.[9] I am only now beginning to regain my composure, since this summer flew by for me in a very disturbing manner.[10]

Farewell, and gladden me soon with a letter.

All the best to Herr Marx.

Yours truly,

Beethoven[11]

1. Schlesinger had met with Beethoven during the last week in September. The Berlin publisher replied to this letter on November 11, 1826 (No. 443 below).

2. Beethoven's brother Johann's estate.

3. Adolf Bernhard Marx (1795–1866), editor of the *Berliner Allgemeine musikalische Zeitung*, 1824–1830.

4. The parts for Op. 135 in Beethoven's hand are in the Beethoven-Haus, Bonn.

5. Seemingly WoO 19–20 and 24 and possibly a revised version of WoO 18.

6. Probably an essay about his life, correcting misrepresentations about his parentage (see Wegeler to Beethoven, December 28, 1825, No. 422 above).

7. Dr. Samuel Heinrich Spicker (or Spiker) (1786–1858), librarian of the Royal Library, Berlin.

8. Symphony No. 9, Op. 125, dedicated to King Friedrich Wilhelm III of Prussia (see Anderson, III, p. 1413), and sent to Berlin on about September 27, 1826. For the royal reply of November 25, 1826, see No. 445 below.

9. Possibly Grillparzer's libretto for *Die schöne Melusine*, much discussed (see Nos. 429 and 430 above) but never set.

10. A reference to Karl's attempted suicide. Karl himself was taking Beethoven's dictation of this passage!

11. Dictated to his nephew Karl; signed by Beethoven.

Incipit: Endlich kam ich dazu. . . .

Sources: Landon, "Two New Beethoven Letters," pp. 218–220; Michael Ladenburger, ed., *Zimelien aus den Sammlungen des Beethoven-Hauses: 21 ausgewählte Neuerwerbungen der letzten drei Jahrzehnte* (Bonn: Beethoven-Haus, 1991), pp. 30–31 (facsimile). Autograph in the Beethoven-Haus, Bonn, since 1991.

440. Tobias Haslinger to Carl Friedrich Peters, Leipzig

Vienna; October 18, 1826[1]

Herr C. F. Peters, Leipzig

The account of your fine journey has given Herr Steiner and me extraordinary delight; but the assurance of your restored health — for which I sincerely wish you the best — gave us even more joy.[2] Of course, we poor Viennese music dealers (the rich Italians excepted)[3] must obligingly do without that kind of pleasure and be happy when we can just get by in life and sometimes spend a Sunday enjoying the [fresh] air a little bit outside the city walls.[4]

Now to a topic upon which I also wrote *exactly the same thing* to Herr Härtel (senior),[5] in order, through mutually beneficial discussion and action, to be able to reach our goal all the more quickly and surely. Specifically, as I have learned from authentic sources, Beethoven wants to arrange an edition of his collected works by subscription[6] in conjunction with *Schott* or *Schlesinger.*[7]

We may anticipate with certainty that the preliminary arrangements will certainly be made in such a way that it [the collected edition] can be undertaken in an untroubled way, because the former as well as the latter will doubtless use his Paris firm as a cloak to hide his shame. If we do not make up our minds now to work together against [this prospect], our interests will be diminished in no small way. My tentative proposal would now be this: that we issue all works by Beethoven that have appeared from our publishing houses—namely from you, Breitkopf und Härtel and me (perhaps also Mollo)—under one pleasing cover, on which we mutually agree to indicate all three firms, at a price as inexpensive as possible (ca. 10 kreuzer C.M. per sheet), and announce beforehand in all the customarily read journals: "that we three publishers have united to issue the Works of Beethoven, complete, in a tasteful and inexpensive edition." Piano works can constitute the beginning, because the edition can proceed the fastest in regard to these and because these are the works that are most sought by the public. We can come to an agreement about the terms among ourselves later.

This is only a project drafted in all haste, which I place before you for further scrutiny and consideration.[8]

With greatest esteem,

Cordially yours,

Tobias Haslinger

[Exterior address:]
Herr C. F. Peters
Bureau de Musique
Leipzig

1. Peters's annotation indicates that the letter arrived on October 27, 1826.

2. Publisher Peters (1779–November 20, 1827) suffered from severe depression, for which he had to be hospitalized. Possibly he had traveled to some fashionable spa in an attempt to restore his health.

3. Possibly the wealthy Artaria family, among others.

4. The Glacis, an open area between the city walls and the suburbs, had been planted with trees and became a pleasant and popular promenade. Beethoven's apartment in the Schwarzspanierhaus overlooked the Glacis, with a view of the city.

5. Härtel, senior, is Gottfried Christoph, as distinguished here from the younger Wilhelm Härtel, also in the publishing business.

6. Orel discusses extensively the concept of composers' collected works, those previously issued by Breitkopf und Härtel and projected collected editions of Beethoven's music in particular.

7. Beethoven's letters to Schott (Anderson No. 1535) and to Adolf Martin Schlesinger (No. 439 above), both dated October 13, 1826, inquire about such a project. Schlesinger's reply on November 11 (No. 443 below) indicated that the Berlin publisher was interested but likewise advised Beethoven to obtain consent from previous publishers of his music. On November 28 (No. 447 below), Schott declined to make any determination; doubtless, such a project was beyond his capabilities at the time.

8. Shortly after Beethoven's death, Haslinger began a collected edition to include such works as piano sonatas, various piano music, the violin and violoncello sonatas, piano trios, string quartets and so forth. Although the project was never completed, the presence of editors such as Carl Czerny for the piano sonatas makes the edition worthy of some consideration when discussing authentic performance practices.

Incipit: Die Beschreibung Ihrer schönen Reise. . . .

Sources: Orel, "Ein Verlegerbrief," pp. 29–35. Facsimile of the recto (with partial transcription) in Hilmar, *Musikverlag Artaria,* pp. 92–93, 176. By 1930, the autograph was in the Wiener Stadtbibliothek (today's Stadt- und Landesbibliothek), Städtische Sammlungen, HIN 6852.

441. Gesellschaft der Musikfreunde, Vienna, to Beethoven (Honorary Membership Diploma)[1]

Vienna; October 26, 1826[2]

The Society of the Friends of Music

most graciously sanctioned by
His Majesty, Emperor Franz I,

which counts among its obligations to demonstrate its great esteem
for men who have rendered exceptional services in the realm of Music,

has elected

Herr Ludwig van Beethoven
as its Honorary Member

147

and issued to him the present diploma. It feels itself honored
to number among
its members a composer of such exceptional fame.

Vienna, October 26, 1826

Count P. von Goess,[3]
President

Baron Anton Carl von Bartenstein,[4]   Baron Emanuel von Doblhoff,[5]
Member of Executive Committee   Member of Representative Body

Joseph Sonnleithner,
Secretary[6]

1. Frimmel's description of the diploma: "Printed laudatory text, with names and date entered in handwriting. Large oblong format, with an engraving of the Muse of Music (the work of S. Langer) at the top. Embossed paper seal. Mounted on green silk."

2. According to Pohl, Beethoven, along with Abbé Maximilian Stadler, Joseph Eybler, Joseph Weigl and Carl Friedrich Zelter, was first proposed for honorary membership in the Gesellschaft der Musikfreunde on December 2, 1814. The honorary members named then and in 1818, however, were all aristocrats. Only in 1825, with Vice President Raphael Georg Kiesewetter presiding during a November 29 session, were the names of fifteen musicians suggested: Beethoven, Stadler, Eybler, Weigl, Adalbert Gyrowetz, Michael Umlauf, Ignaz von Seyfried, Franz Krommer, Johann Nepomuk Hummel, Louis Spohr, Johann Friedrich Rochlitz, Luigi Cherubini, Zelter, Carl Maria von Weber and Gioacchino Rossini. These were confirmed at a subsequent meeting of the Executive Committee under newly elected president Peter von Goess.

During the session of January 31, 1826, Joseph Sonnleithner had to remind the Representative Body that Beethoven and the others had been named as honorary members at the previous meeting. Months passed, and nothing happened, except that Weber died in England on June 5, 1826, without ever having received a diploma. Beethoven's diploma, which Pohl personally examined in a private collection in 1870, was not prepared until October 26, 1826, roughly midway in the composer's two-month visit to his brother Johann's estate at Gneixendorf with his nephew Karl. Even so, the diploma remained in the Gesellschaft's possession until at least March 7, 1827 (less than three weeks before Beethoven died), when Kiesewetter finally wrote a letter (No. 465) intended to accompany it on its way.

As early as 1871, Pohl found this sequence of events suspect and considered it inexplicable that the Gesellschaft's invitation to the requiem Mass that it sponsored for the recently departed Beethoven never mentioned that he had been an honorary member. Furthermore, neither Beethoven nor Weber appeared on the lists of honorary members in the Gesellschaft's *Monatsberichte* of 1829 and 1830, much less in the annual reports of the Gesellschaft from 1828 to 1847. Not until the annual report of 1851 did Beethoven and Weber suddenly appear among the deceased honorary members.

In carrying Pohl's argument one step further, I suggest that Beethoven, like Weber, never received the diploma. There is no record of his sending the Gesellschaft a letter of thanks, a courtesy he would surely have performed, even if he merely signed a letter penned by Schindler. None of the surviving letters after March 7, 1827 — whether written by Schindler, Rau or Streicher — mention the Gesellschaft's honoring Beethoven. Streicher's defense of the Viennese on March 28, 1827 (No. 473 below), would surely have provided him opportunity and motivation for such a reference, but none appears in his letter, nor does Schindler mention the honor in any edition of his *Biographie*. Likewise, Johann Aloys Schlosser was a worshipful observer of the posthumous ceremonies and concerts celebrating Beethoven in both Vienna and Prague, and his *Ludwig van Beethoven: Eine Biographie* (1827 or 1828) never refers to any honor conferred by the Gesellschaft. The Gesellschaft's own failure to mention Beethoven's honorary membership in its invitation to the requiem likewise suggests that Beethoven's circle did not know of the intended honor and would have been offended to learn of it under such circumstances, especially if it had gone undelivered. Similarly, the omission of both Weber's and Beethoven's names from the Gesellschaft's lists of deceased honorary members until 1851 indicates that their diplomas might have suffered a similar fate — nondelivery. By 1851, the details of procrastination in 1826 and 1827 would have receded into the past and been forgotten, while organizational pride could have fostered a certain "revisionist" version of history that few if any would dare contradict.

3. Count Johann Peter von Goess (1774–1846), *Landmarschall* of the Lower Austrian regional government, was president of the Gesellschaft der Musikfreunde, 1825–1832. Frimmel transcribes the initial appearing on the diploma as "J."

4. Bartenstein, a court councillor, was an amateur violinist in the Gesellschaft.

5. Probably related to Baron Karl von Doblhof-Dier (1762–ca. 1845), a former student of Albrechtsberger's and Salieri's; as owner of the Sauerhof, a well-known inn in Baden, Doblhof served for a time on the Gesellschaft's governing board. Another

Doblhof, Baron Anton (1800–1872), was a close friend of Schubert's. Perhaps Anton and Emanuel were sons of Karl.

6. Sonnleithner had served as Beethoven's first librettist for *Fidelio* (1804–1805). *Incipit:* Die von Sr. Majestät dem Kaiser Franz I. . . .

Sources: Pohl, *Gesellschaft der Musikfreunde,* pp. 14–15. When Pohl examined the document, it was in a private collection, presumably in Vienna. Frimmel's "Verzeichnisse," pp. 110–111, reported the diploma in the Bibliothek und Museum der Stadt Wien (Städtische Sammlungen), today's Stadt- und Landesbibliothek. He may have confused the location with that of Kiesewetter's letter of March 7, 1827 (No. 465 below). In any case, by 1991, its whereabouts were unknown.

442. Marie L. Pachler-Koschak to Beethoven

Graz; November 5, 1826[1]

Herr van Beethoven!

Through a most peculiar collection of circumstances, which the bearer of these lines can explain more fully, you are only now receiving my letter that should have already been in your hands more than a year ago. I am not taking it back because the one part of its contents, namely the expressions of my respect for you, as well as that which is said in recommendation of the person named therein, is always valid. Concerning the invitation, on whose acceptance I so joyously counted, I merely carry it forward until the next time when we again get such a pleasant, comfortable country estate for our summer vacation, which I shall probably succeed in doing also this coming year. If, however, you would resolve yourself to traveling in the present season, it would please us very much to receive you in our house here. We have a spacious dwelling of 12 rooms and our family is small. Think over my proposal, H[err] v[an] Beethoven, and reconcile the discontent that the unfortunate fate of my letter caused me, by not sending a refusal.

Marie L. Pachler

1. This letter arrived in Vienna while Beethoven and his nephew Karl were still visiting Beethoven's brother Johann in Gneixendorf. It was delivered, after the composer's return, by Johann Baptist Jenger on around December 19, thus before Beethoven's first operation. Along with it, Jenger brought Frau Pachler's letter to

Beethoven of August 15, 1825 (No. 416 above), which had been lost for over a year. Excerpts from the conversation books, ca. December 19, can be found in Thayer-Deiters-Riemann (cited below), and Jenger's report to Frau Pachler of December 29 is No. 451 below.

Incipit: Durch ein höchst sonderbares Zusammentreffen. . . .

Sources: Thayer-Deiters-Riemann, V, 433, with extensive commentary. Autograph in the Staatsbibliothek zu Berlin–Preussischer Kulturbesitz, Mus. ms. autogr. Beethoven 35, 57b; listed in Kalischer, "Beethoven-Autographe," p. 51, and Bartlitz, p. 136. Further commentary in Faust Pachler, *Beethoven und Marie Pachler-Koschak: Beiträge und Berichtigungen* (Berlin: B. Behr, 1866), pp. 22–24.

443. Adolf Martin Schlesinger to Beethoven

[Berlin;] November 11, 1826[1]

I very much enjoyed your honored letter of October 13, in which you expressed your satisfaction now, having returned to the country,[2] again to be able to live for the Muse. How eager I am to see your new masterwork brought to light soon.[3]

Concerning the marches,[4] I request you to make the address to the King;[5] I shall deliver them with pleasure and make every effort for their publication soon. You can expect no fee from me, though, since the marches appear by order of His Majesty, and since I was furnished the manuscript by His Majesty, because marches are H.M.'s favorite music. Thus they will certainly be very well received, and I shall put in a word on behalf of the wish you expressed to me at the suitable places and hope for its fulfillment.

It would certainly give me much pleasure to publish your complete works, as I already told you in Vienna, and we would in any case come to terms about the fee, but you would have to have the consent of the various previous publishers beforehand, since otherwise I would be attacked from all sides, and would find myself in the awkward position of not being the rightful publisher.

In order to speak suitably about you in the newspapers, I request that you send me the impression of the medal and a copy of the letter from the King of France[6] as soon as possible; also give me several pointers if possible; you can entirely count on my discretion in this matter.[7]

Gladden me soon with a letter about you and your works, my very worthy Herr von Beethoven, and accept the assurance of my greatest respect.

[A. M. S.]

1. Replies to Beethoven's letter to Schlesinger, October 13, 1826 (No. 439 above). There survive related letters to Tobias Haslinger, October 13 (Anderson No. 1536); Tendler & Manstein, October 30 (Anderson No. 1537); Moritz Schlesinger, ca. October 30 (Anderson No. 1538) and undated October (Anderson No. 1538a); and Haslinger, November 11 (Anderson No. 1539).

2. Schlesinger had met Beethoven in the last week of September, just before the composer and his nephew Karl set off for Beethoven's brother Johann's country estate at Gneixendorf.

3. The String Quartet, Op. 135, sent from Gneixendorf, via Johann, on or shortly after October 30 (see Anderson No. 1537). It was published by Moritz Schlesinger (A. M. Schlesinger's son), Paris, in September 1827.

4. WoO 19–20 and 24, possibly a revised version of WoO 18.

5. King Friedrich Wilhelm III of Prussia, to whom Beethoven also sent the dedication of the Symphony No. 9 on around September 27, 1826 (Anderson, III, 1413).

6. See the letters from the duke de La Châtre, February 20, 1824 (No. 343 above), and from Schwebel, April 4, 1824 (No. 353 above).

7. Beethoven intended submitting material to the *Berliner Allgemeine musikalische Zeitung*, probably concerning his life and, in particular, his parentage. See Beethoven to Schlesinger, October 13, 1826 (No. 439 above).

Incipit: Sehr erfreute mich Ihre geehrte Zuschrift. . . .

Sources: Unger, *Beethoven und seine Verleger* (1921), p. 97; taken from a copybook then in the possession of the Schlesinger Musikhandlung, Berlin.

444. Prince Nicolas Galitzin to Beethoven

Kharkov; November 22, 1826[1]

My dear and worthy Monsieur van Beethoven!

You must believe me very inconsistent and very thoughtless to leave you hanging for such a long time without a response, especially since I have received from you two new masterpieces[2] of your immortal and inexhaustible genius. But the unfortunate circumstances in which I found myself, as much due to some great losses that have caused me several bankruptcies as to some other circumstances that I cannot explain to you, have all diverted me from my usual pursuits.

Now I am living in the country in the heart of Russia, and in a few days I shall depart for Persia to take part in the war there.[3] Before this I shall definitely dispatch to Messrs. Stieglitz the sum of 125 ducats to be remitted to you,[4] and I can only offer you my thanks for your masterpieces and my excuses for having been such a long time without giving you any sign of life. Please continue to give me your news, which I very much enjoy; write to me still at the same address, and, I pray, indicate to me in detail what you are composing.

Accept the esteem and respect of one of your greatest admirers,

P[rin]ce Nicolas Galitzin

[On the exterior, probably written by Stephan von Breuning:]

On January 10, 1827, inquiry sent concerning this matter to the banking house Stieglitz and Company, and requesting the delivery of the monetary sum of 125 ducats or a report.[5]

1. Schindler gives the letter's place of origin as Charkoff (Kharkov); Thayer gives no location. The letter is dated November 10/22, citing the old style date as well as the new style (used in the present chronology).

2. String Quartets, Opp. 132 and 130.

3. As late as January 1827, Galitzin seems to have been in Koslov (Tambov District). The Russian war against Persia began in 1827 and concluded with the Treaty of Turkmanchai on February 22, 1828.

4. Fifty ducats for each of the two quartets and 25 ducats for the dedication of the *Consecration of the House* Overture, Op. 124.

5. This inquiry evidently reached St. Petersburg in good time, occasioning Stieglitz and Co.'s letter to Beethoven of January 18, 1827 (No. 456 below).

Incipit: Vous devez me croire. . . .

Sources: Thayer-Deiters-Riemann, V, 569–570; Thayer-Forbes, p. 980. Extensive excerpts in Schindler (1860), pt. 2, pp. 137, 300–301; Schindler-MacArdle, pp. 321–322; Nohl, *Beethoven's Leben* (1877), III, 758, 954. When Thayer and Nohl made their copies, the autograph was in the possession of Beethoven's nephew Karl's widow, Caroline, Vienna. It has since disappeared.

445. King Friedrich Wilhelm III[1] of Prussia to Beethoven

Berlin; November 25, 1826[2]

To the Composer Ludwig van Beethoven

In view of the acknowledged value of your compositions, it gave me great pleasure to receive the new work that you have sent me.[3] I thank you for sending it and dispatch to you the accompanying brilliant ring[4] as a token of my sincere appreciation.

Friedrich Wilhelm

1. The son of Friedrich Wilhelm II, this monarch (1770–1840) has been described by the historian Hans Herzfeld thus: "The king's personal character was so devoid of interest that even at the height of 19th-century Prussian historiography no one felt tempted to write his complete biography" (*Encyclopaedia Britannica* [1965], IX, 836). The circle around Beethoven, however, considered him a greater patron of music than the Hapsburg emperor.

2. Follows in sequence Beethoven's letters to Prince Franz Ludwig Hatzfeld, February/March 1826 (Anderson No. 1508), and to Karl Holz, September 9, 1826 (Anderson No. 1521). Answered by Beethoven's (draft) letter to Hatzfeld, December 1826 (Anderson No. 1546).

3. Symphony No. 9, Op. 125, dedicated to the king, for whom a copy was still being prepared and corrected in September 1826.

4. *Brillantring.* This term has often been translated as "diamond ring," and indeed Beethoven (or Schindler on his behalf) expected one. But the monarch may have intended *Brillant* simply to mean the noun "brilliant," a generic term for a precious stone (Lady Wallace translated *Brillantring* as "a ring of brilliants" in 1867). When the ring finally arrived, evidently some time after this letter, Beethoven was disappointed to find a reddish stone, valued at 300 florins in paper money, the sum for which the indignant composer then sold it. Beethoven seems to have been expecting a decoration instead.

Incipit: Bei dem anerkannten Werte. . . .

Sources: Nohl, *Briefe* (1865), p. 328; Nohl-Wallace, p. 228; Thayer-Deiters-Riemann, V, 369; Thayer-Krehbiel, III, 233–234; Thayer-Forbes, p. 1002; Kalischer (German), V, 270–271; Kalischer-Shedlock, II, 448; Kastner (1910), p. 924; Nohl, "Beethoven widmet," p. 42. Autograph in the Staatsbibliothek zu Berlin–Preussischer Kulturbesitz, Mus. ms. autogr. Beethoven 35, 1; listed in Bartlitz, p. 117.

446. *Johann van Beethoven to Beethoven, Gneixendorf*

[Gneixendorf; late November 1826][1]

My dear Brother!

I cannot possibly remain quiet any longer about the future destiny of Karl. He is getting completely away from all activity, and will become so accustomed to this life that he will be brought to work again only with the greatest difficulty, the *longer* he lives here so unproductively. Upon his departure, Breuning gave him only 14 days to recuperate, and now it is 2 months.[2] You see from Breuning's letter that it is absolutely his intention that Karl *shall hasten* to his profession; the longer he is here, the more unfortunate *for him,* because work will come all the harder to him, and therefore we may experience something else bad.

It is a thousand pities that this talented young man wastes his time so, and who but the *both of us* will be blamed for it, because he is still too young to guide himself. Therefore it is *your* obligation, if you do not want to be reproached by yourself and others later on, to induce him to his profession very soon. Once he is there, much can be done for him and his future; as it is now, though, nothing can be done.

I see from his behavior that he would gladly remain with us, but then his future would be lost, so *this is impossible,* and the longer we hesitate, the harder it will be for him to go away; I therefore implore you to make a firm resolution and not to let Karl dissuade you from it. I therefore believe it should be *by next Monday,*[3] for in no case can you wait on me, since I cannot depart from here without *money,* and it will be a long time yet until I receive enough that I can go with you to Vienna.

[Added pencil marks, perhaps after or as part of some conversation:]
Let us leave this until the day when you depart. The old woman: she has her share, she will get no more.[4]

1. This letter, written while Beethoven was staying with his brother Johann in Gneixendorf, was probably written a few days before Monday, November 27, judging by the reference in the final paragraph. It may actually have been written before either

or both of the letters dated November 22 and 25 (Nos. 444 and 445 above) in the present collection.

2. Stephan von Breuning had accepted guardianship of Karl after his attempted suicide and arranged for the nephew to become an army cadet after a reasonable period of recuperation. Beethoven, Karl and Johann had set out for Gneixendorf on September 29.

3. Probably Monday, November 27.

4. On this letter Anton Schindler made a long annotation merely excerpted here: "The above letter shows that Johann van Beethoven must have had one or another good side, so that one feels somewhat reconciled to him. I can assure with certainty that Ludwig van Beethoven became very angry at his brother's request, and that a most disagreeable scene took place between the two brothers, before Ludwig's departure from Gneixendorf, over the inheritance, upon Johann's death, in favor of nephew Karl. The final words, written in pencil, concern Johann's wife and pertain to the dispute. Beethoven demanded that his brother repudiate and disinherit his wife, but Johann refused. This was the primary cause of dispute between the brothers in the last five or six years of Ludwig's life. Truth to tell, the primary fault was Ludwig's."

As Thayer-Forbes notes, the inheritance passed naturally. Therese van Beethoven died on November 20, 1828, Johann van Beethoven on January 12, 1848, leaving a net sum of 42,000 florins to Karl.

Incipit: Ich kann unmöglich länger mehr ruhig sein. . . .

Sources: Thayer-Deiters-Riemann, V, 411–412; Thayer-Krehbiel, III, 269–270; Thayer-Forbes, pp. 1013–1014; Kalischer (German), V, 275–277; Kalischer-Shedlock, II, 453. Autograph in the Staatsbibliothek zu Berlin–Preussischer Kulturbesitz, Mus. ms. autogr. Beethoven 35, 61; listed in Kalischer, "Beethoven-Autographe," p. 51, and Bartlitz, pp. 137–138.

447. B. Schotts Söhne to Beethoven

Mainz; November 28, 1826[1]

Herr L. v. Beethoven
Vienna

Highly esteemed *Kapellmeister!*

Out of duty and obligation we should have already answered your worthy letter of October 13 earlier, but we hope that you will excuse us this time, as there has been a great deal of work late this year; and since you were also away from Vienna,[2] we did not rush unduly to reply.

We hope that the air in the beautiful countryside did you much good; we wish it from the bottom of our heart, and at the same time assure you that you would also say the same about our Rhenish region, if you would only once give its inhabitants the pleasure of having you live among them for a while.

We have received the new Quartet[3] that you sent, and shall get to work on it shortly.

The Mass is finally in press,[4] and we shall dispatch *copies* by the end of this year. Since we wish to prepare as beautiful a title page for it as we did for the Symphony,[5] and since we are still lacking [His] I[mperial] H[ighness], the Archduke Rudolph's coat of arms for that purpose, please be so kind as to send this by the first post, so that we may have it engraved. We only wish to remind you that we strongly urge your attention to this matter, since you yourself are anxious to see the title page laid out very beautifully, and we hope thereby to receive the desired coat of arms all the more quickly.

We are also still awaiting your reply to our specific questions concerning the *corrections* that you made for us (although not clearly enough) for the Symphony.[6]

The *metronome markings* for the *Symphony* have reached us in good order, and ought to be made known as quickly as possible.[7]

If you also send us the *metronome markings* for the *Quartet* very soon, and for the Mass especially soon, we would be greatly obliged to you.[8]

As to the publication of your collected works, we still cannot make any determination[9] now, since we still need to have time free for other obligations.

We look forward to your obliging reply soon, and send you greetings in all esteem and friendship.

B. Schotts Söhne

P.S. We just now received the Paris *Journal général d'annonces*, No. 94, of November 25. An article in it says:

> Vienna. There has just appeared here a new
> quartet by Beethoven, entitled
> "Grand quatuor pour deux Violons, alto et
> Violoncelle, composé et dédié a S. A.
> Mgr le prince de Galitzin par Beethoven,
> *Oeuvre 127.*"[10]

Please be so kind as to give us some information about this immediately, whether a music publisher there has pirated this Opus 127, i.e., a quartet that is our property, and which gentlemen have undertaken this, so that we may be able to take measures against them. If it is a newer quartet purchased from you, then please send us the *themes* from it and the publisher's name, so that we can make it properly known in the *Caecilia*.

We greet you repeatedly,

B. Schotts Söhne

[Exterior:]

Herr Ludwig van Beethoven

Alser-Vorstadt

Schwarzspanier Haus

Vienna

1. Answers Beethoven's letter of October 13, 1826 (Anderson No. 1535); answered by Beethoven's letters of December 9, 1826 (Anderson No. 1544), December 18, 1826 (Anderson No. 1545), and January 27, 1827 (Anderson No. 1548).

2. Beethoven had been in Gneixendorf on an excursion after his nephew Karl's attempted suicide.

3. String Quartet, Op. 131, published in June 1827.

4. *Missa solemnis,* Op. 123. The proofreading process, however, took until March 1827.

5. Symphony No. 9, Op. 125.

6. A reference to a point made in Beethoven's letter of September 29 (actually 27/28) (Anderson No. 1531).

7. See the *Cäcilia* 6 (1827), 158.

8. In his letter of March 28, 1826 (Anderson No. 1472), Beethoven had promised metronome markings for the Ninth Symphony, the *Missa solemnis* and the String Quartet, Op. 127. Schott may also have meant the Quartet, Op. 131, here.

9. The original reads "keinen Entschluss fassen," terminology perhaps coincidentally similar to "Der schwer gefasste Entschluss," written as an epigram to the Finale of the String Quartet, Op. 135.

10. There is no evidence of a printing or pirate reprinting of Op. 127 in Vienna at this time. The article, printed in Paris, may have referred to Schott's own publication, issued in Mainz and Paris (therefore "here"). See also Schott's letter of December 18 (No. 450 below).

Incipit: Dero sehr werthe Zuschrift vom 13ten Oct. . . .

Sources: Unger, "Beethoven und B. Schott's Söhne," pp. 289–290; Staehelin and Brandenburg, *Briefwechsel,* pp. 67–69. Autograph in the Staatsbibliothek zu Berlin–

Preussischer Kulturbesitz, Mus. ms. autogr. Beethoven 35, 72f; listed in Kalischer, "Beethoven-Autographe," pp. 52–53, and Bartlitz, p. 143.

448. *Xaver Schnyder von Wartensee*[1] *to Beethoven*

Frankfurt am Main; December 12, 1826[2]

Highly honored Friend!

I very gladly take advantage of this opportunity to give you once more a sign of life from me and a token of my respect. I am very diligently continuing to learn and to take joy in your works. Everything new that you fashion from your rich creative power is a festival for me to become acquainted with. I try to grab hold of every bit of your music that I can, and there is only *one* work that, in spite of every special order, I have not yet been able to obtain: your *Prometheus,* of which the piano reduction is out of print, and the score with parts, I believe, cannot be obtained at all.[3] Therefore I prevailed upon the Pichler Music Shop here to [agree to] do a new edition of the piano reduction, and would like for the subject matter of the ballet to be added to each musical number. You would make me *very* happy if you would most kindly let me know if and where I can get the score of this beautiful work, and further, if and where one could obtain the subject matter of the ballet.

I have especially studied the last movement, initially $\frac{9}{16}$ time in variation form, of your highly ingenious Sonata, Opus 111, in C major,[4] with great interest, and I take the liberty to pose a question that I would be especially glad for you to answer, because its subject produces various opinions here and occasions an aesthetic dispute. Specifically, in the second variation, which you designated $\frac{12}{16}$ and wrote "l'istesso Tempo,"[5] did you mean it in regard to the beat and want, in the figure

for the sixteenth with the thirty-second

to be played exactly as fast as the eighth with the sixteenth

in the [original] theme; or did you want the whole figure

played just as fast as

where "l'istesso Tempo" then does not designate individual notes but the primary division of the bar. Likewise, in the third variation, which is designated $\frac{12}{32}$, in the figure

where "l'istesso Tempo" occurs again, did you want the two notes

played exactly as fast as the aforementioned figure

in your [original] theme; — or did you want the whole passage

played in the same time?

My last and most urgent request in this letter full of requests is that you do not take offense at all the previous requests and that you might still remain kindly disposed toward me.[7]

Last year I wrote a large-scale comic opera in three acts — and am presently writing a large-scale romantic opera.[8] I am now struggling with all sorts of difficulties and devilment that stand in the way of the person who wants to bring a work to the stage for the first time, and of which the conceited *Kapellmeister* Guhr[9] here already gave me an excellent foretaste.

Farewell indeed, dear splendid Beethoven! May heaven continue to send you its melodies through an angel, and allow you to sing for a long time in that voice, through which it gives the world an intimation of its blessedness!

With the greatest possible respect, I remain

Your friend,

Xaver Schnyder von Wartensee

[Address:]
Herr Ludwig van Beethoven
Famous Composer
Vienna

1. Franz Xaver Schnyder von Wartensee (1786–1868), a Swiss composer, went to Vienna in 1811, planning to study with Beethoven, who did not accept him as a pupil (see Schnyder's letter to Nägeli, December 17, 1811, No. 157 above). He returned to Switzerland in 1812, moving to Frankfurt as a music teacher five years later. Presumably in 1817, Schnyder wrote to Beethoven, but the composer's reply on August 19 (Anderson No. 803) indicates that even then he did not recall their acquaintance.

2. In the autograph, the date clearly reads "12ten 1ober. 1826"; thus the month is correctly interpreted as "Decem-ber," not October, as all previous publications have indicated. Schnyder's letter would therefore have arrived in Vienna at about the time of Beethoven's first tapping for dropsy, December 20.

Anton Schindler later noted: "This letter remained without a reply. The fact, however, that an 'aesthetic dispute' could arise over a passage that was not read correctly perplexed the Master. Also he no longer remembered from when this friendship with Schnyder von Wartensee dated."

3. The piano reduction of *The Creatures of Prometheus*, Op. 43, was published by Artaria (Vienna) in 1801. A reprint appeared from Cappi and Co. in the mid-1820s.

Although the overture appeared earlier in orchestral parts (1804) and later in score (1855), the entire ballet was not published until 1864.

4. The Sonata, Op. 111, is actually in C minor, although the movement in question is in C major.

5. This passage is actually in $\frac{6}{16}$ time.

6. These four notes are quoted an octave higher than written and in the wrong clef.

7. Schindler's note provides an indication of Beethoven's reaction to this overfamiliar stranger who, as indicated above, managed to misquote this sonata in at least two places.

8. Probably his *Estelle, oder leichter Sinn und Liebesmacht* (1825) and *Fortunat mit dem Säckel und Wünschhütlein* (1827–1828, performed in Frankfurt in 1831), respectively.

9. Karl Guhr (1787–1848), conductor in Frankfurt, 1821–1848, one of the leading music directors of his time, praised by Spontini, Berlioz and Wagner.

Incipit: Sehr gerne benütze ich. . . .

Sources: Geiser, *Beethoven und die Schweiz*, pp. 133–137. Contents briefly mentioned in Nohl, *Neue Briefe* (1867), p. 143, and Thayer-Deiters-Riemann, IV, 45. Autograph in the Staatsbibliothek zu Berlin–Preussischer Kulturbesitz, Mus. ms. autogr. Beethoven 35, 65; listed in Kalischer, "Beethoven-Autographe," p. 52, and Bartlitz, p. 139.

449. Count Alphonse de Feltre[1] to Beethoven

Paris; December 12, 1826[2]

Monsieur,

Although I do not have the honor of being known to you, I cannot resist the desire that I have felt for a long time to prove to you the ardent admiration that I feel for your many works. You are accustomed to inspiring such admiration, Monsieur; therefore, you will not be surprised at all at the step that they made me take to approach you, and the profound regret that I cannot do so in person.

From my early childhood I have found inexpressible pleasure in occupying myself with music, and now, [while I am] still young, this pleasure has become a passion that only leaves me another regret, that I cannot occupy myself solely with an art that I place above all the others. You have already grasped, Monsieur, that your works are those that have the greatest interest for me. Their pointed originality, their broad and audacious construction are beauties of the first order; and the gracious songs, which you have written with so much art intermingled with their correctness, place them above all praise.

With your music ceaselessly before my eyes, I could not help developing a desire that you alone can satisfy.

Persuaded that your obligingness is equal to your reputation, I have the boldness to address myself with confidence to you.

I delight in collecting, with much care, some fragments of music sketched by the hands of the most celebrated composers. I hope that you would be willing to send me a line of your music, *written and signed by your hand*. I have already adorned the interesting collection that I have started with the names of your most distinguished fellow countrymen; the premiere place, however, still remains vacant, and your name alone ought to occupy it.

I venture to hope, Monsieur, that you would be willing to comply with my request. Permit me to give you in advance my most ardent thanks. Please accept the great esteem with which I have the honor to be, Monsieur,

Your very humble and very obedient servant,

Count Alphonse de Feltre

Paris. Rue de la Barouvillère No. 10

1. Count Alphonse Clarke de Feltre (1806–1850) had entered the École Militaire des Pages du Roi in 1824, studied composition with Reicha and Boieldieu on the side and graduated as a second lieutenant in late 1826. Three years later, he gave up his commission and devoted his life to composing light opera (see François-Joseph Fétis, *Biographie Universelle des Musiciens*, 2d ed., 10 vols. [Paris: Firmin-Didot, 1883], III, 203–204).

2. This letter would have reached Beethoven at about the time of his first operation on December 20. He kept the letter but seems not to have answered it.

Incipit: Malgré que je n'aie pas l'honneur. . . .

Sources: Summarized in Thayer-Deiters-Riemann, V, 423–424. Autograph in the Staatsbibliothek zu Berlin–Preussischer Kulturbesitz, Mus. ms. autogr. Beethoven 35, 64; listed in Kalischer, "Beethoven-Autographe," p. 52, and Bartlitz, p. 138.

450. B. Schotts Söhne to Beethoven

Mainz; December 18, 1826[1]

Most Honored Friend and Benefactor!

We have received your honored letter of Dec[ember] 9th, and learned with pleasure that you will take care of the coat of arms very soon. We must repeat, however, since we already have this work in press and will be able to have it published soon, that you must very much hasten in sending the coat of arms. We need this very much, and therefore ask you again to send to us here the drawing or an impression of a seal with the complete coat of arms as soon as possible.[2]

In reference to our question concerning the pirated Quartet, Op. 127,[3] about which a *Paris* journal made an announcement (with a dateline from *Vienna*), specifically that this new Quartet, Op. 127, composed by you, was newly published in *Vienna*. For this reason we inquired whether the Quartet, Op. 127, which we [bought] from you in *Vienna* and printed as our property, had actually been pirated in *Vienna* and by whom?

It may not be reprinted by anyone in Paris, and therefore not even by Schlesinger; nor even by Schlesinger in Berlin, according to contract.

We ask, in a very friendly way, that you send a specific answer, and report this to us in good faith.[4]

While we send you the friendliest greetings, we do not want to neglect, on the occasion of the upcoming New Year, requesting the continuation of your valued friendship, and wish you not only a long life, but also health, happiness, and everything else that can bring satisfaction and pleasure to your life.

Sincerely yours,

B. Schotts Söhne

P.S. Be so kind as to send us the Opus number and the dedication for the newest Quartet.[5]

[Exterior:]
Herr Ludwig van Beethoven

living in the Schwarzspanier Haus
Alser Vorstadt
Vienna

1. Refers to Schott's previous letter, November 28, 1826 (No. 447 above); answers Beethoven's letter of December 9 (Anderson No. 1544); crossed in the mails with Beethoven's of ca. December 18 (Anderson No. 1545); answered by Beethoven's of January 27, 1827 (Anderson No. 1548).

2. The coat of arms of Archduke Rudolph was needed for the title page of the *Missa solemnis*, Op. 123.

3. Schott's original reads "Op. 27" at this point, simply a slip of the pen.

4. Schott had brought up this question in his November 28 letter; on December 9, Beethoven hinted that the reference might have been to Schlesinger (Berlin [and Paris]) or even to Schott's own branch in Paris; on January 27, however, Beethoven dismissed the report as "mere gossip." The last appears to be the case.

5. Opus 131 was originally dedicated to Johann Nepomuk Wolfmayer. Beethoven did not send the information until February 22, 1827 (Anderson No. 1553). Ultimately, however, this quartet was dedicated to Baron Joseph von Stutterheim, Beethoven's nephew Karl's military commander (see Beethoven's letter of March 10, 1827, Anderson No. 1561), and Wolfmayer received the dedication of Op. 135.

Incipit: Wir haben dero geehrte Zuschrift vom 9ten Dec. erhalten. . . .

Sources: Thayer-Deiters-Riemann, V, 396–397 (first paragraph incomplete); Unger, "Beethoven und B. Schott's Söhne," p. 290; Staehelin and Brandenburg, *Briefwechsel,* p. 71. Autograph in the Staatsbibliothek zu Berlin–Preussischer Kulturbesitz, Mus. ms. autogr. Beethoven 35, 72g; listed in Kalischer, "Beethoven-Autographe," p. 53, and Bartlitz, p. 143.

451. Johann Baptist Jenger to Marie L. Pachler-Koschak, Graz

Vienna; December 29, 1826[1]

Now I pay to the dear, kind hostess of the Ludlam's Höhle[2] my most heartfelt, obliging thanks for the letter of November 5, which I received through friend Rettig, and which gave me the opportunity I had long wished for to meet the great musical hero van Beethoven, unfortunately, however, in a condition that shocked me deeply. Because of many vexations and illnesses that his nephew Karl caused the great master, he set out with the nephew on a journey to Upper Austria, intending to visit Beethoven's brother, and remained away from here for over six weeks. Bad treatment at his brother's house in the country, where he had to pay 4 florins C.M. per day for terrible room and board to his brother—who had invited him to visit the country—and then the weather, which had already been persistently terrible, cast him on his sickbed, where I found him about ten days ago. He asked for me because he had heard from my friend Schindler, in whom Beethoven places much stock, that I had a letter from Graz for him.[3]

I was alarmed upon entering his room, where everything lay in disorder, as though in an old storeroom.[4] He himself lay in bed suffering greatly, and since he had not shaved in at least three weeks, you can easily imagine, madam, what he looked like. He greeted me in a very friendly way, and I had to sit with him on his sickbed. I wrote out what was necessary and delivered both your letters, which he read through carefully and which he enjoyed thoroughly. Then he thanked me for the letter and charged me, likewise, to thank you very sincerely, dear lady, with the addition that, as soon as he was in a condition to do so, he would write to you himself. Afterward he spoke of your special musical talents with great joy and concluded that it would have been more sensible for him if he had gone to [visit] you in Graz than to his brother in Upper Austria. Nonetheless, he hopes, however, still to see you sometime in Graz. This will perhaps take place next year; I shall advise him very frequently to do so, and perhaps make the journey there with him.

A week ago today[5] he was tapped for the first time, because he suffered from dropsy in the chest. The operation was not successful, and therefore he will have to be tapped again soon. Would to God he were already healthy again! So much the news of B.

1. Reporting on and in part replying about Frau Pachler's letters to Beethoven of August 15, 1825, and November 5, 1826 (Nos. 416 and 442 above). This item is an extended excerpt from a longer letter, whereabouts unknown.

2. *Ludlams-Herbergs Mutter:* A reference to the Ludlamshöhle, a loose organization of over one hundred artists, writers and musicians that met at various taverns in Vienna in the 1820s. It took its name from *Ludlams Höhle,* a play by A. G. Öhlenschläger that was produced at the Theater an der Wien in 1817. The singer Ignaz Castelli, a friend of Beethoven's, was active in the group; so too, although to a lesser extent, was Franz Schubert. Several members were active in presenting Beethoven the petition from Musicians and Music Lovers on February 26, 1824 (No. 344 above). The organization was terminated through a raid by Prince Metternich's police, on suspicions of sedition, in 1826. Frau Pachler had evidently associated with

the Ludlam's Höhle group when she visited Vienna in the summer of 1823 and in September 1827 hosted Jenger, Anselm Hüttenbrenner and Franz Schubert for three sociable weeks of music making in Graz.

3. Jenger's opinions of both Beethoven's brother Johann and his nephew Karl may have been greatly influenced by Schindler.

4. *Rüstkammer*, a storage room for armaments.

5. The operation actually took place on December 20. A literal interpretation of "heute vor 8 Tagen" (eight days ago) is just slightly closer to the date.

Incipit (this excerpt): Nun entrichte ich der lieben guten. . . .

Sources: Thayer-Deiters-Riemann, V, 434–435; Thayer-Forbes, p. 1025. Thayer presumably found the autograph in the possession of Marie's son, Faust Pachler.

1827

452. Stephan von Breuning to Beethoven

[Vienna; ca. January 3, 1827][1]

Dearest Friend!

I am still too weak to write much to you, but I believe that the following few words from a candid heart should be said to you. Since you told me through Gerhard[2] that I should read the letter to Herr Dr. Bach, I have done so and return it to you provisionally with the following observations. That you name Karl as heir, in the event, hopefully still far distant, that we all have to leave this life[3] — your opinion is in keeping with what you have already done for him. But since Karl up to now has shown himself to be very irresponsible, and since one does not know how his character will develop from his present life,[4] I would be of the opinion that for his own good and for the security of his future you limit his authority to dispose of the capital either for his whole lifetime or at least for several more years, until he has attained his majority of 24 years. With his yearly income, he would in any case have enough for the present, and the limitation would protect him against the consequences of irresponsible actions before he fully reaches maturity. Speak about this with Herr Dr. Bach. I believe it best that you should have him come to visit you; he will arrange everything in the simplest way. I would be happy to speak with you or with Herr Dr. Bach about my observations, for I fear that a mere temporal limitation is no means to restrain Karl from incurring debts, which he will have to pay later from his whole inheritance.

I embrace you warmly.

1. The autograph is without place or date but seems to refer to Beethoven's letter to lawyer Johann Baptist Bach, January 3, 1827 (Anderson No. 1547). Kalischer and Bartlitz, however, both believe the letter to have been written in March 1827.

2. Breuning's son Gerhard (born August 28, 1813) met Beethoven in the fall of 1825 and by January 1826 was sufficiently accomplished on the piano to play Haydn sonatas. The composer developed a fondness for the intelligent, communicative youngster, who became a frequent and welcome guest at the Schwarzspanierhaus apartment. In 1874, Gerhard published *Aus dem Schwarzspanierhause,* reminiscences of his youthful acquaintance with Beethoven. He died in 1892.

3. Breuning suffered from a recurring liver ailment; this disease and, reportedly, pneumonia caused his death on June 4, 1827.

4. Beethoven's nephew Karl had attempted suicide probably on August 6, 1826 (see Köhler et al., *Konversationshefte*, X, 84–95), and on January 2, 1827, had left Vienna to join Baron von Stutterheim's regiment in Iglau.

Incipit: Ich bin noch zu schwach. . . .

Sources: Thayer-Deiters-Riemann, V, 440; English in Thayer-Forbes, p. 1027; summary only in Thayer-Krehbiel, III, 279. Autograph in the Staatsbibliothek zu Berlin–Preussischer Kulturbesitz, Mus. ms. autogr. Beethoven 35, 38; listed in Kalischer, "Beethoven-Autographe," p. 48, and Bartlitz, p. 128.

453. Johann Baptist Streicher[1] to Johann Andreas Stumpff, London

Vienna; January 5, 1827[2]

In accordance with your wish, we arranged it so that the 40 volumes of Handel's *Works,* which you sent us as a gift for L.v. Beethoven, were delivered to him free of all charges, and you will be greatly pleased to learn that your gift gave the greatest joy to poor Beethoven, who is confined in such misery to his sickbed, and made him forget his woeful situation. A book by one of his London acquaintances[3] was delivered to him at the same time as your Handel; he took it in his hand and laid it aside without uttering a syllable. Then he pointed with his finger to Handel's works, and with feeling and exaltation he said, "*This is the Real Thing!*"[4]

Beethoven is ill with dropsy, and although he has been operated on to tap the fluid, his doctors declare that he is in extreme danger. Under these circumstances you will excuse him for not thanking you himself, but he asked me to do so for him, and I hope that I have carried out the whole matter to your satisfaction.

I am, etc.

1. Johann Baptist Streicher (1796–1871), son of Johann Andreas Streicher, had been active in the family piano manufacturing firm since 1823 and took it over on his father's death in 1833.

2. Replies, indirectly, to Stumpff's dedication in the Handel *Works* (Arnold ed.), sent as a gift to Beethoven. See August 24, 1826 (No. 435 above), and Stumpff's reply,

March 1, 1827 (No. 462 below). Receipts for the shipment, December 14, 1826, are in MacArdle & Misch Nos. 462 and 463, and Anderson, III, 1433.

3. Chrysander notes in brackets that Streicher meant compositions. It could also mean, as given in the *Harmonicon,* "A book *from* one of his London acquaintances."

4. Original: "Das ist das Wahre!" *Wahre* can also mean here the "Truth" or the "Genuine Article."

Incipit: Ihrem Wunsche gemäss richteten wir. . . .

Sources: Chrysander, "Beethoven's Verbindung," pp. 450–451; English translation by Johann Reinhold Schultz published in *Harmonicon* 5 (February 1827), 23. For more information on Schultz, see the notes to Schindler to Moscheles, March 24, 1827 (No. 469 below).

454. Johann Baptist Jenger to Marie L. Pachler-Koschak, Graz

Vienna; January 12, 1827[1]

Highly honored Gracious Lady,

Yesterday a consultation about Beethoven was held, which I wanted to wait for in order to be able to give you, in reply to your kind letter of the 1st of this month, as much exact information as possible about the illness of the great master.

Professor Wawruch[2]—who is said to be fairly clever as a doctor—has treated B[eethoven] until now. At the consultation, however, the very renowned Dr. Malfatti[3]—who in earlier times had treated B[eethoven] and is alleged to know his disposition very well—declared that B[eethoven] has been treated very incorrectly in his present illness until now. Then he prescribed for B[eethoven] nothing but frozen fruit punch[4] and massaging the stomach with ice-cold water, a treatment with which Malfatti is said to have just restored a similar patient to full health.

Whether B[eethoven] can endure this treatment, however, is a question that only time will tell. Upon the second tapping, about 5–6 days ago,[5] B[eethoven] was indeed somewhat better, but there is only little—though always some—hope for his complete recovery.

I would, according to your wish, visit B[eethoven] more often, and his other acquaintances really suffer in the same way, but Beethoven will admit no one, not even his most intimate friends, and therefore only my good intentions remain in the matter. If something unusual ensues, most gracious lady, I shall give you news of it immediately, because you take such sincere interest in B[eethoven's] fate, which gladdens me and all of B[eethoven's] friends greatly.

In any case, Beeth[oven] is now in the best medical hands and otherwise wants for nothing. If, therefore, it is possible to save him, then he will be saved. Without knowing you, gracious lady, Schubert sends his greetings and is also glad to make the acquaintance of such an ardent admirer of Beethoven's creations.

May God grant that our mutual wish, to be able to come to Graz this year, is fulfilled.[6]

1. Continues Jenger's correspondence from December 29, 1826 (No. 451 above). Jenger usually refers to Beethoven by the initial B.

2. Dr. Andreas Johann Wawruch (1771–1842) had been a professor at the University of Prague (1812–1819) before coming to Vienna, where he established an enviable reputation as a physician and surgeon.

3. Dr. Johann (von) Malfatti (1776–1858), born in Italy, had resided and worked in Vienna since around 1795. He became Beethoven's doctor for a period of several years after the death of Dr. Johann Adam Schmidt on February 19, 1808.

4. *Obst-Gefrorenes*, a fruit sherbet, probably laced with alcohol of some sort.

5. Schindler states that the second operation took place on January 8.

6. Ultimately, Schubert and Anselm Hüttenbrenner visited Graz with Jenger.

Incipit: Gestern ist über Beethoven *Consilium.* . . .

Sources: Pachler, *Beethoven und Marie Pachler-Koschak* (1866), p. 25 (material serialized in *Neue Berliner Musikzeitung* [1865]); Thayer-Deiters-Riemann, V, 444. Thayer presumably found the autograph in the possession of Marie's son, Faust Pachler.

455. *Karl van Beethoven to Beethoven*

Iglau; January 13, 1827[1]

My dear Father,

I have received your letter, written by Schindler; I ask only that in the future you have the date added so that I may judge the speed of the mails. Concerning the state of your health, I am glad to know that you are in good hands. The method of your earlier doctor (or still the present one?) had also aroused some distrust on my part;[2] hopefully, it will now go very well.

Several days ago I wrote to the Court Councillor[3] and notified him of what I still wish to have. I would have written to you yourself if I had not wanted to spare you from all trouble. Herr von Breuning will take care of everything in the best way possible.

You wish specific reports about my circumstances. The captain under whom I serve is a very educated man with whom I hope to get along very well.[4] I do not know whether I have already written that I am living in a nice room with the sergeant of the company, a very well behaved young man. There is nothing by way of an officers' mess here; everyone goes to eat where he prefers. Out of economic considerations, I myself have already changed my eating location a couple of times; now, however, it is said that a communal mess for cadets will be established—if it comes to that. In the evenings, however, everyone must leave the *Kaserne*[5] and find something elsewhere. I have a little orderly as a servant, who gets 1 florin C.M. monthly, besides expenses for white lead and chalk to clean the uniforms. The washing also costs a few gulden if one wants to have it clean. There is likewise a theater here that I also attend with the permission of the captain. So these are the principal conditions about which I can give you news now.

Concerning things that I still need and have already indicated in the letter to the Court Councillor, the captain naturally can procure nothing before he has the approval from you in his hands; I therefore request you to speak about this with Herr von Breuning. And if you want to send me a bit more of a subsidy on account of the expenses that I could not avoid and likewise have indicated, I would appreciate it. I had also calculated that I would receive my pay from the day that I was declared fit for military service (December 12, 1826); this has not happened, however, since the record of the declaration lay in Vienna. I must therefore live even more frugally now.

And now another request. A first lieutenant of the regiment, who loves music and especially your works, wants to produce the *Concert pour le Piano Forte dédié à M. Charles Nikel, Oeuvre 19. Vienne chez Hoffmeister et Comp^{ie}.*[6] at his quarters in the near future. Through an accident, however, the flute part has been lost, and so he has turned to me. I request you therefore to have the flute part procured and sent to me very soon. My address is of little concern. I receive letters through the regiment's adjutant. Write me again very soon. I embrace you sincerely. My compliments to the Court Councillor.

> Your son who loves you,

> Carl

P.S. Do not believe that the little privations to which I am now subjected make me dissatisfied with my situation; rather, be all the more convinced that I am living quite satisfactorily, and only regret that I am separated so far from you. In time, however, things will change.

> As you can see,
> I have provided myself
> with a seal with my name.

1. Karl had left Vienna for Iglau on January 2. Beethoven's letter, mentioned here, seems not to have survived. Nearly four decades later, the army post where Karl had been stationed would become part of the childhood memories of Gustav Mahler.

2. Karl, then, seemingly distrusted Wawruch and placed more confidence in Malfatti.

3. Stephan von Breuning, who had been appointed guardian after Karl's attempted suicide, probably on August 6, 1826 (see Köhler et al., *Konversationshefte,* X, 84–95).

4. Possibly Captain Bruno de Montluisant, who wrote to Schindler concerning Karl on June 9, 1827 (No. 484 below).

5. Barracks.

6. While not copied with modern scholarly accuracy, this citation for the first edition of the Piano Concerto, Op. 19, indicates that Karl had at least some eye for detail as he looked at a title page.

Incipit: Deinen durch Schindler geschriebenen Brief. . . .

Sources: Thayer-Deiters-Riemann, V, 440–441; excerpt and summary only in Thayer-Forbes, p. 1027. Autograph in the Staatsbibliothek zu Berlin–Preussischer Kulturbesitz, Mus. ms. autogr. Beethoven 35, 60a; listed in Kalischer, "Beethoven-Autographe," p. 51, and Bartlitz, p. 137.

456. Stieglitz and Co. to Beethoven

St. Petersburg; January 18, 1827[1]

On August 13 of last year we had the honor to answer your first letter[, which we] received then. Now we are in possession of a second from January 10, about the same subject that the earlier one concerned. In reply to it, we are notifying you that we have already written on your behalf to Prince Nicolas Galitzin in Koslov in the Tambov District and reminded him of your demand for 125 ducats.[2] We are therefore still awaiting his answer, of which we shall not fail to notify you after its receipt.

With greatest esteem, we have the honor to be

Your most obedient servant,
[illegible]

1. Answers a letter from Beethoven, January 10, 1827 (presumed lost), the dispatch of which was annotated (by Breuning) on the exterior of Galitzin's letter of November 22, 1826 (No. 444 above). It seems almost miraculous that a letter from Vienna would reach St. Petersburg in eight days. In copying this letter, Thayer's pen may have slipped: if the month is indeed January, then a dating of the 28th would seem more likely. One must also consider the possible discrepancy between old-style and new-style dating. Without further evidence, however, the date shall remain here as given: January 18. See also Stieglitz's letter of August 13, 1826 (No. 434 above).

Beethoven wrote to Stieglitz again on his deathbed, March 21, 1827 (Anderson No. 1567), and in any case received neither reply nor full financial settlement to his estate until a quarter century later, with Galitzin correspondence extending sporadically until 1858. A full account of this prolonged affair, including an early partial payment, more unfilled promises and evasions, is included in Thayer-Deiters-Riemann, V, 571–578, summarized in Thayer-Forbes, app. H, pp. 1100–1102.

2. Fifty ducats each for composing the String Quartets, Opp. 132 and 130, and 25 ducats for the dedication of the *Consecration of the House* Overture, Op. 124.

Incipit: Unterm 13 August vorigen Jahres. . . .

Sources: Thayer-Deiters-Riemann, V, 570. When Thayer copied it, the autograph was presumably in the possession of Beethoven's nephew Karl's widow, Caroline, Vienna. It has since disappeared.

457. Anton Schindler to Beethoven

Vienna; January 19, 1827[1]

My great Master!

Because I have a rehearsal today at 8:30, from which I cannot be absent,[2] I must report to you herewith in writing the result of my second visit to Malfatti.

Consequently, he is coming to [see] you today already at 9:30. Knowing well that the Professor[3] has lecture until 10 o'clock, I told him [Malfatti], however, that we were inviting him to come by 9:30. So that the both of us don't get in a pickle, you merely have to offer the excuse to Malf[atti] that the Prof[essor] only told you today that, because of the lecture, he could not come until 10 o'clock. Malf[atti] has a consultation in the city at 10 o'clock: you therefore have the opportunity that you wanted, to speak to him alone.

What I am asking, however, is that you do not pass up this opportunity to reconcile with him completely about the past, for it still irritates him, although [he expresses it] in very gentle words; even today he again gave me to understand that he could not forget this instigated offense, as he called it.[4] A few words of explanation from you will put everything right and get it back on the old, friendly track.

Around 2 o'clock I shall again have the honor of being with you. Meanwhile, *summa cum reverentia,*

Your obliging,

Ant[on] Schindler

1. Schindler discusses the circumstances surrounding this letter in his *Biographie* (1860), pt. 2, p. 135 (Schindler-MacArdle, p. 320).
2. Schindler was a violinist and conductor at the Josephstadt Theater.
3. Dr. Andreas Wawruch.
4. The earlier break with Dr. Malfatti seems to have taken place in 1815, when Beethoven supposedly accused him of obtaining results too slowly in his treatment.
Incipit: Weil ich heute schon um halb 9 Uhr. . . .
Sources: Thayer-Deiters-Riemann, V, 447–448; English translation in Thayer-Forbes, pp. 1031–1032. Autograph in the Staatsbibliothek zu Berlin–Preussischer

Kulturbesitz, Mus. ms. autogr. Beethoven 36, 76; listed in Kalischer, "Beethoven-Autographe," p. 61, and Bartlitz, p. 176.

458. Beethoven, Contract with Ignaz Pleyel & Son, Paris[1]

Vienna; January 24, 1827[2]

I the undersigned, Louis van Beethoven, declare, in the presence of a notary, that I have sold, as entirely their property for the full extent of the kingdom of France, to Messieurs Ignace Pleyel & Elder Son in Paris, my three musical compositions, as follows:

Opus 130. Quartet in B♭ for two violins, viola & violoncello, being the third quartet of the quartets dedicated to Prince Nicolas de Galitzin.

Opus 133. Grosse Fuge in B♭ for two violins, viola & violoncello, dedicated to Archduke Rudolph of Austria.

Opus 134. The same Grosse Fuge in B♭, arranged for piano, four-hands, by myself.

Messieurs Ignace Pleyel & Son, publishers of music in Paris are therefore the only persons authorized to publish them in any manner. They intend [to publish] my aforementioned musical compositions in France, and my intention is that, not knowing the laws of France on this matter, my present declaration be regarded in France as conforming to the laws of France on this matter.

In confidence thereof, I sign the present declaration myself, as well as two requested witnesses to this matter.

Vienna, January 24, 1827

Beethoven, m.p.

[Witnesses:]
  Mathias Artaria
  Jean Traeg[3]

1. The Austrian-born composer Pleyel (1757–1831) studied with Haydn, journeyed to Italy and England and in 1795 settled in Paris, where he established a music

publishing firm. In 1815, he was joined in partnership by his son Camille (1788–1855).

2. A French-language document in another hand, signed by Beethoven and his witnesses.

3. As witnesses, Beethoven enlisted Mathias Artaria (who held the Viennese publication rights to these works) as well as music publisher-dealer Johann Traeg. Thus, the composer's honesty cannot be questioned in such a transaction.

Incipit: Moi sousigné Louis van Beethoven, declare. . . .

Sources: Unger, *Eine Schweizer Beethovensammlung,* no. 289, pp. 82–83; Kinsky-Halm, p. 407; Schmidt, "Beethovenhandschriften," pp. 136–137. Autograph in the Beethoven-Archiv, Bonn, Br 289, since 1956. Sieghard Brandenburg, Beethoven-Archiv, Bonn, kindly supplied the body of the text; Joan Falconer, University of Iowa, generously sent a copy of Unger's entry that included the names of the witnesses.

459. Franz Gerhard Wegeler to Beethoven (with postscript from Eleonore Wegeler)

Koblenz; February 1, 1827[1]

Dear old Friend!

A shipment of several musical pieces from Schott in Mainz has given us the joyous conviction that you remembered us in friendly kindness.[2] Your persistent silence after my last letter nearly had me fearing the contrary. Now I tell myself that I have been no diligent correspondent. And indeed no one would take you back to your years of youth, no one could remind you of a hundred occasions with happy and sad images as I, especially since my wife faithfully assists my memory with tales of Fräulein Westerholdt, Jeanette Hohnrath and whatever the *et ceteras* were named.[3] On the whole, my two children (20 and 23 years old) know you so intimately that, if you came to visit us, they would try to arrange everything in a manner that they thought pleasing to you.

The word *visit* reminds me painfully, however, of your illness, although I see in it a means of realizing one of my most ardent wishes. You will recover from the illness from which you presently suffer in the next months; for me this is not so much indicated by your vigorous manhood, your entire constitution or the passing causes of [the disease], as it is by the nature of the illness itself, which indeed is persistent and lengthy, but nevertheless yields to unweakened nature and the endeavors of art.[4] Now, however, a convalescence will be necessary, and you will find this, if I do not entirely mistake your malady, in Carlsbad. There are now so many express coaches going from here to the country that I can be in Carlsbad in four, at most five days, or I [can] send one of my patients there and accompany him, that is, if one determines that Carlsbad is superior for his needs. We shall then spend three weeks there; and then a little journey through part of southern Germany and finally the happiness and youthful reminiscences upon being in our homeland and the caring circle of my family, of which you are even now virtually a member, ought to fill in what's missing and strengthen your recovery. This is a fond image for me, one with which my fantasy is very happily occupied. If a person is happy only once, and indeed in his most innocent youth, then the stones of his native city and every tree of the surrounding region and every tower of the neighboring villages must be for him hooks upon which to hang pictures of his youth and take pleasure in them.

With us everything is well; I have promised my son, in case he is very diligent, permission to visit Vienna. You will then take pleasure in his athletic workingman's stature. Your old rival Steffan may tell you about my daughter, who continually sins against your works; as a father I can be entirely satisfied with her; she is skillful, clever and, most importantly, always cheerful.[5] Adieu! If my letters please you, then more will follow.

[Wegeler]

[P.S.] I can only concur with everything that Wegeler has written to you, my dear Beethoven[6] — indeed I cannot deny myself requesting most sincerely, in heartfelt words, that, as soon as possible, you attend to everything that concerns a journey here, be it understood, to visit us. I have the greatest hope that you would soon recover completely here, and your visit would grant me the fulfillment of one of my greatest wishes. Why then should the journey to a spa precede it? Come here first and see what influence the happiness of being in your homeland will have upon you.

E. Wegeler

1. Beethoven had recently written to Wegeler on December 7, 1826 (Anderson No. 1542 gives this corrected date, rather than October 7); Beethoven answered Wegeler on February 17, 1827 (Anderson No. 1551).

2. For a list of these works, see Beethoven's instructions to Schott of ca. December 18, 1826 (Anderson No. 1545).

3. Wegeler refers to Beethoven's youthful romances with Anna Maria Westerholt and Jeannette d'Honrath and alludes to more. His spellings of their names are given in the text above.

4. Wegeler's meaning here is not entirely clear: he probably means *natural* recuperation assisted by the *art* of medicine.

5. The Wegelers' daughter Helene was born in 1803, was still living at home and was an amateur pianist. Their son Julius, born in 1807, was a medical student in Berlin. Eleonore Wegeler was the sister of Beethoven's friend Stephan von Breuning.

6. Wegeler here writes with the familiar *Du*, Eleonore with the formal *Sie*.

Incipit: (a) Aus einer Zusendung einiger Musikalien . . . ; (b) Allem, was Wegeler Ihnen. . . .

Sources: Thayer-Deiters-Riemann, V, 456–457. Thayer made his copy from the original then in the possession of Karl van Beethoven's widow, Caroline. Also given by Ludwig Nohl, "Beethovens Tod," in his *Musikalisches Skizzenbuch* (Munich: C. Merhoff, 1866), p. 251.

460. Anton Schindler to Ignaz Moscheles, London

Vienna; February 22, 1827[1]

Dearest Friend!

Upon reading through the letter of our unfortunate Beethoven, you will see that I have reserved for myself directing a few lines of my own to you. Certainly I have very much to tell you, but I prefer dwelling only on Beethoven, because he is now the most important topic occupying my heart.

From his letter to you, you will find expressed his request and his most ardent wish. The same contents are also in the letter to Sir Smart, as well as an earlier one, written in my hand, to the harp maker Stumpff.[2]

Already during your last visit here I described to you Beethoven's financial circumstances and could not predict that the time was so near when we would see this worthy man meet his end in such a lamentable manner.[3] For one can indeed say his end, because as the matter presently stands with his illness, a recovery cannot be considered; although he does not know this for sure, he already suspects it.

On December 3, he arrived from the country with his worthless nephew.[4] On the journey here, because of bad weather, he had to spend the night at a miserable inn, where, due to these circumstances, he caught a cold, which immediately became an inflammation of the lungs, and arrived here in this condition. Hardly had this passed when all the symptoms of dropsy also appeared, which increased so severely that, as early as December 18, he had to be operated upon for the first time, otherwise he would have burst. The second operation followed on January 8, and the third on January 20. After the second and third, the water was allowed to flow from the wound for eleven days, but hardly had the wound healed than the pressure of the water built so terribly quickly that I often feared that he would have to suffocate before another operation could be performed. Only now do I notice that the pressure of the water is not as severe as it was earlier, and, as it looks now, if it continues in this manner, 8–10 more days may pass before the fourth operation.[5]

Now, my friend! Just imagine Beethoven, with his impatience and with his temperament in general, in such a fearful illness! Imagine him placed in such a situation by the meanest of men, his nephew, and also partially by his brother; for both doctors, H[err] Malfatti and Professor Wawruch declare that the cause of the illness was the fearful emotions to which the good man was exposed for a long time by his nephew, as well as too long a stay in the country during the wet season. This was not easy to change because the young man dared not remain in Vienna because of police mandate,[6] and a place in a regiment could not be found immediately. Now he is a cadet with Archduke Ludwig and still behaves toward his uncle as he did before, although, as ever, he is entirely dependent upon him. Beeth[oven] sent him the letter to Sir Smart for translation into English two weeks ago, but as of today there has been no reply, although he is only a few [postal] stations from here, in Iglau.

Should you, my magnificent Moscheles, in conjunction with Sir Smart, induce the Philharmonic Society to comply with his wish, you would certainly perform the greatest benevolence thereby. For the expenses in this protracted illness are extraordinary, indeed such that the conjecture that he will have to suffer want in the future torments him day and night, for he would rather die than have to accept anything from his abominable brother.

As it now appears, there will be emaciation from the dropsy, for he is already skin and bones. But his constitution will still resist this horrible end for a very long time.

Another thing that makes him very ill is that absolutely no one here is concerned about him, and this apathy is really very remarkable. In earlier times, people would drive by in carriages when he was merely indisposed; now he is completely forgotten, as if he had never lived in Vienna. I have the greatest torment because of this, and wish most ardently that his condition might soon change, one way or another, for I am losing all my time, since I alone have to do things for him, because he wants to have no one else around him; but to abandon him in this completely helpless condition would be inhuman.

He now speaks frequently of a journey to London when he is well, and already is calculating how the two of us will live most economically on the journey. But, dear God! I fear that the journey will go further than to England. When he is alone, his entertainment consists of reading the ancient Greeks;[7] he has also read several of the Walter Scott novels with pleasure.

When you are certain, my dear friend, that the Philharmonic Society intends to carry out this long-expressed design,[8] do not fail to notify Beethoven about it immediately, for this will give him a new lease on life. Also, try to induce Sir Smart to write to him, so that he receives a double assurance.

May God be with you! Please give my kindest regards to your excellent wife.[9]

With all imaginable respect,
As always,
Your most obedient friend,

Ant. Schindler

[P.S.]
Do not laugh at the address to Sir Smart, for neither Beeth[oven] nor I know it otherwise.

[P.P.S.]
The piano maker Graf sends most friendly greetings. A short time ago he made Beethoven a gift of a fortepiano.[10] If the matter on behalf of Beethoven materializes, then several of these gentlemen should express to Beeth[oven] without reservation, upon delivery of the money, that the Society wishes that

he might apply this money to his own good, and not to the advantage of his outlandish relatives, especially his ungrateful nephew, who has incurred only the general animosity of other acquaintances in London as well as in Vienna. This would be very advantageous, for otherwise he would give it to his nephew, who would only squander it while [Beethoven himself] suffers privation.

1. Accompanied Beethoven's letters of the same date to Moscheles (Anderson No. 1554) and Sir George Smart (Anderson No. 1555), both dictated to Schindler and signed by the composer. The postal stamp indicates that the three letters arrived in London on March 8.

On March 9, 1827, Moscheles wrote in English to Smart: "My dear Sir. Allow me to give you in a few words the contents of Beethoven's letter to you as I am extremely busy and have not enough time to translate it entirely. He first thanks for the nice present you made to his nephew, then apologizes for writing to you in German instead of English in consequence of his nephew not being with him at present (fortunate for him — remarque of the translator [i.e., Moscheles]), as he, the nephew, used to translate his letters. The remaining part of the letter is a repetition of the one sent to Mr. Stumpff [February 8, 1827, Anderson No. 1550] containing the request of the Philharm. Soc. giving a concert for his benefit . . ." (International Autographs, *Autograph Letters, Manuscripts and Documents*, Catalog] no. 18 [New York, 1967], item 5, pp. 3–4).

2. Anderson No. 1550, dated February 8, 1827.

3. Schindler uses the now archaic intensive phrase "his last end" meaning "his final goal," here and in the next sentence. Moscheles had been in Vienna for a brief visit during October 1826 and gave concerts at the Kärntnertor Theater on October 21 and 25; he did not see Beethoven, who was in Gneixendorf at the time.

4. In the *Harmonicon* translation, Karl was called "his ungrateful and depraved nephew" at this point.

5. The fourth operation took place on February 27.

6. Karl's temporary banishment was due to his attempted suicide the previous summer.

7. Johann Reinhold Schultz, who spent a day with Beethoven in Baden in 1823, translated portions of this letter in the *Harmonicon* and added his own footnote: "He mentioned to me, that of all the classics, he admired none so much as Plutarch and Homer, particularly the *Odyssey*."

8. The Philharmonic Society sent Beethoven £100.

9. This complimentary paragraph, referring in part to Moscheles's wife Charlotte, was omitted from Ley.

10. Conrad Graf (1782–1851) took Beethoven's Broadwood piano for repairs in the fourth week of January 1826, probably on Tuesday, January 24 (Köhler et al., *Konversationshefte*, VIII, 288–289); as a substitute, he brought an instrument of his own manufacture, which is now associated with the composer and owned by the Beethoven-Haus, Bonn. At what point during Beethoven's fourteen-month custody the instrument passed in status from loan to gift — or if it ever did — is difficult to determine. Graf apparently still had the Broadwood piano as late as September 1826, just before Beethoven departed Vienna for two months in Gneixendorf. Moscheles had left Vienna around October 30, 1826, and therefore the "gift," as reported by Schindler, must have taken place after that date. In any case, Graf reclaimed his own piano within three days after Beethoven's death and may actually have removed it while the composer lay comatose, after March 24 (see No. 477 below).

Incipit: Bey Durchlesung des Briefes. . . .

Sources: Ley, *Beethoven als Freund*, pp. 226–228, indicating that the autograph was then in the Wegeler family collection. Slightly different version in Charlotte Moscheles, *Life of Moscheles*, I, 145–149; Smidak, *Moscheles*, pp. 49–50. Described in Nohl, *Beethoven's Leben* (1877), III, 765–766, 955–956. Portions translated and inserted into versions of Schindler's letter of March 24, 1827 (No. 469 below), published by Johann Reinhold Schultz in the *Harmonicon* and by Moscheles in his edition of Schindler's biography.

461. Beethoven to Gottlieb von Tucher, Nürnberg[1]

Vienna; February 28, 1827[2]

[Beethoven gratefully accepts Tucher's dedication of his *Kirchengesänge der berühmtesten älteren italienischen Meister*.[3]]

1. Baron Christoph Carl Gottlieb Sigmund von Tucher von Simmelsdorf (1798–1877), the son of the mayor of Nürnberg, studied law, mathematics, natural sciences and philosophy at the Universities of Heidelberg, Erlangen and Berlin, all concurrently with his musical studies under Anton Friedrich Justus Thibaut (who awakened his love for Renaissance and Baroque music) and Bernhard Klein. On passing his examinations, he traveled through Italy in 1824, collecting early church music. He met the papal musical administrator and Palestrina biographer Giuseppe Baini in Rome and obtained copies of works in the music library of Abbate Fortunato Santini. After returning to a municipal position in Nürnberg in 1825, Tucher sent a

two-volume collection of music by Palestrina and his school to the publisher Mathias Artaria in Vienna.

In a conversation book entry of ca. February 15–17, 1826, Carl Holz told Beethoven: "Artaria has several vocal pieces by the oldest composers, Palestrina, for example, in score. He asks you to look through them and give him your opinion, whether he should publish them or not." At some point during the first few days in March, Beethoven's nephew Karl jotted in the conversation books a translation of passages from two motets, *Pueri hebraeorum vestimenta prosternebant in via* and *Adoramus te Christe*, both attributed to Palestrina in Tucher's collection. At the end of March, Carl Holz again wrote: "Artaria asked about the vocal pieces. . . . He wants to have the texts translated. If you want them later, he will gladly send them to you. The translator has time just now" (Köhler et al., *Konversationshefte*, IX, 31, 83, 125 and notes).

Although Beethoven's interest (but, with it, his approval) supposedly "delayed publication," Tucher (on September 21, 1826) dedicated the first volume of his collection to the composer. This volume was advertised in the *Wiener Zeitung* on March 19, 1827, and was reviewed favorably in the *Allgemeine musikalische Zeitung* 29 (May 1827), cols. 378–382. Beethoven must have received his printed copy as soon as it was off the press, for he conveyed his thanks to Tucher on February 28, 1827. Tucher spent part of 1827–1828 in Anhalt, but we may assume that Beethoven would have addressed his letter to Nürnberg. The second volume in Tucher's collection (dedicated to Thibaut) appeared later in 1827, and the success of this venture encouraged him to spend the rest of his life (although employed in various governmental positions in Germany) collecting and publishing early church music, both Catholic and Lutheran.

2. The noted hymnologist Johannes Zahn (1817–1895) recorded the date and content of this letter in his article on Tucher in the *Allgemeine deutsche Biographie*. Since Zahn had known and worked with Tucher since at least 1850, one may assume that he himself examined the letter, which he described as "eine eigenhändig unterzeichnete Zuschrift," probably an indication that (as with so many letters during Beethoven's final illness) Schindler wrote the note for the composer's signature.

3. Tucher's collection — issued in score — contained five works by (or attributed to) Giovanni Pierluigi da Palestrina (1525/26–1594), three by his successor Felice Anerio (ca. 1560–1614) and two by Tomás Luis de Victoria, here called Vittoria (1548–1611). At some point in the 1820s, possibly in connection with his examination of Tucher's collection, Beethoven made a pencil copy of the "Gloria patri" from the *Magnificat tertii toni* (published in parts in 1591); the copy is presently housed in the State Public Library, St. Petersburg. Nathan Fishman described it briefly in 1967; ten years later, his Soviet colleague Abraham (Avram) Klimovitsky hypothesized that it might have served as a model for the "Heiliger Dankgesang" in Beethoven's String Quartet, Op. 132, a question contested by Sieghard Brandenburg in 1982. To

be sure, the early sketches for Beethoven's quartet movement date from around May 1825, and the "Gloria patri" does not appear in Tucher's collection as published. When Beethoven examined Tucher's material in February–March 1826, he was probably working on the String Quartet, Op. 131, and envisioning the Quartet, Op. 135, as well as the new finale to Op. 130. If the "Heiliger Dankgesang" does not fit into this chronology, the fact remains that Beethoven must have been extremely receptive to antiquarian influence at this period, a phenomenon that merits further investigation. See Fishman (cited below); Abraham Klimovitsky, "Ein 'Gloria' von Palestrina als Modell des 'Heiligen Dankgesanges' aus Beethovens Streichquartett op. 132," in *Bericht über den internationalen Beethoven-Kongress, Berlin 1977*, ed. Harry Goldschmidt, Karl-Heinz Köhler and Konrad Niemann (Leipzig, 1978), pp. 513–517, 223–229; Sieghard Brandenburg, "The Historical Background to the 'Heiliger Dankgesang' in Beethoven's A-Minor Quartet Op. 132," in *Beethoven Studies 3*, ed. Alan Tyson (Cambridge: Cambridge University Press, 1982), pp. 161–191, esp. p. 163; and Johnson-Tyson-Winter, pp. 315–317.

Incipit: Unknown.

Sources: Johannes Zahn, "Tucher," in *Allgemeine deutsche Biographie* (Leipzig, 1894; reprint, Berlin: Duncker & Humblot, 1971), pp. 38, 767–770; Nathan Fishman, "Beiträge zur Beethoveniana," trans. Dagmar Beck, *Beiträge zur Musikwissenschaft* 9, nos. 3/4 (1967), 323–324.

462. Johann Andreas Stumpff to Beethoven

London; March 1, 1827[1]

Herr Lud[wig] v[an] Beethoven, Vienna

Very esteemed Sir![2]

 I cannot express in words how very much the report alarmed me and pierced me with pains, that you suffer from a painful and lengthy illness,[3] of which you now told me yourself in a letter of February 8.[4]

 Indeed, the first report of it that I received through the kindness of Herr B. Streicher,[5] few days have passed when I have not thought very vividly of you, my noble friend!:[6] often I stand in spirit in your room, at the bed of the suffering one,[7] and so often and so anxiously ask the doctor his views about your recovery,[8] and want to extort from him the assurance that the illness is not critical and that the patient will soon be completely restored to health.

Indeed, most affectionately admired friend! If sincere and ardent wishes of a friend could bring about your recovery, the hearts of your admirers would soon be uplifted on the waves of a Symphony of Thanks streaming from your breast to him who alone can help, who leads his creatures in a strange but fatherly way toward the final goal set by him.[9]

That the *Works* of Handel[10] that I sent you gave you great joy is reward enough for me, because such[11] was my only intention. According to your wishes, I interested Messrs. G. Smart and Moscheles in the worthy cause without delay;[12] the Directors of the Philharmonic Society likewise received the report, about which they were then immediately advised,[13] and it was thus resolved: that for the present a sum of 100 pounds would be delivered to Baron Rothschild here with the request to remit it by the first post to the Rothschild [Banking] House in Vienna,[14] with the instruction that the money, when your needs required it, could be withdrawn by you in smaller or larger sums through Herr Rau, steward in Baron Eskeles's [Banking] House.[15] Herr Moscheles, who very much interested himself in the matter, had the kindness to accomplish this because he was in touch[16] with both houses and, at my request, sent letters containing instructions to the previously named persons[17] by today's post.

I thank you sincerely for your friendly offer to be of service to me in Vienna, and to request only a few notes in your kind hand as a remembrance is the object of all my wishes. With the sincere wish to hear of your recovery soon,[18] I have the honor to remain, with greatest esteem,

Your most sincere, most faithful servant,[19]

J. A. Stumpff

Great Portland Street
Portland Place

1. Along with Moscheles's letter of the same date (No. 463 below), this letter replies to Beethoven's letter of February 8, 1827 (Anderson No. 1550). It arrived in Vienna on March 17 (see Streicher's letter to Stumpff of March 28, No. 473 below).

This letter exists in two versions: the draft, as published by Chrysander, and the letter actually sent, preserved in Schindler's *Nachlass* and copied independently by both Nohl and Thayer. The version given here represents the letter sent to and received by Beethoven; the notes cover any translatable variants found in the draft.

2. "Hoch und sehr werthgeschätzter Herr!" in the version sent, "Sehr hochgeschätzter Herr und Freund" in the draft. Stumpff uses the word *friend* in both the salutation and the close of his draft but in neither in the version sent, although the word appears three further times (once placed slightly differently) in both versions. On the whole, however, the wording in the version sent is slightly more restrained than that of the draft.

3. The words "painful and" do not appear in the draft.

4. Dictated to Schindler, signed by Beethoven.

5. Johann Baptist Streicher; see Streicher's letter to Stumpff of January 5, 1827 (No. 453 above).

6. The words "my noble friend!" do not appear in the draft.

7. "At the bed of my suffering friend" in the draft.

8. The draft reads "improvement."

9. The draft reads "to *Him,* who alone can help, who leads his creatures in a fatherly way through inexplicable paths toward the final goal set for him."

10. Arnold's edition; see Stumpff's earlier correspondence.

11. The draft reads "it."

12. Sir George Smart and Ignaz Moscheles; Smart's first name is written out in the draft but not in the letter sent. In his letter of February 8, Beethoven had told Stumpff that he recalled that several years before the Philharmonic Society wanted to give a concert for his benefit and that he was writing to Smart and Moscheles to instigate such a concert now.

13. The draft adds "because such an undertaking could not be accomplished at a moment's notice," a reference to the proposed benefit concert. The phrase "for the present" in the resolution indicates that the £100 represented an advance on the proceeds from the benefit concert if and when it came to pass.

14. From the Frankfurt-based banking family, Nathan Mayer Rothschild (1777–1836) settled in London; Solomon Rothschild (1774–1855) went to Vienna.

15. Judging from a letter written by Simrock to Ries (June 30, 1809, No. 142 above), Beethoven may have had dealings with the Eskeles banking house as early as 1809. For further information on Daniel Bernhard (von) Eskeles (1753–1839) and his elder associates, Nathan Adam Arnstein (1743–1838) and Salomon Herz (1743–1825), see Frimmel, *Handbuch,* I, 127; Staehelin and Brandenburg, *Briefwechsel,* p. 55; and Anderson No. 1485 (n. 3). Although Sebastian Rau becomes active in settling the Philharmonic account, Beethoven seems not to have known him before mid-March 1827. (See Beethoven to Moscheles, March 18, 1827, Anderson No. 1566; and Rau to Moscheles, March 17, 1827, No. 468 below.)

16. The letter sent reads "in Verbindung"; the draft says "in Bekanntschaft" (in acquaintance).

17. The draft specifies their names: "to Barons Rothschild and Eskeles and Herr Rau."

18. The foregoing phrase is not in the draft.

19. The draft's close reads: "I have the honor to remain, Your most obedient friend and servant."

Incipit: Wie sehr mich die Nachricht erschreckt. . . .

Sources: Draft given in Chrysander, "Beethoven's Verbindung," pp. 451–452; version sent to Beethoven transcribed from Schindler's *Nachlass* by Nohl, *Neue Briefe* (1867), pp. 299–300, and, somewhat differently, Thayer-Deiters-Riemann, V, 460–461. All but the final paragraph (possibly based on Nohl) in Kalischer (German), V, 290–291; quoted and summarized in Kalischer-Shedlock, II, 462. Kastner (1910), pp. 934–935, follows Thayer's version. Autograph seemingly in the Österreichische Nationalbibliothek, Vienna. Copy in the Staatsbibliothek zu Berlin–Preussischer Kulturbesitz, Mus. ms. autogr. Beethoven 35, 59; listed in Kalischer, "Beethoven-Autographe," p. 51, and Bartlitz, p. 136.

463. Ignaz Moscheles to Beethoven

London; March 1, 1827[1]

The Society therefore resolved to express to you its good will and active sympathy, while requesting you to accept 100 pounds sterling (1,000 gulden C.M.), in order to provide thereby all necessary comforts and conveniences during your illness. Herr Rau of the House of Eskeles will deliver this money to you in portions, or, if you wish it, all at once, against your receipt.[2]

1. Along with Stumpff's letter of the same date (No. 462 above), this letter replies to Beethoven's letter to Stumpff of February 8, 1827 (Anderson No. 1550). Beethoven, in turn, replied on March 18 (Anderson No. 1566).

2. Only this excerpt is quoted directly by Schindler, who added the following paraphrase of another passage: "Moscheles added that the Philharmonic Society was willing to extend their good offices still further, and that Beethoven had only to write, if he needed their assistance."

Incipit (this excerpt): Die Gesellschaft beschloss daher. . . .

Sources: Schindler (1840), p. 187; Schindler-Moscheles, II, 68–69; Hellinghaus, pp. 244–245; Thayer-Forbes, p. 1036.

464. *Karl van Beethoven to Beethoven*

Iglau; March 4, 1827[1]

My dear Father!

I just received the boots that you sent me and thank you very much for them.[2]

You will have received the translation of the letter to Smart; I do not doubt that it will have favorable results.[3]

Just today a cadet, who was on leave for some time in Vienna, returned to the battalion; he reports having heard that you were saved by a frozen punch, and that you are feeling quite well.[4] I only wish that the latter is true, whatever the means may have been.

There is little new to say about myself; the service goes along in its usual way, only with the difference that the weather is far milder, thus making guard duty also easier to bear.

Write to me quite soon about your state of health; also give my sincere compliments to the Court Councillor. I kiss you,

Your loving son,

Charl[5]

P.S. I request that you place postage on your letters, because I must pay much postage here and have difficulty stretching [my money] to make my bills.[6]

1. Beethoven had evidently written to Karl during the second week of February (see Schindler's letter to Moscheles of February 22, No. 460 above); that letter seems not to have survived.

2. The footwear was probably sent through Court Councillor Stephan von Breuning (see Karl's letter of January 13, No. 455 above). A typographical error renders this word "books" in the Thayer-Forbes translation.

3. On February 22, Schindler had complained to Moscheles (No. 460 above) that Beethoven had sent Karl a letter to Sir George Smart for Karl to translate into English two weeks before and had not received it back yet. On the same day, and again on March 6, Schindler wrote letters to Smart (in German), signed by Beethoven

(Anderson Nos. 1555 and 1559), both times asking the London Philharmonic Society to hold a concert for the composer's benefit.

4. Karl had departed Vienna for military service on January 2, 1827; the frozen punch remedy, suggested by Dr. Malfatti, had begun on January 11 (see Jenger's letter to Pachler-Koschak, January 12, No. 454 above).

5. The close in German is more intimate: "Dein Dich liebender Sohn" (Your you-loving son); Karl had also used it in his letter of January 13. The abbreviated French form of his name that Karl employs here is the same as that which Ries used in referring to Karl's father, Beethoven's brother Carl, in 1803.

6. With Beethoven housebound, Schindler was presumably the person responsible for sending and franking most of the composer's correspondence. It is possible that the secretary, who bore little love for Karl, intentionally sent his letters "postage due."

Incipit: So eben erhalte ich die mir übermachten Stiefel. . . .

Sources: Thayer-Deiters-Riemann, V, 442; Thayer-Forbes, p. 1028. Autograph in the Staatsbibliothek zu Berlin–Preussischer Kulturbesitz, Mus. ms. autogr. Beethoven 35, 60c; listed in Kalischer, "Beethoven-Autographe," p. 51, and Bartlitz, p. 137. Facsimile in Bekker, *Beethoven*, pl. 133; and Valentin, *Beethoven*, p. 118 (taken from Bekker).

465. Raphael Georg Kiesewetter,[1] for the Gesellschaft der Musikfreunde, to Beethoven

Vienna; March 7, 1827

To Herr Ludwig van Beethoven,
Composer

The Society of the Friends of Music of the Austrian Imperial State wishes to bear witness to you of the exceptional esteem with which it properly values the services, which you have rendered to the Art whose furtherance is its purpose. With this intention, it sends to you herewith the diploma[2] as Honorary Member of the Society.

Kiesewetter
Vice President

1. Kiesewetter (1773–1850), a high official in the War Ministry, vice president of the Gesellschaft, 1821–1843, and one of the signers of the petition, shortly before February 26, 1824 (No. 344 above).

2. This letter was written to accompany the Gesellschaft der Musikfreunde's diploma, dated October 26, 1826 (No. 441 above), and already a month old when Beethoven returned to Vienna in deteriorating health in early December 1826.

For a history of the honorary membership, the diploma, this letter and the possibility that Beethoven never received them, see C. F. Pohl's account (noted below) and my commentary to the aforementioned diploma.

Incipit: Die Gesellschaft der Musikfreunde des österr. Kaiserstaates. . . .

Sources: Pohl, *Gesellschaft der Musikfreunde*, p. 16. When Pohl examined it, the letter was presumably in a private collection in Vienna. Listed in Frimmel, "Verzeichnisse," p. 111, with autograph reported in the Bibliothek und Museum der Stadt Wien (Städtische Sammlungen), today's Stadt- und Landesbibliothek (Handschriftenabteilung), I. N. 99 281.

466. B. Schotts Söhne to Beethoven

Mainz; March 8, 1827[1]

Herr Ludwig van Beethoven
Vienna

We read your very honored letter of February 22 with very great regret, in that you could not inform us of your recovery.

In order to comply as quickly as possible with the wish that you expressed, we have chosen for you, from [the stock of] one of our very good friends, a splendid Rüdesheimer Berg-Wein from 1806, produced by himself and preserved completely clear,[2] and have already sent off 12 bottles to you by freight transport via Frankfurt through Herr Emanuel Müller, in a small chest with the seal *V.B.W.*[3] By these means we wish for their best delivery.

So that a little restorative can reach you even earlier, however, we sent off by post coach today a smaller chest as well as a small packet to your address. This small chest contains 4 bottles,[4] 2 of which with clear wine as described above. Two other bottles of the same wine have herbs[5] added, which, taken according to the prescription, should serve as medication for your illness. In the following you will see the instructions for it, as well as for the packet of roots.

We have had this wine sent to a friend who lives 10 hours from here and who has already cured many of dropsy with his herbal wine.

It is our most ardent wish that it might radically cure you too, and that the herb seeker will receive his reward for his trouble through a remembrance from you.

Have us informed of the results quite soon.

The last folios[6] of your Mass are now going to press and should be ready for shipment soon.

Also the Quartet in C♯ minor[7] is already finished, and will likewise be [ready] in Paris soon. Have the kindness to issue a certificate about this Quartet, and send it immediately, with designation of the key and the opus [number], and transferring to us the exclusive property rights not only in Mainz but in Paris and all other places where we think it appropriate, to produce in engraving as our property, and kindly have your signature legalized.[8]

Regarding Schlesinger[9] and the other Parisian publishers, one cannot sufficiently beware and take security measures.

We are counting upon this favor from you.

As soon as your strength has returned, we are also hoping to receive the metronome marks for the Mass.[10] We live in the happy anticipation of your improvement soon, and with pleasure will seize every opportunity to be useful to you and to convince you of our devotion.

May you live well and in health,

B. Schotts Söhne

[Address:]
   Herr Ludwig van Beethoven
   Alservorstadt No. 200[11]
   Vienna

[On a small sheet:]

Remedy
against Dropsy
Directions for Use

In the morning, noon and evening, take each time a tablespoon full of the herbal wine; should the effect of this be too severe and one feels ill to the point of vomiting, then suspend it for a day and continue again and follow the above [instructions].

When the water is completely gone from the body, either through the urine or stool, then take only 2 tablespoons full each day; a week afterward only 1 tablespoon full.

Take ¾ ounce of root (black orchis),[12] have it washed clean and boil in one quart to three pints of water; drink 3 to 4 cups of it each day.

One can eat everything.

[In left margin, written by a later hand:]

On June 13, sent by Schindler; made out by B. and signed by Breuning.[13]

1. Answers Beethoven's letter of February 22, 1827 (Anderson No. 1553).

2. It is not certain from the phrase "von demselben selbst gezogen" whether Schott's friend produced the wine or simply partook of it himself. The reference to clear or pure wine is in reply to Beethoven's request for unadulterated wine.

3. Probably an abbreviation for *Van Beethoven, Wien.*

4. Schott uses the French term *Bouteillen.*

5. *Kräuter,* "medicinal herbs."

6. *Bögen* in German.

7. String Quartet, Op. 131, which appeared in the summer of 1827.

8. That is, by a notary.

9. Maurice Schlesinger, with whom Beethoven had also had dealings recently.

10. *Missa solemnis,* Op. 123.

11. Following Beethoven's own spelling, Schott writes *Alstervorstadt.*

12. *Männertreu* in the original German: *Nigritella nigra* or *Veronica.*

13. Refers to the publication rights to the quartet.

Incipit: Dero sehr geehrte Zuschrift vom 22. Febr. . . . .

Sources: Thayer-Deiters-Riemann, V, 474–475; Kalischer (German), V, 302–304; Staehelin and Brandenburg, *Briefwechsel,* pp. 79–81. Autograph in the Staatsbibliothek zu Berlin–Preussischer Kulturbesitz, Mus. ms. autogr. Beethoven 35, 72h; listed in Kalischer, "Beethoven-Autographe," p. 53, and Bartlitz, p. 143. Both the Thayer-Deiters-Riemann and the Kalischer transcriptions are inaccurate or incomplete in varying details. *Briefwechsel* provides an illustration of the wine bottle label.

467. Anton Schindler to Ignaz Moscheles, London

Vienna; March 14, 1827[1]

My dearest Friend!

Here also a scrap from me. From his letter you can infer Beethoven's present state. He constantly advances nearer death than recovery, this much is certain, for his whole body is already wasting away. However, it could go on like this for many months, because until now his chest has been as if made from steel.

If the Philharmonic Society fulfills his request, just try to arrange it that the money be transferred to someone respectable here (for example, a large business house), from whom he could then withdraw, little by little, as much as he needs. The Philharmonic Society, however, ought to explain to Beethoven regardless that they are taking this measure only in his best interest, since they know too well that the relatives who surround him do not deal with him honestly, etc. He will certainly be startled by it, but I and others in whom he places his confidence will make him understand that this is a very benevolent measure, and he will thereby be satisfied. For what he leaves behind, in any case, will moreover come into the *most un*worthy hands in the world, and it would be better if it were left to a penal institution.[2]

Hummel is here with his wife.[3] He came with great haste to see Beethoven alive once more, because it is generally rumored in Germany that he is already at the point of death. The reunion of these two this past Thursday was really a touching sight.[4] I had warned Hummel earlier that he ought to prepare himself for Beethoven's appearance; nonetheless he was so astonished at it that, in spite of all effort, he could not restrain himself from breaking out in tears. The elder Streicher,[5] however, prevented him from doing so. The first thing he [Beethoven] said to Hummel was: "Look, my dear Hummel, the house where Haydn was born; I received it today as a gift and it gave me childlike joy. — A rude peasant's hut, where such a great man was born!"[6] Thus I saw two men who, in the past, were never the best of friends, forgetting all the [self-]interests of their lives, in the most affectionate conversation with each other. Both of them have promised a rendezvous next summer in Carlsbad. Alas! alas!

My most sincere regards to your amiable wife![7] Thus God be with you.

Your constantly most devoted friend,

Ant. Schindler

[Receipt stamp:]
London, March 29.

1. Enclosed with Beethoven's letter to Moscheles, March 14, 1827 (Anderson No. 1563), dictated to Schindler, signed by Beethoven. There is no mention of Schindler's own letter in Anderson.

2. This last phrase is omitted in Ley.

3. Johann Nepomuk Hummel (1778–1837) had been *Kapellmeister* in Weimar since 1818; his wife, Elisabeth, née Röckel, had been a well-known singer, admired by Beethoven. They brought with them Hummel's student Ferdinand Hiller (1811–1885), whose account of these visits to Beethoven is quoted liberally, although differently, in Sonneck, *Impressions*, pp. 214–219, and Thayer-Forbes, pp. 1044–1047.

4. Hiller's account differs slightly from Schindler's; Schindler may have telescoped events from two Hummel visits (on Thursday, March 8, and Tuesday, March 13) into one in this letter to Moscheles.

5. Piano manufacturer Johann Andreas Streicher (1761–1833).

6. Thayer-Forbes, p. 1037, indicates that Diabelli gave Beethoven the print of Haydn's birthplace sometime in mid-February. In his recollections of the March 13 meeting, Hiller wrote that Beethoven had received the picture "a short time before."

7. This sentence, referring to Charlotte Moscheles, is omitted in Ley.

Incipit: Hier auch ein Eckchen von mir.

Sources: Ley, *Beethoven als Freund*, pp. 229–230, indicating that the autograph was then in the Wegeler family collection; confirmed by Anderson's annotation to Beethoven's March 14 letter. Fuller versions, differing in details, in Charlotte Moscheles, *Life of Moscheles*, I, 152–153, and Smidak, *Moscheles*, pp. 51–52.

468. Sebastian Rau[1] to Ignaz Moscheles, London

Vienna; March 17, 1827

Dear Friend!

After a very severe inflammation of the eyes that kept me imprisoned for three weeks within the four walls of my bedroom, I have, thank God!, recovered to the extent that I may again — although with trouble and exertion — take pen in hand. Make a guess about what you cannot read, and have indulgence with the illegibility of my writing.

Your letter, which I duly received together with the £100 sent for Beethoven,[2] aroused in us just as much astonishment as it did admiration. This great man, highly praised and justly venerated throughout Europe — this noblest, most kindhearted human being lies on his sickbed in Vienna, between life and death, and in greatest need! And this we must learn from London, from whence people hasten to relieve him of his misery and his grief, to rescue him from despair with their generosity.[3]

I drove to him at once, to convince myself of his condition and to tell him of the assistance at hand. It was heartrending to see him, how he clasped his hands and almost dissolved in tears of joy and gratitude. How rewarding, what a blessing it would have been for you, you magnanimous people, if you could have been witness to this highly touching scene!

I found poor Beethoven in the saddest state, more like a skeleton than a living being. The dropsy had seized him to such an extent that he had already had to be tapped 4 or 5 times. For his medical treatment he is in the hands of Dr. Malfatti, and thus is well cared for. Malfatti gives him little hope. It cannot be determined how long his present condition can still last, or whether he can be saved at all. Meanwhile, the news of the assistance has resulted in a remarkable change, brought on by the joyous emotion: one of his punctures, which had healed, burst open during the night, and all of the water that had collected for two weeks flowed from him. When I visited him the next day, he was strikingly cheerful and felt wonderfully relieved. I hastened to Malfatti to let him know about this. He considered this event to be very reassuring. A hollow probe will be applied [to Beethoven's puncture] for some time, to keep this wound open and to allow the congestion of the water free outflow. May God give his blessing!

Beethoven is [quite] satisfied with his domestic environment and service, which consists of a female cook and a maidservant. His friend, our acquaintance, the excellent Schindler, eats daily with him and takes care of him in a very kindly and upright manner in this respect. Schindler [also] takes care of Beethoven's correspondence and, as much as possible, manages his expenses.

Enclosed you will find, d[ear] fr[iend]!, a receipt made out by Beethoven for the 1,000 florins C. M. given to him. When I suggested to him to withdraw only 500 florins now and to leave the remainder of 500 florins with Baron von Eskeles for safekeeping until he needs it, he confessed to me frankly that when the support in the form of 1,000 florins flowed to him as if from heaven, he was in an embarrassing situation, whereby he would have been forced to borrow money. Therefore, according to his urgent wish, I gave him the entire sum of £100 or 1,000 florins C.M. Beethoven will notify the Philharmonic Society in his own letter as to the manner in which he intends to render his thanks. If you can be of service to Beethoven in the future, and if I can lend my hand in the matter, you may count on my eagerness and willingness.[4]

The entire Eskeles family greets you, your wife and little son[5] just as cordially as do I,

Your sincere friend,

Rau

1. Rau was a steward in the banking house of Eskeles (or Arnstein and Eskeles). His first name appears nowhere in the standard body of Beethoven literature, but in a letter to the Magistrat, dated April 10, 1828 (No. 492 below), in the Landesarchiv, Vienna, Rau signs his first name as Sebastian (see Jäger-Sunstenau, "Beethoven-Akten," p. 30). Rau must have been very closely acquainted with Moscheles, for he addresses the musician in the familiar *du* form. Moscheles had taught piano to an Eskeles daughter, so the two may have become friends through that association. For an earlier reference to Rau, see Stumpff's letter to Beethoven, March 1, 1827 (No. 462 above). Thayer-Forbes, p. 1041, states that Rau received notes from London on March 15 and visited Beethoven that day and that this letter to Moscheles also enclosed Beethoven's receipt, dated March 16.

Rau is not to be confused with the German writer Heribert Rau (1813–1876), the author of the biographical novel *Beethoven: Ein Künstlerleben* (Leipzig: T. Thomas, 1859; 2d ed., 1869; English trans., Boston: Ditson, 1880).

2. Sent by the Philharmonic Society, London.

3. Moscheles's annotation: "I have, however, much evidence that Beethoven's dangerous condition aroused considerable sympathy in Vienna at that time, and that many of his admirers would have hastened to him with aid and comfort, if his seclusion had not made access to him or his closest acquaintances very difficult."

4. In his letter to Moscheles of March 18 (Anderson No. 1566), Beethoven calls Rau "a new friend."

5. Moscheles's wife, Charlotte, and presumably his son Felix.

Incipit: Nach einer bedeutenden Augenentzündung. . . .

Sources: Moscheles, *Life of Moscheles,* I, 154–156; Smidak, *Moscheles,* pp. 52–53; Ley, *Beethoven als Freund,* pp. 230–231; paraphrased English translation in Thayer-Krehbiel, III, 292–293, and Thayer-Forbes, p. 1041; German excerpt in Hellinghaus, pp. 245–246. Ley indicates that the autograph was then in the Wegeler family collection.

469. Anton Schindler to Ignaz Moscheles, London

Vienna; March 24, 1827[1]

My dear Friend!

Do not be confused by the difference of date on the two letters; I intentionally wanted to hold [Beethoven's] letter back a few days, because on the day afterward, that is on the 19th of this month, we feared that our great master would breathe his last.[2] However, up to today, God be praised, this has not been the case; but by the time you read these lines, my good Moscheles, our friend will no longer be among the living. His dissolution proceeds with giant strides, and it is the single wish of us all to see him released from these terrible sufferings soon. Nothing else remains [to be done]. For a week,[3] he has lain near death, but upon several occasions he has gathered his last strength and asked about one thing or requested another. His condition is terrible, and exactly like we read about [in the case of] the Duke of York a short while ago. He is continually lost in empty thought; his head hangs down on his chest, and he stares for hours at one spot. He seldom recognizes his closest acquaintances, except when someone tells him who stands before him. In short, it is horrible to see this, and such a condition can last only for a few more days, because since yesterday all functions of the body have ceased. Thus, God willing, he will soon be released, and we along with him. Now people come flocking to see him once more, although absolutely none are admitted except those who are audacious enough to molest the dying man even in his last hours.

Except for a few words in the introduction, the letter to you was dictated entirely in his own words and, no doubt, will be the last one during his life, although he whispered to me even today in a very broken manner: "write . . . Smart . . . Stumpff."[4] If it is possible for him to put only his name onto paper yet, it will still be done. He feels that his end is near, for yesterday he said to me and Herr von Breuning: "*Plaudite amici, comoedia finita est!*"[5]

We were also fortunate enough yesterday to put his will in order, although nothing is there except several old pieces of furniture and [his] manuscripts. He was working on a quintet for stringed instruments, and the 10th Symphony that he mentioned in his letter to you. Two movements of the Quintet are entirely finished. It was intended for Diabelli.[6]

The day after the receipt of your letter he was extremely excited, and told me a great deal about the plan for the symphony, which would now turn out all the greater because he would be writing it for the Philharmonic Society. Still I would have very much wished that you would have stated positively that he could only withdraw the sum of 1,000 florins C.M. partially,[7] and I had already agreed upon this with Herr Rau, but Beethoven held obstinately to the last part of the sentence in your letter.[8] In brief, his grief and cares suddenly vanished, once the money was there, and he said, overjoyed: "Now we can treat ourselves to many a good day again," for there had been only 340 florins W.W. left in the cash box, and for some time we had limited ourselves to beef with vegetables, which caused him more pain than anything else.[9] On the next day, since it was Friday,[10] he had his favorite fish dish made, if only to be able to nibble on it.[11] His joy at the noble action of the Philharmonic Society at times degenerated into the childish. Also a large so-called grandfather's chair had to be bought immediately, which cost 50 florins W.W.,[12] in which he rests at least half an hour daily while his bed is being put in order.

His stubbornness, however, is as atrocious as ever, and falls particularly hard on me, since he will allow absolutely nobody around him but me. And what was left for me to do then but to give up all my lessons and devote every spare moment to him? I must taste every dish and every drink beforehand to determine whether it might not be harmful to him. As gladly as I do this now, the situation unfortunately is continuing too long for such a poor devil as I am. But, I hope to God that things will return to normal little by little if I remain healthy. [With the part of] the 1,000 florins that remains, we want to have him decently buried, without clamor, in the [churchyard] near Döbling, where he always enjoyed staying.[13] Then, too, the rent comes due on St. George's Day,[14] which must be paid for another half year, and several more small expenditures (the doctors), so that the 1,000 florins will just be enough, without much left over.

Two days after your letter came also one from the worthy Herr Stumpff, who also mentioned you with greatest praise,[15] all of which affected Beethoven too much, since he was already extremely weakened by the discharge of water from the wound that had previously healed for fourteen days. Then he was heard to say aloud countless times throughout the day: "May God reward them all a thousandfold."

You can imagine that this noble action by the Philharmonic Society aroused a general sensation here, and in general people highly praise the noble-mindedness of the English, and grumble aloud about the behavior of the local rich people. The *Beobachter* has published an article about this, as has the *Wiener Zeitung*. It is enclosed here![16]

Pause of a few hours. — — —

I have just come from Beethoven. He is already dying, and before this letter is beyond the walls of the capital, the great light will have been extinguished forever. He is still fully conscious, however. I hasten to dispatch this letter, in order to run to him. I have just cut these hairs from his head and am sending them to you. God be with you!

Your most obliging friend,

Ant. Schindler

[Receipt stamp:]
London, April 5

1. Accompanied Beethoven's letter to Moscheles, March 18, 1827 (Anderson No. 1566), written by Schindler and signed by Beethoven.

2. A rhetorical reference to Beethoven's "great soul" breathing its last in the original German does not translate smoothly into English.

3. Literally, "for eight days" in German.

4. Sir George Smart and Johann Andreas Stumpff, London supporters active in arranging the Philharmonic Society's gift of £100 to the dying Beethoven.

5. Gerhard von Breuning recalled that he (then aged thirteen), his father Stephan and Schindler were present when Beethoven uttered this dramatic close "in his favorite sarcastic, humorous manner." In this letter, Schindler implies the presence of the elder Breuning; in his April 12 letter to Schott (No. 479 below), he specifies the younger, indicating that Gerhard's recollection in *Aus dem Schwarzspanierhause* (Vienna: Rosner, 1874), pp. 104–105, is accurate in this respect.

6. Scattered sketches exist for both these works.

7. Schindler had specified his preference for withdrawal in installments in his letter to Moscheles on March 14; on February 22, he had asked that the Philharmonic Society stipulate that the money be used for Beethoven's benefit, to the exclusion of his relatives.

8. Moscheles's letter to Beethoven, March 1, 1827 (No. 463 above).

9. It is not clear whether Schindler means that this diet caused Beethoven mental grief or abdominal distress.

10. The banking steward Sebastian Rau therefore notified Beethoven of the bequest on Thursday, March 15.

11. In translating and editing this passage for the *Harmonicon*, Johann Reinhold Schultz noted: "Trout was, as I heard him say, the only thing in the way of eatables that he really was fond of."

12. Ley read this figure as 30 florins W.W.; both Moscheles and Schultz read it as 50, the latter adding, to confirm his reading, "rather more than 5£ in English money."

13. The bracketed words in this sentence are places where Ley indicated holes in the paper of the autograph in recent times. The earlier transcriptions and translations by Schultz and Moscheles have helped in filling these gaps.

14. April 23, one of the traditional semiannual rent payment days.

15. Stumpff's letter of March 1, 1827 (No. 462 above).

16. The clipping is lost.

Incipit: Lassen Sie sich durch die Verschiedenheit. . . .

Sources: Harmonicon 5 (May, 1827), 84–85 (article signed by "J.R.S."); Schindler-Moscheles, pp. 275–277; Ley, *Beethoven als Freund,* pp. 235–237; Charlotte Moscheles, *Life of Moscheles,* I, 159–163; Smidak, *Moscheles,* pp. 54–56. Brief excerpts in Thayer-Krehbiel, III, 293; Thayer-Forbes, pp. 1041–1042; Hellinghaus, pp. 249–251. Ley indicates that the autograph was then in the Wegeler family collection.

Note: During the first half of 1827, both Ignaz Moscheles and Johann Andreas Stumpff made some of the letters that they received from Beethoven, Schindler and Johann Baptist Streicher available to Johann Reinhold Schultz, a Prussian merchant living in London, so that Schultz might translate and edit them for publication in the *Harmonicon*. Schultz had met Beethoven briefly in 1816 and then had spent the day with him in Baden on September 28, 1823, publishing his account in the *Harmonicon* 2 (January 1824), 10–11. This Schultz has often been confused in the literature with the English pianist Edouard Schulz (1812–1876), who had reputedly met Beethoven as a youth in Vienna. See Köhler et al., *Konversationshefte,* VII, 370–371, n. 216, for correct identification.

In an article entitled "Hopeless State of Beethoven," *Harmonicon* 5 (February 1827), 23, Johann Reinhold Schultz published Streicher to Stumpff, January 5, 1827 (No. 453 above). In "Beethoven's Last Illness and Death," *Harmonicon* 5 (May 1827), 84–87, he published Beethoven to Moscheles, March 18, 1827; Schindler to Moscheles,

March 24, 1827 (with excerpts of February 22, 1827) (this letter), and April 4, 1827 (No. 477 below); and Streicher to Stumpff, March 28, 1827 (No. 473 below).

Schultz's translation of the March 24 letter omits more than a paragraph of the original but adds substantial excerpts from the February 22 letter in two places. Schindler-Moscheles has different cuts and shorter insertions and varies (sometimes to the better) in details of translation. Ley presents essentially the full text in German.

470. Stephan von Breuning to Anton Schindler

Vienna; March 27, 1827

The announcement of the hour of our departed friend's funeral will appear tomorrow or certainly the day after tomorrow in the *Beobachter,* and perhaps also in the *Wiener Zeitung,* instead of any other obituary notice. I have written about it [the funeral] to Herr v[on] Rau and received his acceptance.[1]

Tomorrow morning a certain Danhauser wishes to take a plaster cast of the body; he will be done with it in 5, at most 8 minutes.[2] Write and tell me yes or no as to whether I should allow it. Such casts are often permitted in the case of famous men, and not to permit it could later be grieved as an insult to the public.[3]

Breuning

1. Schindler's printed transcription indicates that Breuning had received a "zustimmende Antwort" (consent) from Rau, but an examination of the facsimile in the same volume reveals that Breuning actually indicated Rau's "zusagende Antwort" (an acceptance) of the invitation to the funeral. Sebastian Rau was an acquaintance of less than two weeks but was the representative of the banking house of Eskeles and therefore (like his employers) possibly of the Jewish faith or origin. It seems likely that Breuning singled him out for a special invitation so that he would feel welcome (or, if he were Christian, that he would represent the Jewish banking house) at the Catholic funeral. For Rau's given name, see Rau to Moscheles, March 17, 1827 (No. 468 above).

2. Josef Danhauser (1805–1845), a Viennese artist who would occupy a prominent position among Biedermeier painters. With his brother Carl and a plasterer, Hofmann, he took Beethoven's death mask (face only, as was customary, not the entire body) and made two oil sketches of Beethoven's face and hands, the former being used as the basis for a published lithograph.

3. Schindler's printed transcription indicates the participle "angesehen" (viewed), while the autograph reads "angeklagt" (grieved).

Incipit: Die Ankündigung der Stunde. . . .

Sources: Schindler (1860), pt. 2, p. 150 and plate; Schindler-MacArdle, p. 332, facsimile on pp. 330–331. Autograph in the Staatsbibliothek zu Berlin–Preussischer Kulturbesitz, Mus. ms. autogr. Beethoven 36, 79; listed in Kalischer, "Beethoven-Autographe," p. 61, and Bartlitz, p. 177. For Carl Danhauser's memoir of the above event, see Landon, *Beethoven: A Documentary Study,* pp. 396–397; and Alessandra Comini, *The Changing Image of Beethoven* (New York: Rizzoli, 1987), pp. 72–73 and pls. 5 and 9 (between pp. 16 and 17).

471. Magistrat,[1] *Vienna, Receipt of Beethoven's Will*

Vienna; March 27, 1827[2]

B.

This Testament of Herr Ludwig van Beethoven, brought unsealed *today* to the Court by Dr. Bach, and proclaimed in the presence of the same, is to be retained, and copies to be given.

By the Viennese Magistrat
March 27, 1827

Schütz m.p.

1. *Magistrat* (not to be confused with the English word *magistrate*) was the collective term for the offices and departments that administered the affairs of the city. For a more extensive definition, see Schindler-MacArdle, p. 341. Schütz was probably a records clerk.

2. Appended to Beethoven's letter of January 3, 1827, to the lawyer Dr. Johann Baptist Bach (Anderson No. 1547), which constituted his semifinal will.

Incipit: Dieses vom Dr. Bach *heute* offen. . . .

Sources: Thayer-Deiters-Riemann, V, 439; Thayer-Forbes, p. 1027; Kalischer (German), V, 288–289; Kalischer-Shedlock, II, 461.

472. *Johann Baptist Streicher to*
Johann Andreas Stumpff, London

Vienna; March 28, 1827[1]

Most estimable Friend!

I have promised to report to you everything that might happen to the man about whom you have concerned yourself with such warm sympathy, and I would keep my word—but for the last time: Beethoven is no more!

Already when I delivered to him the letter that you had enclosed with the one to me of March 1 (it was on March 17, a half hour after receipt of your letter), I found the patient very weak but fervently touched and pleased by the magnanimous gift, as he called it, received from London.[2] He told me what I already knew from your letter, but he had learned it a day earlier through the house of Arnstein and Eskeles.[3] The joy over this event caused a spontaneous rupture of water and made unnecessary an operation that had already been agreed upon. Although the sufferer took this to be a good sign, and believed that it was Nature helping itself, it soon appeared to be a reduction of his general strength, because from this time on, he became visibly weaker, and since Sunday had been unconscious. I found him early on Monday the 26th, already in the throes of death. Convulsively he rolled his wide-open eyes, and beat an indentation into the pillows with his head; but the doctor's assistant, who had kept watch during the night, assured me that the dying man felt nothing more. In the afternoon, about 2 o'clock, when Herr Schickh[4] came to Beethoven, the latter was nearing death: his eyes were closed, and the breathing alone indicated that the person still lived who, we would have wished, might never have died.

It truly appeared as if Nature had chosen to distinguish the day on which we were deprived of this extraordinary genius, for while he was in the agonies of death, there were three flashes of lightning and three violent claps of thunder, accompanied by hail and snow, as if to announce the loss that the world was about to suffer. At 5:45 P.M., Beethoven suddenly and violently sat up in bed, and passed away in the arms of his brother, in the presence of Herr Hüttenbrenner[5] and a painter who still attempted to draw the great artist in his last moments.[6]

I need not tell you especially how widely and deeply this irreplaceable loss is felt and mourned here, but I may not leave unmentioned the fact that our entire public, although long accustomed to Beethoven's peculiarities, are not only surprised but grievously hurt by the last example of his eccentricities—his turning to England for assistance.

Was it excessive anxiety, created by his illness, that in the end he might, perhaps, suffer from want? Had he been ill advised by a hasty friend? Or what else could have moved him to take such a step that portrays those in whose midst he had lived for thirty-four years,[7] his friends, his second fatherland, indeed all of Germany in a bad light?

Beethoven appears to have felt this himself later, for when I delivered your enclosure to him he carefully avoided mentioning that, through you, he had induced the Philharmonic Society to render this assistance, and, on the contrary, told me that people in London must be of the opinion that, hindered from composing because of his illness, he finds himself in financial difficulty. "I shall provisionally accept the thousand gulden from them (these were his own words), which they in London may then deduct from the proceeds of the concert organized for me. If they will send me the surplus, then, when I am capable of working again, I shall write them something for it."

Had Beethoven expressed even the least of his needs to one of his friends and admirers; had he turned to his patron, the Archduke Rudolph; had he expressed here in Vienna the wish that someone might organize a concert for his benefit, not hundreds, but thousands would have been ready to fulfill this wish, and would have supported him with all their powers. Lastly, believe me that if Beethoven could not have counted upon all these resources, my father,[8] Beethoven's friend for thirty-four years, would surely have shared everything with him immediately if he could have believed that the sick man lacked even the slightest comfort! Who would guess then that Beethoven—while the patient's reticence never allowed him to accept the medical help of the famous physician Staudenheim,[9] because the latter had declined beforehand any fee for his efforts (Beethoven told me this himself); while Beethoven refused all relief or attention offered by my father, and was induced only with difficulty to accept two bottles of old wine[10]—would have indulged his idiosyncracy so far as to solicit in London assistance that he did not at all need!

How hasty, how unnecessary this request was is confirmed by Beethoven's estate, which consisted (as the public knew before)[11] of bank shares totaling 10,000 florins C.M. or £1,000 sterling. If you reckon, in addition to this, three pensions from the Archduke Rudolph, Prince Lobkowitz and Count Kinsky, amounting on the whole to an annual yield of about 720 florins or £72 sterling, you will easily judge that with *this* sum, particularly in Vienna, Beethoven could have lived for several more years without finding himself really in need of assistance.[12]

The 1,000 florins C.M. raised by Beethoven[13] remain untouched, with the rest of his estate. His sole heir is his nephew Karl, whom I believe you know. Without indulging myself in an opinion of his character, I mention only that the legal authorities have taken great pains to modify or turn the will [of Beethoven] in such a way that the property may become a *fidei commissum*,[14] and that the heir shall receive only the interest of the capital, by which means it will be protected for him, to his real benefit.

You may be assured, however, that the readiness with which Beethoven's wish was fulfilled, through your endeavors as well as those of Herr Moscheles, [Sir] G[eorge] Smart and the Philharmonic Society, is universally approved here, and it is only regretted that, in consequence of this totally unnecessary request of the deceased, we should have been falsely judged. In the next days something concerning this will be mentioned publicly in the *Wiener Zeitschrift*, and you would render your fellow countrymen [i.e., Germans] a substantial service if you would save their honor by placing the essay, which will follow shortly, in an English journal.

Since Herr Schickh has eagerly taken responsibility for Beethoven's funeral, he is prevented at the moment from writing to you and Herr Schultz himself. Meanwhile, he sends you the enclosed lock of Beethoven's hair, cut after his death, as well as a little piece of manuscript; a larger will follow.

Beethoven could no longer carry out his intention to write something exclusively for you; he mentioned you very often with love and friendship, and always called you a true and honest German, and assured me that he would never part with your precious gift of the Handel *Works*.[15] Until shortly before his end, he mentioned that he still wanted to come to England, in which case he would certainly spend much time with you, but Heaven had other plans for him!

After Beethoven's funeral, a concert will be organized to erect a suitable monument to the great man. If enough remains after this purpose has been attained, it ought to be designated for a foundation [to assist] a talented young musician.

These, most valued friend, are the most necessary things that I have to report to you at this tragic time. If the intended *Akademie*, which was spoken of earlier, now takes place there [i.e., London], I need to learn about it, through your kindness, as soon as possible.

Farewell, with sincerest greetings to you from my parents, my wife, sister and brother-in-law, but especially be embraced with esteem and warm friendship by

Your

J.B.S.

1. Responding partially to Stumpff's letter to Beethoven, March 1, 1827 (No. 462 above), and continued in correspondence between Stumpff and Streicher from March 28 to June 9 (Nos. 473, 480 and 485 below).

2. The gift of £100 from the Philharmonic Society, London.

3. The banking firm's representative was Sebastian Rau, who figures importantly in the correspondence beginning March 17, 1827 (No. 468 above).

4. Johann Schickh (1770–1835), a longtime friend of the composer's; silk dealer, writer and editor of the *Wiener Zeitschrift für Kunst, Literatur, Theater, und Mode.*

5. Anselm Hüttenbrenner (1794–1868), who in 1860 supplied Thayer with his own account of Beethoven's death.

6. Josef Teltscher (1802–1837), like Hüttenbrenner, essentially a member of Schubert's circle of friends. All three of Teltscher's surviving sketches are reproduced in Otto Erich Deutsch, "Die wiedergefundenen Bildnisse des sterbenden Beethoven," *Die Musik* 9, pt. 1 (1909), 64–67, and illustrations. Hüttenbrenner (quoted in Thayer-Forbes, p. 1050) indicated that Stephan von Breuning became indignant at Teltscher's sketching and induced him to leave the room, evidently earlier in the afternoon.

7. Unger gives this figure as "36 years," the manuscript "34."

8. Piano manufacturer Johann Andreas Streicher (1761–1833).

9. Dr. Jakob von Staudenheim (1764–1830) had treated Beethoven for a period up to early 1825 but had become dissatisfied when Beethoven did not follow his regimen, which included the prohibition of alcohol. In early December 1826, Staudenheim for some reason failed to come when summoned to Beethoven but later consulted with Dr. Wawruch prior to the first operation for dropsy. The *Harmonicon* and the manuscript gave his name as "Staudenheimer," Unger as "Landesheimer."

10. These seemingly have nothing to do with the Rhein wine that Beethoven requested from Schott.

11. Johann Reinhold Schultz, translating and editing for the *Harmonicon,* annotated the foregoing passage: "This is an extraordinary parenthesis, and I leave it to explain itself." He, too, may have been skeptical of Streicher's defensive tone and line of reasoning.

12. For a relatively commonsense alternative view of this financial situation, although expressed in emotional terms, see Schindler to Moscheles, April 4, 1827 (No. 477 below), and subsequent letters.

13. That is, from the Philharmonic Society, London.

14. A trust fund.

15. Stumpff's gift to Beethoven; see Streicher to Stumpff, January 5, 1827 (No. 453 above), concerning their delivery. Schultz's edited version added, "these works were his last joy," and thus concluded the excerpt.

Incipit: Ich habe versprochen, Ihnen alles mitzuteilen. . . .

Sources: Harmonicon 5 (May 1827), 86–87, translated and edited by Johann Reinhold Schultz (see the source note to Schindler to Moscheles, March 24, 1827, No. 469 above). Transcription up to final four paragraphs, Max Unger, "Neue Kunde vom Totenbette Beethovens," *Deutsche Musiker-Zeitung* 58 (March 26, 1927), 276–280. Brief excerpt and discussion of later ownership of the Handel *Works* volumes in Chrysander, "Beethovens Verbindung," p. 452. Autograph (or draft) in the Österreichische Nationalbibliothek, Vienna, cataloged as 126/78–1. The *Harmonicon* version is largely complete, except for the final three paragraphs, although both Schultz and Unger (at least as far as he transcribes) omit different phrases on occasion.

473. Sebastian Rau to Ignaz Moscheles, London

Vienna; March 28, 1827[1]

Dear Friend!

Beethoven is no more. He departed this life on the evening of March 26, between 5 and 6 o'clock, amidst the most dreadful death struggle and terrible suffering. Since the day before, however, he had been totally unconscious.

Now a word or two about his estate. From my last letter, you learned that Beethoven, according to his own statement, found himself without assistance, without money, and therefore in greatest need. But at the inventory, at which I was present, 7 bank shares were found in an old half-moldy box. Whether Beethoven intentionally kept them secret (for he was very mistrustful, and hoped for a speedy recovery), or whether he himself did not know that he possessed them is a problem that I cannot solve.

The 1,000 florins C.M. sent by the Philharmonic Society were found still untouched. According to your instructions, I reclaimed them;[2] but until more specific directions are received from the Philharmonic Society, I had to deposit the sum with the Magistrat. I could not consent to the costs of the funeral being defrayed from this money without authorization from the Society. I would venture to ask, however, if it can be effected from there, that something might be done in favor of the two poor servants, who attended the sick man with infinite patience, love and loyalty,[3] since they were not mentioned with a single word in the will. Beethoven's nephew is the sole heir.[4] Herr Schindler will communicate particulars to you in due time concerning the gift that Beethoven intended for the Philharmonic Society. Write to me soon, telling me for certain what I am to do, and be convinced of my punctuality in carrying it out.

Beethoven will be buried on the 29th. An invitation went out to all the artists, orchestras[5] and theaters. Twenty virtuosos and composers will accompany the body with torches; Herr Grillparzer[6] has prepared a most touching address, which Herr Anschütz[7] will deliver at the grave. On the whole, preparations are being made for a solemn funeral worthy of the deceased.

The entire Eskeles family sends greetings to you and yours, as do I with all my heart.

Your friend,

Rau

[P.S.] In haste and with continuing pain in the eyes.[8]

1. As in his letter of March 17, Rau addresses Moscheles with the familiar *du* in the original German.

2. Rau was the representative of the banking house of Arnstein and Eskeles, through which the gift from London had originally been sent.

3. One of these was Beethoven's faithful housekeeper Sali (a diminutive for Rosalie), whose surname seems not to be known.

4. Moscheles later commented: "In answer to the above, I informed Mr. Rau, in the name of the Philharmonic Society, that the money having been sent for the express purpose, and on condition that Beethoven himself should make use of it,

the Society would, now that the event had taken place before the end in view could be achieved, expect the money to be returned" (Schindler-Moscheles, p. 278). For further developments, see Thayer-Krehbiel, III, 293–294.

    5. *Kapellen* in the original, probably included orchestras and various chapel choirs.

    6. The poet Franz Grillparzer (1791–1872), whose name Rau spelled "Krillpatzer."

    7. The actor Heinrich Anschütz (1785–1865).

    8. Rau spoke of his eye troubles in his March 17 letter (No. 468 above).

Incipit: Beethoven ist nicht mehr; er verschied. . . .

Sources: Schindler-Moscheles, pp. 277–278; Charlotte Moscheles, *Life of Moscheles,* I, 163–165; Smidak, *Moscheles,* pp. 57–58 (in English); Ley, *Beethoven als Freund,* pp. 237–238; excerpted extensively in Thayer-Krehbiel, III, 293–294. Ley indicates that the autograph was then in the Wegeler family collection.

474. Magistrat, Vienna, Receipt of Codicil to Beethoven's Will

Vienna; March 29, 1827[1]

Z. 15254

   38

B.

    This testamentary instruction of Ludwig Beethoven, brought to the Court in an unsealed envelope through official channels, and proclaimed *today,* is to be retained, and copies to be given.

By the Viennese Magistrat

March 29, 1827

Schütz m.p.

    1. Receipt for Beethoven's last handwritten will (Anderson No. 1568). See the Magistrat's receipt of March 27 (No. 471 above) for a similar document.

Incipit: Diese in offenem Umschlage. . . .

Sources: Thayer-Deiters-Riemann, V, 485.

475. B. Schotts Söhne to Beethoven

Mainz; March 29, 1827[1]

Dear Herr v[an] Beethoven,

We are very sorry that no satisfying reports concerning your health (which is so dear to us) have as yet reached us, although we have not given up hope that we will receive news of your recovery, as well as the safe arrival of the wine,[2] very soon.

In answer to your worthy letter of the 10th of this month, we can report to you that we shall use the recently sent *dedication* to Baron von Stutterheim for the title page of the Quartet,[3] and as soon as the engraving is done in Paris, we shall dispatch it.

In our last letter we asked you for a proprietary contract for the Quartet, in which you have to state the opus number specifically and expressly transfer to us the publication rights in Germany, *France* and all other places. We would like it even more if you would also mention the first Quartet in it.[4] Schlesinger in Paris[5] shows signs of wanting to engage our publishing house in court, so one cannot take sufficient caution against such a rival.

With all our heart, we wish for the improvement [of your health], and send most friendly greetings,

B. Schotts Söhne

[Exterior:]
    Herr Ludwig van Beethoven
    Alservorstadt No. 200
    Vienna

1. Replies to Beethoven's letter of March 10, 1827 (Anderson No. 1561). Answered by Schindler's letter to Schott, April 12, 1827 (No. 479 below).

2. The Rüdesheimer wine arrived on the afternoon of March 24, according to Schindler's April 12 letter.

3. String Quartet, Op. 131. The dedicatee was Baron Joseph von Stutterheim (1764–1831), a lieutenant field marshal who had accepted Beethoven's nephew Karl into the "Archduke Ludwig" Regiment at Iglau.

4. The declaration, dated March 20, 1827, was written by Schindler and signed by Beethoven, with Schindler and Stephan von Breuning as witnesses (Anderson, III,

1452–1453). It specifies only Op. 131, with no mention of Op. 127, the other quartet sold to Schott.

5. Moritz (Maurice) Schlesinger.

Incipit: Dass uns noch keine befriedigende Nachrichten. . . .

Sources: Max Unger, "Beethoven und B. Schott's Söhne: Mit zwei ungedruckten Briefen des Verlags an den Meister," *Die Musik* 34 (June 1942), 291; Staehelin and Brandenburg, *Briefwechsel,* p. 84. Autograph in the Staatsbibliothek zu Berlin–Preussischer Kulturbesitz, Mus. ms. autogr. Beethoven 35, 72; listed in Kalischer, "Beethoven-Autographe," p. 53, and Bartlitz, pp. 143–144.

476. Anton Schindler to Sir George Smart, London

Vienna; March 31, 1827[1]

Sir!

Beethoven is no more! On the 26th of this month at a quarter to 6 in the afternoon, he breathed his last.[2] At the hour of his death there was a great storm here with thunder and lightning. As late as the morning of the 24th, when his weakness became so severe that he himself felt his end approaching, he requested me, when he was no more, to send to you and Herr Stumpff in his name, and through you to the Philharmonic Society and the entire English nation, his sincerest thanks for the demonstrated regards given him in life as well as now, near his end. I hasten herewith to carry out the earnest instructions of my dying friend, and request you, Sir Smart, to make these sentiments of our immortal Beethoven known in London.

His grave is in Währing, a village not far from Vienna, where he lies next to the young Lord Ingestre,[3] who drowned here last summer. And so it came to pass that he has something in common with an Englishman, even in his grave.

Herr Rau also wrote to Moscheles this week, and reported to him everything that has happened concerning the 100 pounds.[4] It is only to be wished that the Philharmonic Society dispose of it in a manner worthy of the English nation. Meanwhile, the two of us, Court Councillor von Breuning and I, covered the costs of the funeral with it, pending reimbursement. Otherwise we would not have been able to have him buried respectably, without having to sell one of the 7 bank shares that make up his entire estate.[5]

The acquaintance with your countryman Mr. Lewisey makes it easier to write all of this to you in the English language. Concerning the works that Beethoven offered as a return gift to the Philharmonic Society in his *very* last letter to Herr Moscheles,[6] we will take care that if *only one* entirely unknown work is found in the estate, then this shall be given over to the Philharmonic Society as a remembrance.

Otherwise accept the assurance of my esteem and respect, with which I remain

Your most obedient,

A. Schindler

1. Schindler retained this German-language letter in his possession, while Lewisey prepared a translation, dated and sent on April 2. Smart received it on April 17 (see Young in the source note to this letter). The present text is my translation of Schindler's draft.

2. Schindler used the same metaphor here as he did anticipating Beethoven's death to Moscheles (see March 24, 1827, No. 469 above, n. 2).

3. Charles Thomas Talbot, Viscount Ingestre (1802–1826), educated at Eton and Christ Church, Oxford.

4. Rau to Ignaz Moscheles, March 28, 1827 (No. 472 above).

5. Schindler exaggerates to some degree, but the £100 (1,000 florins) in cash was more readily available to the executors than the bank shares when they needed to cover immediate funeral expenses. Fischhof noted the expenses as 650 florins (Thayer-Krehbiel, III, 293–294).

6. March 18, 1827 (Anderson No. 1566). Beethoven mentioned "a new symphony, . . . a new overture, or something else."

Incipit: Beethoven ist nicht mehr! am 26. dies. . . .

Sources: Mentioned briefly in Thayer-Krehbiel, III, 294; otherwise previously unpublished. Autograph in the Staatsbibliothek zu Berlin–Preussischer Kulturbesitz, Mus. ms. autogr. Beethoven 35, 72c; listed in Kalischer, "Beethoven-Autographe," p. 53, and Bartlitz, p. 145. Lewisey's translation is partially reproduced in Percy M. Young, *Beethoven: A Victorian Tribute* (London: Dennis Dobson, 1976), p. 17, and is in the collection of the British Library, Add. MS. 41771, fol. 81.

477. Anton Schindler to Ignaz Moscheles, London

Vienna; April 4, 1827

My noble Friend!

I take the occasion to write to you again, in order to be sure that the enclosed letter gets to Sir [George] Smart.[1] It contains Beethoven's last thanks to Smart, Stumpff and the Philharmonic Society, as well as the whole English nation, which he most sincerely asked me to do in the last moments of his life. I very much request you to deliver it to them soon. Herr Lewisey of the English legation was kind enough to translate it into English immediately.

Thus it was, on March 26 at a quarter to 6 in the afternoon, during a great thunderstorm, that our immortal friend breathed his last. From the 24th, toward evening, until his last breath, he was almost constantly in delirium. Still, in the terrible battle between life and death, he did not forget the benevolence of the Philharmonic Society when he had a lucid moment, and praised the English nation, which always showed him so much consideration.

His suffering was indescribably great, especially since the time when his incision broke open by itself and the flow of water ensued so suddenly. His last days were extremely remarkable for the way that his great spirit prepared itself for death with a truly Socratic wisdom. I shall probably also write this down and make it known publicly, for it is of inestimable value for his biographers.[2]

The funeral was only that as befits a great man. About 30,000 people assembled on the Glacis and in the streets where the procession was to pass.[3] This really cannot be described, but think of the *Praterfest* at the Congress in the year 1814 and you will get the idea.[4] [It is to be regretted that there were no means of preserving uniform good order among so great a mass of people; but in the immediate neighborhood of the procession the most solemn silence prevailed.[5]] Eight *Kapellmeisters* were pallbearers, among them Eybler, Weigl, Gyrowetz, Hummel, Seyfried, etc.,[6] [and] thirty-six torchbearers, among them Grillparzer, Castelli, Haslinger, Steiner, etc., etc.[7] Yesterday, Mozart's *Requiem* was given in the Augustinerkirche for him. The great church could not contain all the people who pressed in. Lablache sang bass.[8] The Board of Art Dealers sponsored this memorial service. You have Beethoven's last letter, that of March 18, and Schott in Mainz has his last signature.

Among his property were seven bank shares and several hundred gulden W.W. And now the Viennese write and cry aloud in public, "he did not need the assistance of a foreign nation," etc.,[9] but [they] do not consider that Beethoven, fifty-six years old and anxious, could expect to live to age seventy. If now he was not to do any work for years, as his doctors advised him, he would be compelled to sell one share after the other, and how many years could he live on seven shares without finding himself in the greatest need? Briefly, dear friend, Court Councillor von Breuning and I very much request, if horrible arguments of this sort spread to England, that you honor Beethoven's Manes and publish the letters that you have from Beethoven on this subject in one of the most widely read German journals, for example the *Allgemeine Zeitung* in Augsburg. The Philharmonic Society could do this on their own initiative, all the better to instruct these scribblers here about it.

The Philharmonic Society has the honor to have buried this great man with their money, for without it we could not have done so respectably. Everyone cried, "What a shame for Austria! This should not be allowed to happen, for everyone will contribute to it," but theirs remain only [empty] cries. On the day after his burial, the *Musikverein* resolved . . . to have a *Requiem* performed for him, and that is all. We of the Kärntnertor Theater,[10] however, shall hold a grand concert during the course of April in order to have a nice gravestone made for him.

I must still report to you that the grave digger of Währing, where he lies buried, visited us yesterday and told us that someone, in a note that he showed us, had offered him 1,000 florins C.M. if he would deposit the head of Beethoven at a specified location. The police are already engaged in an investigation of this matter.[11]

The funeral cost somewhat over 300 florins C.M. Friend Rau will already have written you about it. If the Philharmonic Society wanted to leave the remaining money here, for example, to give me a small portion of it as well, then I would consider it as a bequest from my friend Beethoven, for I really did not receive the least remembrance of him, nor did anyone, for death took him by surprise, as it did those of us who were close to him.

Write to me, even if only a few lines, about whether you received my letters of February 22, March 14 and March 18, and likewise Sir Smart.

Toward the end, Beethoven's relatives behaved themselves in the basest manner: he was not even dead yet when his brother came and wanted to haul everything away, even the 1,000 florins from London, but we threw him right out the door.[12] Such were the scenes that took place at Beethoven's deathbed. Make the Philharmonic Society aware of the golden medallion from Louis XVIII, however; it weighs 5 ounces[13] and would be the finest remembrance of this great man.

Thus God be with you!

Your old friend,

A. Schindler

[P.S.] Hummel plays tomorrow at the Kärntnertor Theater. Mr. Lewisey sends greetings to Herr Neate.

1. Schindler to Smart, March 31, 1827 (No. 476 above).

2. At this time, therefore, Schindler seems not to have considered himself Beethoven's biographer.

3. The Schwarzspanierhaus faced the Glacis, the open area between the city wall and the suburbs. The cemetery was some distance further out in the suburb of Währing.

4. On October 18, 1814, a festival was held in the Prater to celebrate the anniversary of the Battle of Leipzig, a major turning point in the victory of the allies over Napoleon. For an illustrated title page by Diabelli commemorating the festival, see Michael Ladenburger, "Der Wiener Kongress im Spiegel der Musik," in *Beethoven: Zwischen Revolution und Restauration,* ed. Helga Lühning and Sieghard Brandenburg (Bonn: Beethoven-Haus, 1989), pp. 289–290.

5. This sentence appears in Johann Reinhold Schultz's English-language version in the *Harmonicon* but not in the versions given by either Ley or Moscheles.

6. Joseph Eybler (1765–1846), Joseph Weigl (1766–1846), Adalbert Gyrowetz (1763–1850), Johann Nepomuk Hummel (1778–1837) and Ignaz von Seyfried (1776–1841).

7. The poets Franz Grillparzer (1791–1872) and Ignaz Franz Castelli (1781–1862) and the publishers Tobias Haslinger (1787–1842) and Sigmund Anton Steiner (1773–1838).

8. Luigi Lablache (1794–1858), a well-known Italian operatic bass, also associated with Schubert.

9. See Streicher's letter to Stumpff, March 28, 1827 (No. 473 above), for just such protestations.

10. Schindler had been appointed a conductor at the Kärntnertor Theater in 1825.

11. For a similar plan that did succeed in the case of Haydn, see "The Diaries of Joseph Carl Rosenbaum (1770–1829)," trans. Eugene Hartzell, ed. Else Radant, *Haydn Yearbook* 5 (1968), 148–150, 156–158. Phrenologist Rosenbaum's diary reveals no attempt on his part to purchase Beethoven's head (Österreichische National-bibliothek, Handschriftin-Sammlung, Ser. N. 204, ff. 44r–45v, with gratitude to Dr. Rosemary Moravec-Hilmar).

12. Possibly the piano maker Conrad Graf accompanied Johann to reclaim the four-stringed instrument that he had loaned Beethoven in January 1826 (see No. 460, n. 10, above). In any case, only the composer's Broadwood piano can be seen in drawings of the death room made by Joseph Teltscher (while Beethoven lay comatose) or by Johann Nepomuk Hoechle (on March 29, 1827). For Teltscher, see Otto Erich Deutsch, "Die wiedergefundene Bildnisse des sterbenden Beethoven," *Die Musik* 9, pt. 1 (1909), 64–67 and illustrative supplement; for Hoechle, see Bory, p. 203.

13. Ley transcribes the weight as "50 #," and Charlotte Moscheles interpreted the phrase as "it weighs 50 ducats." Mandyczewski, however, gives the medal's weight as 143½ grams, which converts to 5 ounces avoirdupois. Thus Schindler may have meant "5 Oz." since he was describing the medal to a resident of England. See Eusebius Mandyczewski, Richard von Perger and Robert Hirschfeld, *Geschichte der K. K. Gesellschaft der Musikfreunde*, 2 vols. (Vienna, 1912), II (*Zusatz-Band*), 151, which also describes the medal's harrowing odyssey on its way from Beethoven's estate to the Gesellschaft's archives.

Incipit: Ich finde mich veranlasst, abermals. . . .

Sources: Translated, abridged, edited and annotated by Johann Reinhold Schultz, *Harmonicon* 5 (May 1827), 85–86. Moscheles, *Life of Moscheles*, I, 168–172; Smidak, *Moscheles*, pp. 59–61. Fuller version in German, Ley, *Beethoven als Freund*, pp. 238–240. Excerpt in Hellinghaus, p. 254. Ley indicates that the autograph was then in the Wegeler family collection.

478. Anton Schindler to Ignaz Moscheles, London

Vienna; April 11, 1827

My noble Friend!

You will be alarmed at my many fat-bodied letters.[1] But my good fellow! Read on! and be amazed! To save the honor of yourself, of our friend

Beethoven, and of the Philharmonic Society, there remains nothing for us to do but to report everything to you exactly and in detail.

Already in my last letter [April 4], I told you that people here write and cry about the noble action of the [Philharmonic] Society. Now, however, the *Allgemeine Zeitung*[2] contains an article that must arouse each person to the highest indignation. We have taken as our obligation to reply to it, and Court Councillor von Breuning undertook to draw up this article (enclosed) in pursuit of truth, and Pilat[3] is sending it today to the Editor of the *Allgemeine Zeitung*. Without being acquainted with the article in the *Allgemeine Zeitung,* you will immediately guess its content and purpose when you read through our reply. It only remains for you and Smart to make your two letters known publicly so that these people, the scum of the earth, will be humbled with a vengeance. Rau[4] and Pilat think that our essay is too polite, but the two of us—Breuning and I—did not want to tell any more of the facts than we had to, and which one would be obliged to tell the world; for, in any case, I—as a friend of Beethoven's and as advocate of his cause—have already made many enemies, but it would be low of me to remain silent if his memory were still insulted in the grave, and [if] his well-meaning friends should be publicly attacked for their noble endeavors. I already wrote you in my last letter that the Philharmonic Society should enter the fray in your names by making public your and Smart's letters, and now it is not only my wish, but the wish of us all. The Philharmonic Society should say that it is well known in London that, after his first *Akademie* in the Kärntnertor Theater two years ago, after deducting all the expenses, which came to 1,000 florins, and which he had to pay to the Administration for the Theater, Beethoven had only 300 florins W.W. left over, for not a single one of the subscribers paid him so much as a *heller* for his *loge,* and not one of the Court was to be seen at this *Akademie,* although Beethoven, accompanied by me, personally invited all of the members of the Imperial House, and all promised to come; and in the end, not only did they not appear, but they sent him nary a *groschen,* something they would not have done even to their most ordinary beneficiaries.[5] At the second concert in the same month[6] in the Redoutensaal, the Administration, who undertook it for their receipts [as projected profit], had to pay out about 300 florins C.M., and I had the greatest difficulty in restraining Beethoven from paying this deficit out of the 300 florins C.M.[7] guaranteed him by the Administration, since it most deeply pained him that the Administration should suffer a loss because of him.[8]

Upon the subscription for his recent grand Mass,[9] no one here, not even the court, wanted to subscribe. And innumerable other base acts and humiliations, which the poor man had to endure. All of this should now be made known, because now is the best occasion to do so. All Vienna knew that Beethoven already lay ill two, then three months, and no one concerned himself either with his health or with his economic circumstances. After such sad experiences, would he then have sought further assistance here? And by God! if the Philharmonic Society had not given the impulse by their noble gift and aroused the Viennese, then Beethoven would have died and been buried like Haydn, behind whose bier perhaps fifteen people walked.[10]

As for the *Akademie* that the collected personnel of our Theater wants to give [to raise money] for the grave monument, it looks this way. The Ferial Day [*Norma-Tag*] after Easter has been moved to this week, consequently [there are] no more days when the theaters will be closed to stage performances [*Spielfreie Tage*] in this month.[11] Weigl[12] advises not to give the concert at noon, and he also recommends not carrying out this plan until next fall. But by then the little enthusiasm [for the plan] will have completely cooled, and no one will think any longer about doing something on its behalf.

I must also tell you something about his medical treatment. At the very beginning of his illness, Beethoven had his earlier doctors called to look after him. Dr. Braunhofer begged to be excused, since the distance was too great for him; and Dr. Staudenheim finally came after three days of requests, but he left and did not come a second time. He [Beethoven] therefore had to entrust himself to a Professor of the *Allgemeines Krankenhaus*,[13] whom he contacted in a most unusual fashion. Namely, Gehringer, a coffeehouse proprietor on the Kohlmarkt, had a sick domestic servant, whom he wanted to entrust to this professor in his clinic. For this reason, he [Gehringer] wrote to this Professor Wawruch, saying that he wanted him to take the servant's case, and, at the same time, requested him to go to Beethoven, who needed a doctor, and to say only that he sent him there. After a long time, I was finally able to discover that the amiable nephew Karl v[an] Beethoven gave the coffee brewer instructions to do this while he was playing billiards there one day. The professor knew neither Beethoven nor his nature and therefore treated him in a completely orthodox manner; in the first four weeks, he had him take no fewer than 72 bottles of medicine, many days three different kinds, so that by the first days in January, Beethoven was already more dead than alive. Finally, I could not tolerate this disaster any longer, and went without further ado to Dr. Malfatti, who in former times was his friend. The doctor took a long time in answering the request, and Beethoven himself asked him at the first consultation to look after him, for God's sake! But Malfatti objected that he could not do this, out of consideration for another doctor, and came for consultation once, at most twice, each week until he finally came daily during the last week. In short, I can and will tell you: Beethoven has gone to his grave at least ten years too soon as a sacrifice to the most horrible base actions and ignorance. But a more detailed elucidation about all of this will be reserved for a later time.

Hummel returned to Weimar on the 9th. He had his wife and his student, one Herr Hiller from Frankfurt,[14] with him here. The last sends his enthusiastic greetings to you, as does Hummel.

The expenditures for the funeral have now pretty much ended, and come to about 330 florins C.M. I still have much, very much to tell you, but I must close. Friend Lewinger sends sincere greetings to you both; he is so kind as to expedite this letter through Rothschild. Also Rau sends greetings to you. Write to us very soon. All imaginable felicities to Herr Stumpff, and tell him that it was Beethoven's intention to dedicate to him one of his newest works. This shall still be done if only we find a few that are complete. Otherwise a hearty Farewell! from

Your old friend,

Ant. Schindler

[P.S.] The essay from the *Allgemeine Zeitung* is also enclosed herewith.

    1. Follows on Schindler's letters to Moscheles, March 24 and April 4, 1827 (Nos. 469 and 477 above), among others.

    2. Probably the Augsburg journal to which Schindler referred in his April 4 letter.

    3. Joseph Anton von Pilat (1782–1865), editor of the *Österreichischer Beobachter,* Vienna.

    4. The steward in the Viennese banking house of Eskeles who had delivered news of the Philharmonic Society's gift to Beethoven.

    5. Schindler refers to the *Akademie* of May 7, 1824, on which the Symphony No. 9 was premiered.

6. The repeat performance of the Ninth Symphony, with a slightly changed program, took place on May 23, 1824.

7. Charlotte Moscheles and Smidak (following her) give the figure here as *500* gulden/florins.

8. For slightly different financial figures, possibly more accurate than Schindler's assertion or Ley's transcription, see Thayer-Forbes, pp. 911–913.

9. *Missa solemnis,* Op. 123.

10. Schindler's bitter assertion is confirmed by the observations of Joseph Carl Rosenbaum: Haydn's funeral on June 1, 1809, was poorly attended largely because of the confusion and lack of communication during the recent French occupation of Vienna. Rosenbaum noted: "Not one Viennese Kapellmeister was in the funeral cortège." On June 15, 1809, a memorial service for Haydn was held in the Schottenkirche, consisting of Mozart's *Requiem,* performed by a large group of singers and instrumentalists, attended by "the whole of Viennese society," and with both local militia and French troops as guards. Rosenbaum's verdict on this occasion: "The whole was most solemn and worthy of Haydn" ("The Diaries of Joseph Carl Rosenbaum [1770–1829]," trans. Eugene Hartzell, ed. Else Radant, *Haydn Yearbook* 5 [1968], 149–151).

11. In 1827, Easter fell on Sunday, April 15. Schindler and his associates at the Kärntnertor Theater had evidently counted on being able to give a concert on a *Norma-Tag* (a day when no theatrical production would have been given) after Easter. The shift of that ferial day to the week *before* Easter suddenly meant that all the evenings *after* Easter would be occupied by theatrical performances. Therefore, there would be little or no opportunity for a concert using theatrical space or theatrical music personnel in the immediate future.

12. Joseph Weigl (1766–1846) had been appointed vice-*Kapellmeister* to the court on January 22, 1827.

13. Dr. Andreas Wawruch. Founded by Emperor Joseph II, the Allgemeines Krankenhaus was the foremost hospital in Vienna, not far from Beethoven's lodging in the Schwarzspanierhaus.

14. Ferdinand Hiller accompanied Hummel on his visits to Beethoven and left a firsthand account of them.

Incipit: Sie werden erschrecken. . . .

Sources: Charlotte Moscheles, *Life of Moscheles,* I, 172–177; Smidak, *Moscheles,* pp. 61–63; Ley, *Beethoven als Freund,* pp. 240- 243, indicating that the autograph was then in the Wegeler family collection.

479. Anton Schindler to B. Schotts Söhne, Mainz

Vienna; April 12, 1827[1]

Sirs!

I would gladly have taken the liberty already of forwarding to you this enclosed document[2] in the name of our departed Beethoven, who gave me instructions to do so, even on his deathbed, but there was so much business to attend to after the passing of my friend that I could not think of doing so any earlier. Unfortunately it was not possible to have this document legalized; in this case Beethoven's signature would have had to be written at the [law] court, which was by then the greatest impossibility. Nonetheless, Beethoven requested Court Councillor von Breuning and me, as witness, to draw it up with him, since we both were present. And so, we believe that it will also serve its intended purpose. I must further mention to you that in this document you possess the last signature of this immortal man, for this was the last stroke of his pen.

I cannot refrain from also telling you something about his last hours of consciousness (namely on March 24, from early in the morning until about one o'clock in the afternoon), since it might be of not just a little interest, especially for you, sirs.

When I came to him on the morning of March 24, I found his whole appearance in ruins and him so weak that he could make at most two or three words intelligible only with the greatest effort. Right afterward came the *Ordinarius*,[3] who, after observing him for a few moments, said to me: he is rapidly approaching his end! Since we had already settled the matter of his testament, as well as it would ever be done, the day before,[4] only one ardent wish remained for us, to reconcile him with Heaven and at the same time to show the world that he ended his life as a true Christian. The Professor Ordinarius wrote it out for him and requested him, in the name of all his friends, therefore to receive the Last Holy Sacraments, whereupon he answered in a completely and collected way: "I will."[5]

The doctor went, and left me to take care of this. Then Beethoven said to me: "I now ask you to write to Schott and send him the document. He will need it. And write to him in my name, for I am too weak, saying that I very much desire the promised wine. Also write to England if you still have time today."

The priest came at about 12 o'clock, and the ceremony took place with the greatest edification; and now for the first time he seemed to believe that his end was near, for hardly had the clergyman left, when he said to me and young Herr von Breuning: "*Plaudite amici, comoedia finita est!*[6] Haven't I always said that it would happen like this!" Then he asked me once more not to forget Schott, and also to thank the Philharmonic Society once more in his name for their great gift, adding that the Society had gladdened his last days of life, and that even on the brink of the grave, he thanked the Society and the whole English nation! "God bless them!" and so forth. At this moment Herr von Breuning's Chancellory servant entered the room with the small chest of wine and [medicinal] drink that you sent. This was at about quarter to one o'clock. I placed the two bottles of Rüdesheimer [wine] and the other two bottles with the drink on the table next to his bed. He looked at them and said: "Pity! — Pity! — too late!" These were absolutely his last words. Right afterward he fell into such an agony that he could not utter another sound.

Toward evening he lost consciousness and began to fantasize. This continued until the evening of the 25th, when visible signs of death appeared. Nonetheless he did not die until the 26th at a quarter to six o'clock in the evening.

This death struggle was terrible to behold, for his general constitution, especially his chest, was gigantic. He still drank some of your Rüdesheimer wine in spoonfuls until he passed away.

Thus, in a few words I report to you the last three days of life of our unforgettable friend.

Concerning the dedication of the C♯ minor Quartet to General Stutterheim,[7] Court Councillor von Breuning requests you, please, to send him three copies on nice paper through one of the art dealers here, so that he can deliver them to the General. Concerning the opus number in the declaration, I must beg your pardon, for neither Beethoven nor anyone else could give me definite information about it. I was told only that it comes before the quartet that Schlesinger in Berlin has. I am therefore also writing to Schlesinger today. The opus number is probably 131 or 132.[8]

I received your last letter through Herr Streicher.[9] If you want to write to Court Councillor von Breuning or me again, this can be done either through Streicher or to one of the music dealers here, for example Diabelli & Co.[10] Court Councillor von Breuning lives in the Rothes Haus in the Alservorstadt.[11]

In closing, accept the assurance of my greatest esteem, with which I remain

Yours sincerely,

Ant. Schindler

1. Replies to Schott's letter of March 8, 1827 (No. 466 above).

2. A certificate officially transferring ownership of the Quartet, Op. 131, to Schott.

3. Dr. Andreas Wawruch.

4. The codicil to Beethoven's will, March 23, 1827 (Anderson No. 1568). Beethoven's great weakness and semiconscious state are evident in the many photographic reproductions of this document to be found in the literature.

5. The original German reads "Ich will's."

6. See Schindler's letter to Moscheles, March 24, 1827 (No. 469 above), for a slightly different version of this anecdote, with editorial commentary.

7. Baron Joseph von Stutterheim, who had accepted Beethoven's nephew Karl into his army regiment.

8. Schott's quartet was Op. 131; Schlesinger's was Op. 135. See Schlesinger's letters to his son (April 17, 1827, No. 481 below) and Schindler (April 21, 1827, No. 482 below).

9. Piano manufacturer Johann Andreas Streicher (1761–1833), longtime friend of Beethoven's.

10. Publisher Anton Diabelli (1781–1858).

11. Stephan von Breuning, soon to pass away himself, lived very close to Beethoven, thus his son Gerhard's close acquaintance with the composer.

Incipit: Gern schon hätte mir die Freiheit. . . .

Sources: Cäcilia 6 (May 1827), 309–312; Kalischer (German), V, 311–314; Kalischer-Shedlock II, 474–476. Excerpts in Hellinghaus, pp. 251–252, and Thayer-Forbes, p. 1049. Critical (complete) text in Staehelin and Brandenburg, *Briefwechsel,* pp. 85–87. Autograph in the Stadtbibliothek, Mainz; Schindler's copy in the Staatsbibliothek zu Berlin–Preussischer Kulturbesitz.

480. *Johann Andreas Stumpff to*
Johann Baptist Streicher, Vienna

London; April 16, 1827[1]

Herr B. Streicher
Vienna

Cherished Friend,

The passing of that irreplaceably great German man, our friend Beethoven, pierced me deeply. Here I sit, bent over your dear letter that confirmed the news of it for me, and stare at the lock that adorned the head from which flowed the immortal works, which are and shall remain the admiration of all cultivated nations.

Trembling throughout with a thousand feelings, I would sit here without any thoughts, dumbfounded, and lost as if in a labyrinth, and attempt in vain to give vent to my deeply moved breast. Finally, to soothe my pressing breast, I drafted, a few days afterward, the following essay in the form of a sonnet, with which I wish to do my part in the glorification of the departed great one, to justify its transmission and to take my good intention as the deed when you read the sonnet, "By a Friend from Afar."[2]

> I must weep — Ah, from the dim distance,
> I see your mortal remains — as the sower sows
> On God's acre; noble seeds
> Ripen there, where pure winds abide.
>   Brightly you shine in the host of stars,
>   Now unclouded in those blue heights,
>   Where the seer nightly likes to explore,
>   There, there he saw you arise of late.
> Like Mozart, he drew me to see
> You, in dimness on the Danube shore.
> And once, in such complete trust,
>   Beethoven extended his noble hand to the Pilgrim.

Ah, he listens to you in those meadows,
There, where the bonds of friendship never dissolve.

In the hope that you will forgive me for having taken the liberty without first getting your consent, I have had your letter translated and inserted in the *Harmonicon,* a musical magazine here.[3] This was due to a sudden concern that arose here among several friends (occasioned by an article in an Augsburg newspaper, taken from the *Wiener Zeitung,* and picked up by an English newspaper), and it seemed to me the only way to appease the English who were aroused by that article. I fear, dear friend, that the letter from Beethoven to Herr Moscheles, with the receipt signed by himself, and in which he so animatedly expressed his joy at the delivery of the 100 pounds sterling,[4] and which appeared in several English newspapers, will weaken everything that the Viennese may produce to excuse the alleged neglect of the great man, and even more so since Beethoven had requested me so urgently to try everything to organize a concert for him, and since, from the seriousness of his illness, little hope remained for his recovery, as if the anxious concerns for the future that his mood had uneasily raised had not inflamed me to risk and venture everything for him. In the hope that my friends, through such immediate support, could perhaps have a beneficial effect upon his mood and put a stop to the devastation of his illness, I employed the most urgent representations to win over Herr Moscheles and other members of the Philharmonic Society. I myself wrote to the society's board of directors, and introduced Beethoven's request in such a light that it did not degrade the character of the German, and had to persuade the Englishmen to come to the aid of the great man with assistance. In a general business meeting of the society, I finally sought to refute the unpleasant remarks concerning the alleged neglect of the great man in Germany and especially in Vienna, as follows: that if it became known that Beethoven was ill and in need, all hearts and purses, not only those of his patrons in Vienna, but in all Germany, would have been opened to aid the great man.

Now, my dear friend, I thank you most sincerely for the lock of hair and music of our departed friend that you sent, with the request that you give Herr von Schickh[5] my many regards, and extend my thanks for the tender proof of his friendly sentiments toward me; and should Herr von Schickh not find the above Sonnet unworthy of acceptance into his journal, I would gladly allow it to be inserted under my name.

Now I take the liberty further to mention here that letters that are registered at the Post Office in Germany, as your last one was, just do not go more securely than those that are not — [information] which was furnished to me at the Post Office here — and since it is so troublesome to receive such letters from the Post Office here, and beyond that, that every simple letter costs 5 shillings extra, in addition to the postal fee, I request that you be so kind as to send me your letters at the Post Office in the usual manner.

Again I thank you sincerely for the friendly communications concerning the great man who has been torn from us too soon, as well as for everything that you will have been so very kind to send to me written by the hands of the deceased.

In a letter to his friend Rau in Vienna, Herr Moscheles, in the name of the Philharmonic Society, recently asked for the 100 pounds to be sent back, which was one of the conditions in case Beethoven was already dead or if such support had come from foreign lands and his circumstances no longer warranted it.

Along with my sincere greetings to your estimable parents[6] and relatives, I remain with constant love and friendship,

Yours most truly,

J. A. Stumpff

[P.S.] I still cannot seal this letter without sending you the verse that I wrote for the Englishmen in the English language, and under Beethoven's picture, which I brought with me from Vienna owing to your kindness. I am copying it out because it met with approval here.

> When Jupiter, who from Olympus hurl'd
> This flaming shaft's, th'advancing foes to chase,
> On up-pil'd rocks, their banners stu[c]k unfurl'd,
> To force access — attempted Titans race:
> When tempest-blast's, the roaring mountains dash,
> Form'd by its ire, in gulfs, from whence they spring,
> Wild angry waves, the rock-bas'd Beacon lash
> To which exhausted, oft the ship-wre[c]k clung:

Thus strik's with awe, when Sy[m]phonies proclaim
Beethoven magic powr's, long mark'd by fame.[7]
J. A. St., Feb. 8th, 1827.

[Exterior:]
[Address:]
Herr B. Streicher
No. 371 Ungar-Gasse, his own house
Vienna
Germany

[Streicher's annotation:]
J. A. Stumpff
[Sent:] London, April 16, 1827
Received: May 2,   "
Answered: [no date] " [8]

50

1. Answers Streicher's letter of March 28, 1827 (No. 473 above). Streicher replied, or drafted a reply, on June 9, 1827 (No. 485 below).

2. "Eines Freundes aus der Ferne" in the original German.

3. Streicher to Stumpff, March 28, 1827; *Harmonicon* 5 (May 1827), 86–87.

4. Beethoven to Moscheles, March 18, 1827 (Anderson No. 1566).

5. Johann Schickh, editor of the *Wiener Zeitschrift*.

6. Piano manufacturer Johann Andreas Streicher and his wife, Nannette Stein Streicher.

7. Other than to correct "Syphonies," "wrek" and "stuk," nothing has been done to alter Stumpff's English-language poem.

8. The fact that the date of Streicher's June 9, 1827, letter is not entered here may indicate that it was drafted but never sent.

Incipit: Das Hinscheiden des unersetzlichen grossen deutschen Mannes. . . .

Sources: Excerpt and discussion in Max Unger, "Neue Kunde vom Totenbette Beethovens," *Deutsche Musiker-Zeitung* 58 (March 27, 1927), 279; Unger's transcription varies in several places from the autograph in the Österreichische Nationalbibliothek, Vienna, 126/77–2.

481. Adolf Martin Schlesinger to Moritz Schlesinger, Paris

Berlin; April 17, 1827

You will know that Beethoven is dead. I still have no answer concerning the Quartet. I repeat to you that I am counting on printing it, and publishing it on the same day as you do.[1] I just received the following letter from Music Director Schindler in Vienna:[2] "My departed friend Beethoven requested me, a few days before his death, to write to you and to ask what opus number is affixed to this last Quartet that you got from him and if Beethoven already communicated to you a dedication for this Quartet. Concerning the opus number, he believed that it must be 130 or 131.[3] He asked that the dedication, which he could not remember having sent to you, be made to his friend Johann Wolfmeyer.[4] His estate [*Nachlass*] is now in my and Court Councillor von Breuning's hands, to whom the departed one entrusted everything. Since it now depends upon us to put his estate in order as soon as possible, we both ask you to inform us about the two matters mentioned above, and to kindly indicate to us the time when you intend to publish the Quartet." (Schindler's address is: c/o the Chancellory of the Imperial Royal Court Opera Theater near the Kärntnertor.) I am writing him tomorrow concerning the estate and shall communicate the results to you; write immediately concerning the dedication of the Quartet.

1. Father and son operated cooperative publishing houses in Berlin and Paris, respectively. Moritz became known as Maurice after he moved to France.

2. Schindler's letter to Schott, April 12, 1827 (No. 479 above), indicated that he would write to Schlesinger that same day; Schlesinger's letter of April 21 (No. 482 below) confirms this.

3. It was Moritz Schlesinger who had purchased the Quartet in F, which ultimately became Op. 135. For more confusion in opus numbers, see Beethoven's letter to Schott, February 22, 1827 (Anderson No. 1553).

4. Wolfmeyer, a Viennese cloth merchant who had attempted to commission a *Requiem* from Beethoven in 1818 (see the letter of April 9, 1818, No. 247 above), was supposed to receive the dedication of the Quartet, Op. 131. A dedication to Stutterheim must have seemed more urgent, so Wolfmayer's recognition was postponed to Op. 135.

Incipit: (a) Schlesinger: Dass Beethoven todt, wirst Du wissen . . . ; (b) Schindler: Mein verewigter Freund Beeth[oven] ersuchte mich. . . .

Sources: Extract from Schlesinger's copybook in Unger, *Beethoven und seine Verleger,* p. 37. Schindler's letter seems not to have survived except in this quote. Presumably all this material was destroyed during or before World War II.

482. Adolf Martin Schlesinger to Anton Schindler, Vienna

Berlin; April 21, 1827[1]

Sir,

I have received your letter of the 12th of this month and hasten to answer it. My son in Paris bought the Quartet[2] from the departed Herr van Beethoven, whom everyone mourns deeply. It will appear here and in Paris at the same time, but I do not know when, because my son has not yet written me anything about it. I have sent your letter to him and he will send you details by return post.

Should there be anything in the estate [*Nachlass*] that is ready to be published, I shall be very pleased to enter into discussion with you about it, and I am convinced that we shall be able to reach an agreement.[3]

1. Replies to Schindler's letter of April 12, 1827 (lost, but excerpted in Schlesinger's letter to his son Moritz, April 17, 1827, No. 481 above). See also Schindler to Schott, April 12, 1827 (No. 479 above).

2. Op. 135.

3. Schlesinger seems to have received nothing from the *Nachlass.*

Incipit: Ew. Wohlgeb. Schreiben vom 12. d. . . .

Sources: Extract (with run-on abbreviations) from Schlesinger's copybook in Unger, *Beethoven und seine Verleger,* p. 37.

483. *Appraisal of the Value of Beethoven's Library*

Vienna; May 5, 1827[1]

Appraisal Proceedings
May 5, 1827
of the Books belonging to the Estate of
Herr Ludwig van Beethoven, Composer, Alservorstadt No. 200.[2]

Present: Ferd[inand] Prandstetter and Ign[az] Schleicher.[3]

No.	Title of Books[4]	Appraisal in *Wiener Währung*	Sale in *Conv. Münze*
1.	Sailer, *Goldkörner*, Grätz, 1819	— 10	— 6
2.	Kant, *Naturgeschichte*, Zeitz, 1798	— 5	— 30
3.	Forkel, *Allg. Litteratur der Musik*, Leipzig, 1792	— 30	— 52
4.*	Seume, *Spaziergang nach Syrakus*, 1803	1 —	
5.*	" , *Apokryphen*, 1811	— 20	
6.	Türk, *Anweisung zum Generalbassspielen*, Halle, 1791	— 20	— 44
7.	Thomson, *Jahreszeiten*, Altona, 1796	— 15	— 12
8.*	Kotzebue, *Über den Adel* (lacking title page)	— 5	
9.	Hufeland, *Übersicht der Heilquellen*, 1815	— 10	— 12
10.	Liechtenthal, *Ideen zur Diätetik*, Vienna, 1810	— 5	— 4
11.	Sailer, *Kleine Bibel für Kranke*, Gratz, 1819	— 5	— 4
12.	Streckfuss, *Gedichte*, Vienna, 1804, [with] Bouterweck, *Gedichte*, Reutlingen, 1803	— 5	— 4
13.	Schenk, *Taschenbuch für Badegäste Badens*, 1805	— 10	— 6
14.	Fergar, *Kl. prakt.* [= *poet.*] *Hand-Apparat*, Pest, 1823	— 5	— 8
15.*	Müller (W. Chr.), *Paris im Scheitelpunkte*, 1816	— 5	
16.*	Fessler, *Geschichten* [= *Ansichten*] *von Religion*, Berlin, 1805	1 —	
17.	Lafontaine, *Fables choisies*, Vienna, 1805	— 5	— 6
18.	Gaal, *Gedichte*, Dresden, 1812	— 5	— 6
19.	Peucer, *Commentarius* . . . , Wittemberg	— 5	— —
20.	Tiedge, *Elegien*, Halle, 1806	— 20	— 10

21. ", *Urania*, Halle, 1808	—	10	—	10
22. Ramler, *Poetische Werke*, Vienna	—	20	—	12
23. Thomas von Kempis, *Nachfolge Christi*, Reutlingen	—	5	—	8
24. Matthison, *Lyrische Anthologie*, Zürich, 1809	1	30	1	16
25. Goethe, *Sämmtliche Schriften*, Vienna, 1811	2	—	3	15
26. Schiller, *Sämmtliche Werke*	1	—	2	3
27. Campe, *Kinderschriften*, Vienna	—	45	1	4
28. Klopstock, *Werke*, Troppau, 1785	—	20	—	15
29. Hölty, *Gedichte*, Vienna, 1815	—	20	—	10
30. Nägeli, *Liederkränze*, Zürich, 1825	—	20	—	13
31. Heinse, *Linz und Umgebungen*, 1812	—	5	—	6
32. Weissenbach, *Meine Reise zum Congress*, 1816	—	5	—	6
33. Seckendorf, *Prometheus*, Vienna, 1808	—	20	—	12
34. Bode, *Anleitung . . . des Himmels*, Berlin	1	—	—	41
35. *Kalliroe*, Tragedy, Leipzig, 1806, [with] *Polyidos*, Leipzig, 1804	—	20	—	30
36. *Cäcilia*, journal, Mainz, 1824–1826	2	—	3	30
37. A package of Italian grammar	—	20	—	10
38. Many individual parts [*Theile*] of Guthrie and Gray's *World History*. Shakespeare's plays, Cicero's *Epistolae* (with German notes and translation), Plutarch's *Lives*, etc., and many brochures in very bad condition.	4	—	3	13
39. Meissner, *Skizzen*, Karlsruhe, 1782, [and] Klopstock, *Werke*, Vienna	2	—	1	—
40. *Berliner musikalische Zeitung*, many issues from several annual volumes, and other individual issues of old professional newspapers.	1	—	—	40
41. *Neujahrsgeschenk an die Zürcherische Jugend*, for the years 1812–1818, 1820–1824	2	—	—	48
42. Burney, *A General History of Music*, 1789	15	—	19	55
43. Mattheson, *Der volkommene Kapellmeister*; Marpurg, *Abhandlung von der Fuge*; [and] *Missale romanum*, Venice, 1770.	—	45	—	60
44. *Bible*, trans. into French, Liège, 1742	5	—	3	—
Total	45	50	47	9

Franz Joseph Rötzl, member of the Foreign Affairs Council and sworn Auditor-Appraiser; Chr. Gottfr. Kaulfuss, sworn Auditor-Appraiser.

The books crossed out as forbidden [noted with an asterisk above] are, according to the existing instructions of the most honorable Censor, to be delivered for official processing. By the I[mperial] R[oyal] Central Auditing Office, June 6, 1827.[5]

It is hereby confirmed that the above crossed-out books were previously delivered. September 5, 1827.

1. Although this document was prepared on May 5, Jäger-Sunstenau indicates that it underwent several revisions until September 5. The auction of Beethoven's effects took place on November 5, 1827, and is largely documented in Thayer-Forbes, pp. 1061–1076.

This inventory of mostly non-music-related items in Beethoven's library, however, was never included in Thayer's biography or other standard sources, although its existence was implied in the "Sale of Beethoven's Mss. and Musical Library," *Harmonicon* (April 1828), reprinted in Thayer-Forbes, p. 1071, which notes the following sale catalog heading: "7. A small collection of general literature."

2. Several phonetic spellings originally found in this list indicate that one of the appraisers read out names and titles while the other wrote them down: entry 11 spelled Sailer as "Seiler"; entry 20 spelled Tiedge as "Tiedger"; entry 38 spelled Gray as "Grey"; entry 42 spelled Burney as "Burnet." In the case of Burney, one can almost envision the reader calling out "Boor-nay" and then having to show or spell out the English-language title to his colleague. Similarly, in entry 14, the reader called out Fergar, which was then written as "Ferger"; the reader himself probably misread the abbreviation "*poet.*" in the title and called out "*prakt.*," which the scribe then set to paper. Likewise, in entry 16, "*Ansichten*" probably became "*Geschichten*" through some slip of reading or listening; similarly "*Kalliroe*" became "*Kaltiron*" in entry 35. The most important of these and similar errors have been corrected without further comment in the inventory as presented here.

3. The first names of these two men appear on the acts of the civil courts, March 27, 1827; quoted in Jäger-Sunstenau, p. 20.

4. After consulting a facsimile of the front page of this document (including the first eighteen items), I was able to emend Jäger-Sunstenau's transcription and otherwise identify most of the authors and works in the inventory as follows (by item number):

1. Johann Michael Sailer (1751–1832), a popular religious leader whose collected works comprise forty volumes. At one time, Beethoven had hoped to send his nephew

Karl to Sailer's boarding school in Landshut (see Antonie Brentano to Sailer, February 22, 1819, No. 256 above). The present item is his *Goldkörner: Weisheit und Tugend* (Grätz: Ferstl, 1819). See also item 11 below.

2. Immanuel Kant's (1724–1804) *Allgemeine Naturgeschichte und Theorie des Himmels . . .* reached a fourth printing (Zeitz: W. Weber) by 1808.

3. Johann Nikolaus Forkel's (1749–1818) *Allgemeine Litteratur der Musik* (Leipzig: Schwickert, 1792) is still regarded as one of the classics of music scholarship.

4/5. Johann Gottfried Seume's (1763–1810) *Spaziergang nach Syrakus im Jahre 1802* was published in Braunschweig in 1803. His *Apokryphen* also saw a reprinting in Leipzig (Hartknock) in 1819.

6. The classic *Anweisung* (originally *Kurze Anweisung*) of Daniel Gottlob Türk (1756–1813) saw a second, enlarged edition (Halle and Leipzig: Schwickert) in 1800.

7. *The Seasons* by James Thomson (1700–1748) was one of the most popular literary works of the eighteenth century and inspired Haydn's oratorio. The edition in Beethoven's collection was *Die Jahreszeiten, in deutschen Iamben* by Harries (Altona: I. F. Hammerlich, 1796).

8. "Concerning the Nobility," probably *Vom Adel: Bruchstück eines grössern historisch-philosophischen Werkes über Ehre und Schande, Ruhm und Nachruhm* (Leipzig: Kummer, 1792), by August Kotzebue (1761–1819), with whom Beethoven had collaborated on *King Stephan* and *The Ruins of Athens* in 1811–1812. See Kotzebue's letters to Beethoven, April 20, 1812, and September 24, 1813 (Nos. 161 and 177 above).

9. *Übersicht der Heilquellen Teutschlands* (Berlin, 1815), a work by Christoph Wilhelm Hufeland (1762–1836), the author of a popular treatise on prolonging life (*Die Kunst menschliche Leben zu verlängern*), a treatise on nerve fever (1799) and one on homeopathic medicine (*Makrobiotik,* 1796). See Beethoven to Dr. Anton Braunhofer, ca. February 27/28, 1826 (No. 427 above).

10. *Ideen zur Diätetik für d. Beiwohner Wiens,* by Peter Lichtenthal (1780–1853), who wrote books on medicine, music and music therapy. Although he still published German-language books in Vienna as late as 1813, most of his works after about 1815 appeared in Italy in Italian.

11. Another work by Sailer (see item 1 above), his *Kleine Bibel für Kranke und Sterbende, und ihre Freunde,* 3d ed. (Grätz: Ferstl, 1819).

12. A one-volume collection of poetry by Adolf Friedrich Karl Streckfuss (1778–1844), published in Vienna by J. V. Degen in 1804. The other volume of poetry in this item was by Friedrich Bouterwek (1766–1828); the variant spelling of his name in the inventory is common in contemporary sources.

13. Carl Schenk's *Taschenbuch für Badegäste Badens* (Vienna: J. Geistinger, 1805). Although he had spent a month there in 1804, Beethoven came to prefer Baden as a summer resort only after 1817.

14. Probably F. G. Fergar's *Kleiner poet. Hand-Apparat, oder die Kunst, in zwei Stunden ein Dichter zu werden* (Pest: Hartleben, 1823).

15. *Paris im Scheitelpunkt, oder flüchtige Reise durch Hospitäler und Schlachtfelder zu den Herrlichkeiten in Frankreichs Herrscherstaat im August 1815,* 2 vols. (Bremen: [H. Müller(?),] 1816–1818), by Wilhelm Christian Müller (1752–1831). An author of travel books about Germany as well, published in the early 1820s, Müller was the leader of a group of Beethoven enthusiasts in Bremen during this period (see Dr. Karl Iken and Elise Müller to Beethoven, before December 17, 1819, No. 266 above). *Paris im Scheitelpunkt* may well have been a gift from its author.

16. *Ansichten von Religion und Kirchenthum* (Berlin: Sander, 1805) by Ignaz Aurelius Fessler (1756–1839).

17. A popular work by Jean de La Fontaine (1621–1695).

18. A volume of poetry by Hungarian writer Georg von Gaal (1783–1855), published by Walther in Dresden in 1812.

19. Kaspar Peucer (1525–1602), *Commentarius de praecipuis generibus divinationum,* was first published in 1553 and saw at least nine editions before 1607. Five of these appeared in Wittenberg: 1553, 1560, 1572, 1576 and 1580.

20/21. Christoph August Tiedge (1752–1841), *Elegien, und vermischte Gedichte,* 2d ed. (Halle: Renger, 1806–1807); and his *Urania,* 4th ed. (Halle: Renger, 1808). *Urania* was Tiedge's most popular collection of poems, expressing the ideas of Kant; Beethoven probably owned a copy by about June 1804, when he set "An die Hoffnung," Op. 32. He met Tiedge in Teplitz in 1811 and then composed a more extensive setting of the poem, as Op. 94, in 1813.

22. The *Poetische Werke* of Karl Wilhelm Ramler (1725–1798) were published in Berlin (J. D. Sander, 1801–1802) as a two-volume set. Perhaps the Viennese version appeared in a single volume. Ramler is best known to musicians as the poet of Carl Heinrich Graun's popular oratorio *Der Tod Jesu.*

23. Thomas à Kempis's (1379–1471) *De imitatione Christi* (ca. 1415–1424) was one of the most popular inspirational books in Christendom and remains in print even today. Beethoven's copy was one of several German-language editions then available.

24. Friedrich von Matthison (1761–1831), *Lyrische Anthologie,* 20 vols. in 10 (Zürich: Orell Füssli, 1803–1807); Beethoven's copy (complete?) was probably a second printing.

25. Goethe was one of Beethoven's favorite authors (see Goethe to Beethoven, June 25, 1811, No. 155 above); his complete works have seen innumerable printings.

26. As with Goethe (item 25 above), the works of Schiller have been reprinted widely to the present day. Schiller was a favorite of Beethoven's as early as his Bonn days. The Staatsbibliothek zu Berlin–Preussischer Kulturbesitz possesses vol. (*Theil*) 6 of an edition published by Anton Doll in Vienna in 1810.

27. Joachim Heinrich Campe (1746–1818), *Kinder-Bibliothek,* 6 vols. in 3 (Vienna: B. P. Bauer, 1813), included children's adaptations of stories about Christopher Columbus, Hernando Cortez, the discovery of America and Robinson Crusoe. Doubtless these were meant for Beethoven's nephew Karl, as must have been several other books surviving in Beethoven's *Nachlass.*

28. Works of the inspirational author Friedrich Gottlieb Klopstock (1724–1803); see also item 39 below.

29. The Viennese publisher Bauer printed this edition of poetry by Ludwig Heinrich Christoph Hölty (1748–1776).

30. Doubtless this was the copy that Hans Georg Nägeli himself had sent Beethoven (see Nägeli to Beethoven, February 21, 1825, No. 395 above).

31. Beethoven may have bought this guide to Linz by Gottlieb Heinrich Heinse (1766–1832) during his journey there in the fall of 1812. It was published by the Academische Buchhandlung in Linz.

32. Alois Weissenbach (1766–1821), *Meine Reise zum Kongress: Wahrheit und Dichtung* (Vienna: J. B. Wallishauser, 1816). Weissenbach met Beethoven during his journey, and they became friends. His book contains a report about Beethoven, and it became popular reading in the composer's circle (see Weissenbach to Beethoven, November 15, 1819, No. 264 above).

33. Possibly a work by Christian Adolph von Seckendorff (1767–1833).

34. Johann Elert Bode (1747–1826), *Anleitung zur Kenntniss des gestirnten Himmels.* This popular book on astronomy had its fourth printing (Berlin: Himburg) in 1778. It reached an eighth printing (Berlin: Nicolai) in 1808 and a ninth in 1823.

35. *Kalliroe* (or *Kallirhöe*), published by Breitkopf und Härtel in Leipzig in 1806, and the earlier *Polyïdos,* published by Hartnock in Leipzig. Both books were by Johann August Apel (1771–1816), the author of ghost stories, one of which was later the basis for Carl Maria von Weber's opera *Der Freischütz.*

36. *Cäcilia* was the house journal of B. Schott's Söhne, Mainz; its editor was Gottfried Weber.

37. Beethoven could have used such materials during his studies with Antonio Salieri, from around 1793 until 1802.

38. William Guthrie (1708–1770) and John Gray's *A General History of the World from the Creation to the Present Time,* 12 vols. (London: J. Newbery, 1764–1767), was gradually translated into German, by a multiplicity of hands, as *Allgemeine Weltgeschichte von der Schöpfung an bis auf gegenwärtige Zeit,* 17 pts. (*Theile*) (Leipzig, 1765–1808). Beethoven owned the German edition; whether each part (*Teil*) was equivalent to a volume in this case is difficult to determine.

     Beethoven owned Johann Joachim Eschenburg's translation of Shakespeare's *Schauspiele,* itself an expanded revision of a prose translation by Christoph

Martin Wieland (1762–1766). Eschenburg's version had appeared in 13 volumes in Zurich from 1775 to 1782. Beethoven's copies were from a reprint edition published in Mannheim and Strassburg from roughly 1783 to roughly 1804. Surviving composite vols. 3/4 (*The Merchant of Venice, As You Like It, Love's Labors Lost,* and *The Winter's Tale*) and 9/10 (*Othello, Romeo and Juliet, Much Ado about Nothing,* and *All's Well That Ends Well*) in Eschenburg's translation came through Schindler to the Staatsbibliothek zu Berlin–Preussischer Kulturbesitz (see Bartlitz, pp. 210–211). On the whole, the various items in the present inventory seem never to have been in Schindler's possession. Thus, the books here are probably not those now in the Berlin library and may have included at least three composite volumes of Eschenburg in reprint: 1/2, 5/6 and 7/8.

Editions of Cicero's *Epistolae,* such as described above, appeared in Halle in 1771 and Berlin in 1790.

Editions of Plutarch's *Biographien* (as it is termed in the original inventory) appeared in Berlin in 1776–1780 and Vienna in 1809. Other German-language editions (entitled *Lebensbeschreibungen*) appeared in Leipzig in 1745–1754 and Magdeburg in 1799–1806. Beethoven probably owned one of the former versions.

39. August Gottlieb Meissner (1753–1807), *Skizzen,* 6 vols. in 5 (Karlsruhe: C. G. Schneider, 1782–1784), and more works by Klopstock (see item 28 above).

40. The *Berliner Allgemeine musikalische Zeitung,* begun in 1824 and edited by Adolf Bernhard Marx (1795–1866), probably sent to Beethoven by the publisher Adolf Martin Schlesinger. The additional papers may have been issues of Leipzig's *Allgemeine musikalische Zeitung,* sent by publisher Gottfried Christoph Härtel.

41. The Allgemeine Musik-Gesellschaft in Zurich was founded in 1812 and soon began issuing this series of "New Year's Gifts." Beethoven's copies were probably sent by Hans Georg Nägeli (see item 30 above). Most of these early pamphlets concerned Swiss folk traditions. With vol. 18 (1830), the name of the series was changed to *Neujahrsstück,* and each volume now featured the biography of a prominent musician. Beethoven himself was the subject of one of these sixteen-page pamphlets in 1834.

42. The famous *A General History of Music from the Earliest Ages to the Present Period,* 4 vols. (London, 1782–1789), by Charles Burney (1726–1814). Beethoven probably owned a copy of Burney's *History* well before he met the author's granddaughter, Sarah Burney Payne (then about thirty-two), on September 27, 1825. His French note to her ("With pleasure I shall receive a daughter [*sic*] of [Charles Burney]. Beethoven"), dating from around September 25, 1825, is printed in the *Harmonicon* 3 (1825), 222, and MacArdle & Misch No. 427.

43. Johann Mattheson (1681–1764), *Der vollkommene Kapellmeister* (Hamburg: C. Herold, 1739), and Friedrich Wilhelm Marpurg (1718–1795), *Abhandlung von*

der Fuge, probably the edition by A. Haude and J. C. Spener (Berlin, 1753–1754), or possibly the "Neue Ausgabe," published by Ambrosius Kühnel (Leipzig, 1806), standard texts in Beethoven's era. A missal was a commonplace in any Catholic household.

44. A French-language Bible of this vintage may have been among family possessions dating back to Beethoven's grandfather Ludwig (1712–1773), who was born in Malines and came to Bonn in 1733.

5. The books marked by an asterisk therefore seem not to have been sold at the November 5 auction.

Incipit: Schätzungsprotokoll. . . .

Sources: Jäger-Sunstenau, "Beethoven-Akten," pp. 21–23. First page (through item 18) reproduced in Bory, p. 222. Autograph in the Landesarchiv, Vienna.

484. Captain Bruno de Montluisant[1] to Anton Schindler, Vienna

Iglau; June 9, 1827

Sir,

Court Councillor von Breuning's generally excellent instructions and his more-than-fatherly letters that so kindly and congenially reached me concerning the affairs of Cadet Karl van Beethoven imbued me with the feeling of highest esteem for him. Therefore, your kind letter with the unexpected news of his passing[2] not only awakened the true sympathy that he merited, but also decided me, out of personal esteem for the deceased, not only to redouble my efforts for the welfare of this young person, but to make every exertion to achieve all that is connected with his [Breuning's] splendid objective. The young man, who gives the best indication here of acquiring good judgment, feels the loss deeply, and I certainly with him, since I take an active interest in his destiny.

The guilt that he brought on himself earlier through youthful imprudence is indeed, as you said, very great; but the punishment that now has resulted is even greater. Therefore, I believe that it is necessary, so as not to completely remove all support and lessen his confidence, to forget the past and to exert all effort in support of his resolution to do well. If—out of consideration for his famous uncle, whose friendship you shared—you would therefore not deny the Cadet your support, both this young man and I would be doubly obliged to you if you would support the good choice for his future guardianship; [young] Beethoven will certainly overlook nothing in order to make himself worthy of fatherly attention.[3] With this assurance, I have the honor to be, with all esteem,

Yours sincerely,

de Montluisant
Captain of H[is] H[ighness]
Ludwig['s Infantry]

[P.S.] Since I do not know the address of Doctor v[on] Bach,[4] I ask you most kindly to take care of this matter verbally: the prescribed period for the quarterly allowance of 36 florins monthly has expired, but the allowance of 20 florins monthly, which the Court Councillor effected shortly before his death in a letter to [young] Beethoven, has not been carried out instead.

[Exterior:]
   To Herr Music Director
   Anton von Schindler
   to be delivered at
   Krugerstrasse No. 1014
   Vienna

From Captain Montluisant
concerning Karl van Beethoven

1. Köhler et al., *Konversationshefte*, X, 419, identifies Beethoven's nephew Karl's commanding officer as Chevalier Bruno de Montluisant. His advocacy for the young man is touching, especially since Schindler did not have much use for him. Karl's basic contentment with military life is reflected in his letters to Beethoven of January 13 and March 4, 1827 (Nos. 455 and 464 above).

2. Stephan von Breuning, Karl's guardian and a virtual lifelong friend of the composer's, died of pneumonia on June 4, 1827. He had been ill at the beginning of the year but had seemingly recovered. Schindler-MacArdle, p. 332, implied that stress

in his relations with his superior in the War Ministry also contributed to Breuning's death.

3. Schindler's annotation on the exterior of the letter: "Immediately after Breuning's death I suggested to Dr. Bach that he seek Beethoven's old friend and benefactor, the cloth dealer Joh[ann] Wolfmayer to accept the guardianship; out of reverence for Beethoven he surely would not have refused. Dr. Bach promised to do this. I was not a little astonished to learn that he had accepted for that office a total stranger to Beethoven's case, in the person of Court Secretary Hotschevar, who was recommended through the infamous mother of Beethoven's nephew and heir; the man was supposed to have been distantly related to the mother. Doubtless Dr. Bach, through this choice, rendered good service neither to Beethoven's nephew nor to his case, since he cannot have known the man in the least." Jakob Hotschevar was, in fact, the husband of a stepsister of Frau Johanna van Beethoven's deceased mother and had represented Johanna in her litigation with Beethoven in 1818–1819 (see Thayer-Forbes, p. 707).

4. Johann Baptist von Bach (1779–1847), Beethoven's lawyer.

Incipit: Der allgemeine vortreffliche Auf[trag]. . . .

Sources: Autograph in the Staatsbibliothek zu Berlin–Preussischer Kulturbesitz, Mus. ms. autogr. Beethoven 38, 1; listed in Kalischer, "Beethoven-Autographe," p. 74, and Bartlitz, pp. 190–191.

485. Johann Baptist Streicher to Johann Andreas Stumpff, London

Vienna; June 9, 1827[1]

Herr Stumpff
London

Dear best of friends,

Your estimable letter of April 16 has long lain before me to be answered; but I wanted to write you about the much-discussed Beethoven case in considerable detail and to send only authentic news. To this end I wanted to speak to Court Councillor von Breuning, who concerned himself with the affairs of his deceased friend Beethoven, and would thereby be able to give you the true information. I found Herr von Breuning ill and unable to receive anyone. He became progressively weaker, and now he is dead.[2] I must now restrict myself to sending you the enclosed clippings from the *Wiener Zeitschrift* and to note what else I learned indirectly: Beethoven's *Nachlass* in funds is said to have consisted of 7 stock shares at 1,000 florins each; his pension, instead of the 720 florins that I indicated to you earlier, actually amounted to 1,350 florins annually. On that point, the statement in my last letter needs to be corrected, and thus it appears all the clearer how little Beethoven had cause to seek assistance. Otherwise, I have nothing against the fact that you made the aforementioned letter known,[3] since even today, except for the correction in the sums, I can and wish to write not another word about it. The observations of several doctors can serve to excuse Beethoven and to explain his peculiar steps: many patients with Beethoven's disease are given to becoming extremely anxious, indeed miserly, without any cause to do so. Admittedly, [it would have been better] if the friends who surrounded Beethoven during his last illness had been wiser, and had dissuaded him from his intention; only how little these gentlemen[4] considered it is indeed indicated in that—after they read through your letter about the accusation of the English (as if we Viennese neglected Beethoven and surrendered him to privation, and as if we were informed of his condition)—they could still have the unfortunate idea to take the 200 florins C.M. from the money of the Philharmonic Society as a contribution to Beethoven's funeral, and to apply to the aforementioned Society by way of request about giving this sum![5] The bad side to this case is that no one is becoming involved, nor can become involved in this matter without coming into contact with Messrs. so-and-so.[6] A concert by dilettantes—because of a hasty advertisement as if this were only the beginning of a *series* of similar undertakings and because of the unfavorable time of the performance (4 o'clock in the afternoon)—had very little success, for the receipts, which should have served as a contribution to Beethoven's monument, amounted to only 200 florins. The musicians[7] are insulted that the dilettantes beat them to it, and thereby one could not tell them that they had to do something for the sake of appearances, so they now do nothing for the sake of honor. They are allowing public enthusiasm to grow cold, and it appears that nothing more will be done for Beethoven. [Draft ends here.]

    1. Answers Stumpff's letter of April 16, 1827 (No. 480 above). The source of this material is a rambling draft with several passages added, changed and deleted.

    2. Stephan von Breuning died on June 4, 1827.

3. Streicher to Stumpff, March 28, 1827 (No. 473 above).

4. A preliminary version, crossed out, reads "only how little these [friends] were annoyed at it, how little they understood to forge the right path, was proven by the funeral," and ends at this point, resuming with the word "gentlemen" in the final text. This is probably a veiled reference to Schindler and those allied with him.

5. Another phrase, crossed out, was originally added to conclude this sentence: "as if Beethoven could not have been buried here without foreign assistance!"

6. The German reads "Herren so u. so," plural, probably meaning (as in n. 4, this letter) Schindler and his allies.

7. Streicher's term is "Tonkünstler," probably differentiating professional musicians, and even composers, from the amateurs ("Dilettanten"). See Schindler's letters of April 4 and 11 (Nos. 477 and 478 above), which mention benefit concerts. Aloys Schlosser's hastily prepared biography, *Ludwig van Beethoven: Eine Biographie derselben* (Prague: Buchler, Stephani & Schlosser, 1827, 1828), also gives details about early memorial performances for Beethoven.

Incipit: Lange jeher liegt Ihr schätzbaren Brief. . . .

Sources: Excerpt and discussion in Max Unger, "Neue Kunde vom Totenbette Beethovens," *Deutsche Musiker-Zeitung* 58 (1927), 279; Unger's transcription varies in several places from the autograph draft in the Österreichische Nationalbibliothek, Vienna, 126/78–2.

486. Sebastian Rau to Ignaz Moscheles, London

Vienna; June 17, 1827[1]

Do not accuse me of neglect, dear friend, because I have left you so long without information concerning the state of Beethoven's affairs. I already told you that I put in a claim for the 1,000 florins sent by the Philharmonic Society before he died. However, Court Councillor Breuning, the executor of the will, could not and dared not take any steps in the matter until Beethoven's creditors had been summoned publicly in the usual way. They met on June 5. Upon the advice of Baron von Eskeles, I sent a lawyer friend of mine to the meeting, desiring him to renew my claim, but the "public trustee," Dr. Bach,[2] steadily opposed it. In order to expedite matters and bring them to a successful conclusion, I need a power of attorney from the Philharmonic Society, which, duly certified by the Austrian Embassy, may confer upon me full powers to demand back, by legal process, the 1,000 florins, and to appoint my lawyer friend to settle this business. I propose Dr. [Joseph August] Eltz as a suitable person.

After the meeting, I went to Dr. Bach's, to discuss the matter confidentially, for I could not understand the difficulties which people had thrust in the way of this legitimate claim. He answered me honestly and openly that it was his duty, acting on behalf of the nephew, still a minor, to dispute every counter-claim that interfered with that nephew's interests. But his opinion was that a lawsuit and its heavy attendant expenses could best be avoided if the Philharmonic Society would generously be induced to consider [a portion of] this sum as a contribution to Beethoven's monument, the remainder to be lodged in the House of Eskeles or Rothschild for remittance back to the Society. Working on this premise, Dr. Bach would do his best to ensure this remittance. Baron Eskeles and many experienced jurists find this proposal very acceptible, especially because, since Beethoven's death, one of our most important witnesses, namely Court Councillor von Breuning, has also died. This excellent man caught cold while attending the auction of Beethoven's property, and died three days later.[3] He was the single witness who could identify the 1,000 florins as the same that were sent by the Society. We shall be guided by your next letter as to our future conduct of this affair.[4]

The Eskeles family and the Wimpffens, one and all, send kind regards to you and your wife,[5] as do I,

Your friend,

Rau

1. As steward (or even family tutor) in the Eskeles banking firm, Rau had delivered Beethoven news of the arrival of the £100 (1,000 florins) sent by the Philharmonic Society of London, through Moscheles, ten days before his death. This letter is one of several later reports that Rau made concerning the matter.

2. As *Masse-Curator*, especially after Breuning's death, the lawyer Johann Baptist Bach was administrator of Beethoven's estate.

3. Breuning died on June 4, 1827, thus the day before Beethoven's creditors met. The formal auction was held on November 5, 1827, but Schindler's accounts indicate that considerable dispersal of Beethoven's effects among his friends and relatives had taken place before that time.

4. See Hotschevar's and Rau's letters to Moscheles, both February 10, 1828 (Nos. 490 and 491 below), advising, in the face of potentially expensive legal battles, that the Philharmonic's gift should remain as part of the estate.

5. Charlotte Moscheles, who edited Ignaz Moscheles's diaries and correspondence into a biography after his death. Without her efforts, posterity might not possess complete copies of this letter as well as those of September 14, 1827, and February 10, 1828 (as well as details in several others)—see Nos. 487, 490 and 491 below.

Incipit (English translation): Do not accuse me of neglect. . . .

Sources: Charlotte Moscheles, *Life of Moscheles,* I, 177–179; Smidak, *Moscheles,* pp. 63–64.

487. Anton Schindler to Ignaz Moscheles, London

Vienna; September 14, 1827

My dearest Friend!

I am taking the opportunity to write to you upon the departure of the bearer of this letter, the English Ministry courier Lewisey,[1] and through his kindness to send you the enclosed as a remembrance of our friend Beethoven. In your last letter you asked for a manuscript, and particularly of something already known. *Behold*[2] the conclusion of the Scherzo of the last Symphony![3] The second [piece] is one of those noteworthy pocket books in which Beethoven wrote his sketches, usually in the open air, and then [copied] at home in score. I was fortunate enough to rescue several of these, which have the greatest interest for me. No one will be able to decipher it unless he knows the child of which it is the embryo. This one here contains the sketch of one of his last Quartets, and if you ever hear these Quartets, you will surely know to which one it belongs. A few of his thoughts are very clearly written out.[4] I believe that in this I am giving you proof of my friendship, since at the same time I assure you that, other than you, no one has received, or will ever receive, a similar relic—except for a great deal of money.

The portrait of Beethoven has already been sent to you by Lewinger, as he told me yesterday. I only hope it is the lithograph where he is portrayed as writing, for that is the best; all of the others are worthless. On the sheet on which he is writing it says: *Missa solemnis.*[5] I wanted to send you all of this together through Herr Clementi, whose acquaintance I made at Baden,[6] but I missed his departure, of which I was not informed.

Pixis[7] came here from Paris for two weeks, and returned yesterday, traveling by way of Prague. Spontini left yesterday as well. He is on a recruiting trip and, while he was here, gave my sister an engagement.[8] She and I will probably go to Berlin together next Spring, since the Kärntnertor Theater may be closed again, anyway. At least, it is certain that Barbaja's term as manager ends next April.[9] What will happen afterward is open to question. People speak confidently of Madame Pasta's coming here for next winter.[10] I would very much like to hear from you whether this is true. You can easily find out for me. I would be glad for my sister's sake if she could see and hear such an artist. Perhaps you could kindly enclose a note for me in a letter to Lewinger or Rau, and give me information about this matter. I would like, too, to have acknowledgment of the receipt of these papers, sketches, etc. Tell me how you are, as well as all your family.[11]

The transactions concerning Beethoven grind very slowly because so many obstacles have come up. In June, that most worthy man Court Councillor von Breuning died,[12] and now the administrator of Beethoven's estate[13] has been ill for six weeks. I am now curious about what will happen to the English money.[14] The grave monument ought to be erected very soon. Piringer[15] and several others have had it done. I have heard and seen absolutely nothing about it, for they are doing everything in silence, probably to have the glory all to themselves. In Prague, one Herr Schlosser has published a most miserable biography about Beethoven;[16] here they are likewise announcing a subscription to one that, I hear, Herr Gräffer wants to write;[17] and yet the biographer chosen by Beethoven is Court Councillor Rochlitz in Leipzig, for whom he gave Breuning and me very important papers.[18] Now, however, the newly appointed guardian for Beethoven's nephew[19] has given Breuning's papers to Herr Gräffer, which indeed is monstrous, but will not harm anything because these were for the most part family papers,[20] and I have the most important ones in my hands.

For this time, God be with you!

Your most sincere and obliging friend,

Ant. Schindler

[P.S.] My sister sends her greetings in fondest remembrance.

[Exterior:]
Herr I. Moscheles

Norton Street No. 77
London

1. Lewisey (Levisey) had helped Schindler earlier in his correspondence with England, e.g., by translating the letter to Sir George Smart on March 31 (No. 476 above).

2. The original reads "Ecco," the Italian word having Latin/religious connotations (*Ecce homo*). Indeed Schindler later refers to this material as a "Reliquie."

3. The final two leaves of the Scherzo of the Symphony No. 9, after several interim owners, are now in the Bodmer Collection of the Beethoven-Archiv, Bonn. Most of their odyssey can be traced in Kinsky-Halm, pp. 374–375. The leaves have been "restored" to their rightful place in Peters's facsimile reprint of the autograph (1975), pp. 183–186.

4. The sketch is Bonn B Sk 22 and Mh 96 (16 leaves), containing sketches for the Quartet, Op. 131, and described in Johnson-Tyson-Winter, pp. 438–441. Schindler uses the word *Entwurf* to describe this material. Schindler-Moscheles translates the last sentence as, "Some of the passages [are] written down at full length."

5. Schindler's preferred portrait is doubtless the more famous of the two by Joseph Stieler (1781–1858). The version noted here is probably the lithograph by Dürck, published by Artaria in Vienna in 1826. See Theodor Frimmel, *Beethovens Äussere Erscheinung*, vol. 1 of *Beethoven Studien* (Munich: Georg Müller, 1905), pp. 96–97; and Carl Friedrich Whistling and Friedrich Hofmeister, *Handbuch der musikalischen Literatur* (Leipzig, 1827), p. 67.

6. Muzio Clementi (1752–1832), making his last visit to the Continent.

7. Johann Peter Pixis (1788–1874) had moved from Mannheim to Vienna in 1806 and remained there until 1823. He then went to Paris, where he became a successful piano teacher.

8. Gaspare Spontini (1774–1851) had been *Generalmusikdirektor* in Berlin since 1819. Schindler's sister Marie (married name Egloff, died in 1882) was a singer, active in Vienna, Pest, Berlin and Aachen (Köhler et al., *Konversationshefte*, IX, n. 732).

9. After several seasons of managing the Kärntnertor Theater in Vienna, Domenico Barbaja (1778–1841) returned to Milan and Naples in 1826, while also maintaining his Viennese activities through the spring of 1828.

10. Soprano Giuditta Pasta (1797–1865) had recently sung in London, Paris and at home in Italy. She would appear in Vienna early in 1829.

11. Ley omitted the foregoing paragraph, included in Charlotte Moscheles and in Smidak.

12. Stephan von Breuning died on June 4.

13. Lawyer Johann Baptist Bach.

14. The £100 from the Philharmonic Society of London.

15. Ferdinand Piringer (1780–1829), high-ranking Viennese official and musical amateur.

16. Johann Aloys Schlosser, *Ludwig van Beethoven: Eine Biographie derselben* (Prague: Buchler, Stephani & Schlosser, 1827, 1828). The first printing is dated June 1827; the second (enlarged somewhat) dates from 1828. On the whole, this hastily written biography is based on unreliable earlier material; pp. 69–76, however, contain details about concerts and memorial services in Vienna and Prague (April–July 1827) difficult to locate elsewhere.

17. Anton Gräffer (1784–1852), employee of Artaria & Co. For details about the projected "Viennese biography," see Maynard Solomon, "Beethoven's Tagebuch of 1812–1818," in *Beethoven Studies 3*, ed. Alan Tyson (Cambridge: Cambridge University Press, 1982), pp. 194–196; revised in his *Beethoven Essays* (Cambridge, Mass.: Harvard University Press, 1988), pp. 237–240.

18. Friedrich Rochlitz. For a disappointing turn of events in this respect, see Rochlitz to Schindler, September 18, 1827 (No. 488 below).

19. Jakob (Jacob) Hotschevar was appointed guardian on June 26, 1827 (Frimmel, *Beethoven Studien* II [Munich: Georg Müller, 1906], 181).

20. These seemingly included the *Tagebuch* (diary) of 1812–1818, the Heiligenstadt Testament of 1802 and the *Stammbuch* (autograph book) of 1792 (the last of these included in the present collection). See Solomon, "Tagebuch," pp. 193–194 (rev., pp. 237–239).

Incipit: Ich ergreife die Gelegenheit mit dem Überbringer. . . .

Sources: Charlotte Moscheles, *Life of Moscheles*, I, 179–181; Smidak, *Moscheles*, pp. 64–65. The first half translated into English in Schindler-Moscheles, pp. 278–279. Fuller German version (although missing a paragraph) in Ley, *Beethoven als Freund*, pp. 243–245, indicating that the autograph was then in the Wegeler family collection.

488. Friedrich Rochlitz to Anton Schindler, Vienna

Leipzig; September 18, 1827

Dear Sir,

Your letter of the 12th of this month,[1] which arrived yesterday, gave me a great deal of pleasure, and I thank you obligingly for it. From time immemorial, the eccentricities and rough edges in our admired Beethoven's nature have not concealed the splendid and noble in his character from me; and if, when I visited Vienna in 1822, I met him only a few times — although with frankness and trust — this was only because of the malady that oppressed him and made every conversation so difficult.[2] This, in conjunction with happy acknowledgment of his genius and great merit as an artist, was also the reason that I followed the progress of his spirit and inner life, insofar as they were reflected in his works, from his youth until his death, to the best of my ability. And since I took every opportunity, from time to time, to learn some reliable information about his external life, I considered myself, when he died, not entirely incapable of becoming his biographer; which I resolved to do, and indeed to designate Beethoven's life, along with Maria Weber's, as the principal articles of the third volume of my book *Für Freunde der Tonkunst*.[3] Now, in addition, comes your promise to assist me with materials, and the wish of Beethoven himself that you communicated.[4] Judge for yourself, from all of this, whether I might be inclined to accept your invitation as well as those of various other friends of Beethoven's! It is all the sadder for me, then, that I cannot do so. Of late, I have paid rather dearly for the earlier years of my life, spent in almost unceasing exertion. After two years of pining away, I had decided, upon the advice of my doctors, finally to undergo radical treatment and invigoration during the entire spring and summer just past. I have been back for two weeks, having found, instead of relief, a life-endangering illness from which I can never recover. Since I am now forced almost completely to alter my previous lifestyle, and since the most important of these alterations is that I sit and work far less, I will therefore be neither compelled nor enticed into undertaking any new, significant projects. And so, of necessity, I must also refuse the fulfillment of that wish that is yours as well as my own.[5] My desire to do so remains and will always remain, but it would be unfair to you and the Manes of our excellent Beethoven if, because of this desire, I promised you something about which I had the least doubt, and thereby hindered the project because another who was more capable did not carry it out. I cannot tell you how sorry I am to give you this answer, but I must submit to that which is necessary.

Accept once more my thanks for your confidence in me, and the assurance of my great esteem, with which I am

Yours most truly,

Rochlitz

[Exterior postmark:]
  Leipzig, September 18, 1827

Herr Music Director Schindler
Vienna
Krugerstrasse No. 1014
3d floor[6]

1. Schindler's letter to Rochlitz (1769–1842) seems not to have survived. As editor of the *Allgemeine musikalische Zeitung* from its founding in 1798 until 1818, and as a contributor thereafter, Rochlitz had ample opportunity to write about Beethoven and his music.

2. Maynard Solomon doubts whether Rochlitz ever met Beethoven in 1822. See "Beethoven's Creative Process: A Two-Part Invention," in his *Beethoven Essays* (Cambridge, Mass.: Harvard University Press, 1988), pp. 135–138, 328–329.

3. Rochlitz's collections of essays appeared in four volumes (Leipzig: Cnobloch) between 1824 and 1832; the essay on Beethoven appeared in vol. 4 (1832).

4. Solomon, as cited in n. 2, this letter, likewise believes that Schindler fabricated Beethoven's deathbed request to disenfranchise Karl Holz as the potential authorized biographer.

5. Schindler seems not to have taken Rochlitz's refusal at face value, for he inquired again, with the same results. Rochlitz's second refusal, dated October 3, 1827, is quoted in Schindler (1860), p. xx, and Schindler-MacArdle, p. 33, and will not otherwise be included in the present collection.

6. American fourth floor.

Incipit: Ew. Wohlgeb. Gestern eingegangenes Schreiben. . . .

Sources: Extensive excerpts in Schindler (1860), pp. xix–xx, and Schindler-Mac-Ardle, p. 32. Autographs of this and Rochlitz's letter of October 3, 1827, in the Staatsbibliothek zu Berlin–Preussischer Kulturbesitz, Mus. ms. autogr. Beethoven 38, 4; listed in Kalischer, "Beethoven-Autographe," p. 74, and Bartlitz, p. 191.

489. Jakob Hotschevar[1] *to Prince Lobkowitz's Chief Cashier*[2]

Vienna; October 6, 1827

Receipt

for 66 f[lorins] 53 kr[euzer] *C.M.*, that is sixty-six gulden and 53½ kreuzer *Conventions Münze*, which the appointed guardian of the minor Karl van Beethoven, nephew and universal testimentary heir of the composer Ludwig van Beethoven, who died on March 26, 1827, as a back payment of the pension or subsistence granted the latter, of 700 florins *W.W.* or 280 florins

C.M. annually for the period from January 1, 1827, as the back payment day, until and including March 26, 1827, the day of Ludwig van Beethoven's death, at 2 months and 26 days, and thus 167 florins 13⅓ kreuzer *W.W.* or 66 florins 53½ kreuzer *C.M.* from Prince Lobkowitz's Chief Cashier in Vienna, in accordance with the Magistrat's Legitimation Decree, dated September 14, 1827, No. 43990/38, duly received today in cash, and hereby attested.

Vienna, October 6, 1827

> Jakob Hotschevar
> I.R. Court Secretary
> Guardian of Karl van Beethoven

(that is, 66 florins 53½ kreuzer, *C.M.*)

    1. Jakob Hotschevar was the husband of a stepsister of Frau Johanna van Beethoven's mother and had represented Johanna in her litigation with Beethoven in 1818–1819 (see Thayer-Forbes, p. 707). After the death of Stephan von Breuning on June 4, 1827, Hotschevar was appointed Beethoven's nephew Karl's guardian on June 26.

    2. This receipt represents the final installment of the Lobkowitz portion of Beethoven's annual stipend, begun in 1809 and continued after Prince Franz Joseph Lobkowitz's death in 1816. Similar documents must have existed to confirm the final payments from Archduke Rudolph and from Prince Kinsky's estate as well.

    Incipit: Quittung, über 66 f 53 xr K.M. . . .

    Sources: Plevka, "Vztah Beethoven," pp. 331–339; Gutiérrez-Denhoff, " 'o Unseeliges Dekret': Beethovens Rente," pp. 132 (facsimile), 134 (transcription), 145 (listing). Autograph in the Státni oblastní v Litoměřicích, pobočka Žitenice.

1828

490. *Jakob Hotschevar¹ to Ignaz Moscheles, London*

Vienna; February 10, 1828

Herr Ignaz Moscheles
Composer of Music, and
Member of the Philharmonic Society of London

Dear Sir,

After the death of Herr von Breuning, which took place in Vienna on June 4, 1827, I was appointed by the proper authority in that city the legal guardian of Karl van Beethoven, a minor, the nephew and heir of the composer Ludwig van Beethoven, who died — alas! prematurely for the world of art — on March 26 last year. I undertook this heavy responsibility solely for the purpose of trying to lead this highly gifted youth back to the paths of virtue, from which (I say with sorrow) he has to some extent strayed. I did it for the sake of his great uncle, who had befriended him since his childhood, although he had not always availed himself of the most discreet means to insure his welfare. I have yet another reason. The young man has expressed great confidence in me, and has conducted himself with the strictest propriety since he entered upon the military profession as a cadet in an Imperial infantry regiment.

Judging from the legal documents before me, Beethoven's small estate (after deducting sums for payment of some heavy debts, expenses of his illness and funeral) consists of little more than 8,000 florins in Austrian paper money. I am at the point of negotiating the legal registration of this property, because according to the terms of the will my ward is only to receive the lifetime interest from the property, while the capital reverts to his heirs, unless otherwise specified in the will, to whom the property will legally be secured.

In addition to several other debts legally registered and publicly announced at the general meeting of Ludwig van Beethoven's creditors, there is a further claim of 1,000 florins, Austrian money, put forth by the Viennese lawyer Dr. [Joseph August] Eltz, as the representative and nominee of your friend Herr Rau; he is also empowered to act on behalf of the Philharmonic Society of London. This sum is said to be identified as the money sent some time ago, during Beethoven's lifetime, as a gift in the form of financial aid, by the Philharmonic Society of London.

Because it is necessary, before the legal settlement of the testator's property, to prove that this claim on the part of Dr. Eltz has either been settled or withdrawn, and because I, acting as guardian, am most anxious to settle this matter as soon as possible, I write to you, Sir, as one of Beethoven's most intimate and respected friends, as the representative of the magnanimous Philharmonic Society of London, and as our fellow countryman whom we delight to honor, although living far from us. Lastly, in the name of a twenty-one-year-old youth, full of talent and promise, who, when his uncle died, lost his support and is left destitute. I beg you, Sir, to take the necessary steps to induce the Society, which demonstrated its generosity in the past, to withdraw their claim, even assuming it to be a perfectly justified one, through Herr Rau and his representative Dr. Eltz; and that they [the Society] empower Herr Rau to notify the proper authorities concerning their withdrawal of this claim.

I am deeply concerned for the welfare of this most promising youth who, by the death of his uncle Ludwig van Beethoven, who idolized him, has lost his only support. I address myself very confidently to the noble Philharmonic Society, trusting that they will not request the return of the sum given to assist Beethoven — money presented so long ago[2] that it is impossible to say that the identical sum still exists, undisturbed. I would further request the Society, through you, not to reduce further the small sum with which I am to support my ward, for I can hardly hope to get more than 400 florins in the form of annual interest.[3] According to the accounts, more than 1,000 florins have been expended in defraying the expenses of the testator's illness and funeral, in addition to other debts. Thus you can fully believe that I feel great difficulty in keeping my ward free from want until he is fortunate enough to receive his commission as an officer — a position which, in the absence of other support, would actually still leave him short of funds.

For these reasons, Sir, I shall be excused in expressing a hope that the Philharmonic Society, as well as Beethoven's old friends and admirers, will honor his memory by befriending the nephew who very much needs their assistance. I venture to offer my services, and pledge myself to invest any sum as advantageously as I can.

I cannot bring myself to think that the Philharmonic Society would ever persist in enforcing their claim; nor (because the law does not permit such a gift to be revoked, even if it can be identified) do I doubt for a moment that the judge would give a decision in favor of the heir. Moreover, the legal expenses and the delay would seriously embarrass me. The sum left is so small, and I must pay legal expenses, legacy taxes, etc.

Finally, I think I can explain to the Society why Ludwig van Beethoven complained of poverty before his death and asked the Society for their assistance. It was because he considered his nephew as his son and ward, and thought it his duty to provide for his support. Doubtless this is why he looked upon the seven shares of the Austrian National Bank not as his own property, but as that of his favored nephew, for whose support he designated them in his will. It was a matter of religious feeling with him, and he adhered to it faithfully, that the burden of maintaining his poor nephew, for whom he would have sacrificed his own life, imposed such a duty upon him.

I may safely say that the noblest sacrifice to the Manes of Beethoven, and the fulfillment of his fondest wish, for which he labored wholeheartedly during his lifetime, would be the securing of his poor nephew from future hardship. If I myself were in more fortunate circumstances, and if I did not have duties to my own family, I would willingly take the obligation upon myself.

I trust, Sir, that you will recognize the honesty and purity of intention with which I write you, and that you will excuse me all the more readily because I can assure you that, out of pure affection for the great man's nephew, I have undertaken the duties and the cares of a guardian. Herr Rau will give you all the information you might wish concerning this point, as well as about my personal character.

Hoping that I shall soon receive a kind and favorable reply, sent to me directly or through Herr Rau, and commending myself and the cause of my ward to your kind consideration, I remain, Sir, with great respect,

Your most humble servant,

Jacob Hotschevar
I.R. Secretary

Alter Fleischmarkt, No. 695

1. Jacob (Jakob) Hotschevar had been appointed Beethoven's nephew Karl's guardian on June 26, 1827 (Frimmel, *Beethoven Studien* II [Munich: Georg Müller,

1906], 181). This official letter was accompanied by Rau's more personal letter of the same date (No. 491 below).

2. Actually, the money had arrived about March 17, 1827, barely nine days before Beethoven's death.

3. On the basis of an estate valued at 8,000 florins, Hotschevar was evidently reckoning on an annual interest rate of roughly 5 percent.

Incipit (English translation): After the death of Herr von Breuning. . . .

Sources: Charlotte Moscheles, *Life of Moscheles,* I, 182–186; Smidak, *Moscheles,* pp. 65–67.

491. Sebastian Rau to Ignaz Moscheles, London

Vienna; February 10, 1828[1]

Dear Friend,

I send you herewith a letter from the administrator of Beethoven's estate, from which you will see that the legal proceedings are drawing to an end. I was called upon to give an official explanation about the 1,000 florins presented by the Philharmonic Society. Not having received further instructions from you, however, and unwilling to take responsibility myself without them, I requested a delay until I learned your wishes on the matter. The enclosed letter will give you all the facts.

Between us, if you can manage to negotiate the surrender of the 1,000 florins, we shall be spared a great deal of unpleasantness and perhaps even a lawsuit. Dr. [Joseph August] Eltz and Baron Eskeles also think that the 1,000 florins found at Beethoven's death would be identified only with great difficulty, especially since Court Councillor Breuning, who oversaw the inventory, is now dead. Should the money, however, unexpectedly be reclaimed, a power of attorney must be sent to Dr. Eltz by the Philharmonic Society, in order that he might prove his legal claims, *at the expense of the Society.* It is possible, however, that the legal process might eat up the entire sum. Please give me a definite answer soon.[2]

The Eskeles family, the Wimpffens, Ephraims, etc., are well and send kind regards to you and your wife,[3] as do I,

Your friend,

Rau

1. Accompanied Hotschevar's official letter to Moscheles, February 10, 1828 (No. 490 above).

2. On receipt of these letters, Moscheles conferred with the directors of the Philharmonic Society, who then decided to abandon their claim to the £100 (1,000 florins) sent to the dying Beethoven less than a year before. Charlotte Moscheles commented: "The whole business and comments about it gave [Moscheles] a great deal of annoyance and trouble. . . . It was enough for him to have been called 'friend' by Beethoven himself, and to have lightened, in however humble a way, the sufferings of his last days."

3. Charlotte Moscheles.

Incipit (English translation): I send you herewith a letter. . . .

Sources: Charlotte Moscheles, *Life of Moscheles*, I, 186–187; Smidak, *Moscheles*, p. 67; Schindler-Moscheles, pp. 279–280.

492. Sebastian Rau[1] to the Magistrat, Vienna

Vienna; April 10, 1828

Honorable Magistrat!

At the prescribed convocation [of creditors] concerning the estate of Herr Ludwig van Beethoven, I submitted a claim on behalf of the Philharmonic Society of London for 1,000 florins C.M. As a result of the letter from Herr Moscheles directed to Herr Hotschevar,[2] as guardian of the minor Karl van Beethoven, nephew and heir to the aforementioned testator, the Philharmonic Society withdraws this application, and therefore, in order not to delay the proceedings, I hereby withdraw the above application for the 1,000 florins C.M., [providing] that the previously noted letter from Herr Moscheles be duly preserved by the guardian Herr Hotschevar among the documents of the Beethoven proceedings. I therefore request that the honorable Magistrat deign to accept this declaration of withdrawal and notify the [estate's] trustee[3] of this action.[4]

Sebastian Rau

1. Of the several surviving letters and documents from Rau or mentioning him, this letter alone provides his given name. See Rau to Moscheles, March 17, 1827 (No. 468 above, n. 1).

2. The letter from Moscheles to Hotschevar is not present in the archival materials, but its contents may be inferred from the present sentence and the two letters from Hotschevar and Rau to Moscheles, dated February 10, 1828 (Nos. 490 and 491 above).

3. Lawyer Johann Baptist Bach.

4. On April 30, 1828, the Lower Austrian tax assessor issued a statement indicating that the Beethoven estate, valued at 8,738 florins, 58½ kreuzer C.M., would be taxed at 10 percent, resulting in an inheritance tax of 873 gulden (florins), 45 kreuzer C.M. As trustee of the estate and the minor Karl van Beethoven, Dr. Bach was directed to pay the assessed sum by the end of May 1828.

Incipit: Ich habe bei der angeordneten Convocationstagsatzung. . . .

Sources: Jäger-Sunstenau, pp. 30–31. Documents in the Landesarchiv, Vienna: H.-A.-Akten, Persönlichk., 1/2, fols. 136 and 138.

BIBLIOGRAPHY

Allgemeine Musik-Zeitung 27 (1900), 493–494. S.v. "Berichte."

Albrecht, Theodore, and Elaine Schwensen. "More Than Just *Peanuts*: Evidence for December 16 as Beethoven's Birthday." *Beethoven Newsletter* 3 (Winter 1988), 49, 60–63.

Altmann, Wilhelm. "Zu Beethovens 'Fidelio' und 'Melusine.'" *Die Musik* 3, no. 2 (March 1904), 433–437.

Amelung, Heinz. "Beethoven und die Brentanos." *Rheinischer Beobachter* 2 (1923), 501–503.

Anderson, Emily, ed. *The Letters of Beethoven.* 3 vols. London: Macmillan; New York: St. Martin's, 1961. Reprint, New York: W. W. Norton, 1985.

Barber, Elinore L. "Beethoven Writes to the Imperial Prussian Embassy in 1823, Concerning 'A Large Solemn Mass.'" *Bach* 7, no. 4 (1976), 23–25.

Bárdos, K. "Eine späte Quittung Beethovens in Ungarn." *Studia Musicologica* 16, nos. 1–4 (1974), 257–259.

Bartha, Dénes, ed. *Joseph Haydn: Gesammelte Briefe und Aufzeichnungen.* Kassel: Bärenreiter, 1965.

[Bartlitz.] Bartlitz, Eveline. *Die Beethoven-Sammlung in der Musikabteilung der Deutschen Staatsbibliothek: Verzeichnis—Autographe, Abschriften, Dokumente, Briefe.* Berlin: Deutsche Staatsbibliothek, 1970.

Bartlitz, Eveline. "Ein aufgefundener Beethoven-Brief." In *Zu Beethoven 2: Aufsätze und Dokumente,* ed. Harry Goldschmidt, pp. 10–13. Berlin: Verlag Neue Musik, 1984.

Beethoven, Ludwig van. *Sechs Bagatellen für Klavier, Op. 126: Faksimile . . . mit Kommentar.* Edited by Sieghard Brandenburg. 2 vols. Bonn: Beethoven-Haus, 1984.

"Beethoven et son éditeur Steiner." By O.Bn. *Ménestrel* 66 (1900), 269–270.

"Beethoven und Clemens Brentano." *Deutsche Musiker-Zeitung* 60 (1929), 352.

Bekker, Paul. *Beethoven.* Large-format, illus. ed. Berlin: Schuster & Loeffler, 1911.

Biberhofer, Raoul. "Beethoven und das Theater." In *Ein Wiener Beethoven-Buch,* ed. Alfred Orel, pp. 108–131. Vienna: Gerlach & Wiedling, 1921.

"Ein bisher unbekanntes Beethoven-Autograph." *Neue Freie Presse* (Vienna), August 17, 1900.

Blum, Klaus. *Musikfreunde und Musici: Musikleben in Bremen seit der Aufklärung.* Tutzing: Hans Schneider, 1975.

Böckh, Franz Heinrich. *Merkwürdigkeiten der Haupt- und Residenz-Stadt Wien und ihrer nächsten Umgebungen: Ein Handbuch.* . . . Vienna: Böckh, 1823.

Bory, Robert. *Ludwig van Beethoven: His Life and Work in Pictures.* French-, German- and English-language eds. Zürich: Atlantis, 1960.

Brandenburg, Sieghard. "Beethovens politische Erfahrungen in Bonn." In *Beethoven: Zwischen Revolution und Restauration,* ed. Helga Lühning and Sieghard Brandenburg, pp. 3–50. Bonn: Beethoven-Haus, 1989.

Brandenburg, Sieghard. "Beethovens Streichquartette op. 18." In *Beethoven und Böhmen: Beiträge zu Biographie und Wirkungsgeschichte Beethovens,* ed. Sieghard Brandenburg and Martella Gutiérrez-Denhoff, pp. 259–309. Bonn: Beethoven-Haus, 1988.

Braubach, Max. "Beethovens Abschied von Bonn: Das rheinische Erbe." In *Beethoven-Symposion, Wien, 1970: Bericht,* ed. Erich Schenk, pp. 25–41. Vienna: Hermann Böhlaus Nachfolger, 1971.

Braubach, Max, ed. *Die Stammbücher Beethovens und der Babette Koch.* Bonn: Beethovenhaus, 1970.

Brenneis, Clemens. "Das Fischhof-Manuskript: Zur Frühgeschichte der Beethoven-Biographik." In *Zu Beethoven: Aufsätze und Annotationen,* ed. Harry Goldschmidt, pp. 90–116. Berlin: Verlag Neue Musik, 1979.

Brenneis, Clemens. "Versuch einer Rekonstruktion des Skizzenbuches Landsberg 5." In *Zu Beethoven 3: Aufsätze und Dokumente,* ed. Harry Goldschmidt, pp. 83–112. Berlin: Verlag Neue Musik, 1988.

Breuning, Gerhard von. *Aus dem Schwarzspanierhause: Erinnerungen an L. van Beethoven aus meiner Jugendzeit.* Vienna: C. Rosner, 1874.

[Breuning-Solomon.] Breuning, Gerhard von. *Memories of Beethoven: From the House of the Black-Robed Spaniards.* Translated and edited by Maynard Solomon. New York: Cambridge University Press, 1992.

Brilliant, Ira. "Music Auction Report . . . Stargardt/Haus der Bücher, Basel, September 19, 1992." *Beethoven Newsletter* (San Jose) 8, no. 1 (Spring 1993), 26–27.

Chrysander, Friedrich. "Beethoven's Verbindung mit Birchall und Stumpff in London." *Jahrbücher für musikalische Wissenschaft* 1 (1863), 429–452. Periodical reprint, Hildesheim: Georg Olms, 1966.

Comini, Alessandra. *The Changing Image of Beethoven.* New York: Rizzoli, 1987.

Cooper, Barry, ed. *The Beethoven Compendium.* New York: Thames & Hudson, 1991.

Cooper, Barry. *Beethoven's Folksong Settings: Chronology, Sources, Style.* Oxford: Clarendon, 1994.

Cox, H. Bertram, and C. L. E. Cox, eds. *Leaves from the Journals of Sir George Smart.* London: Longmans, Green, 1907. Reprint, New York: Da Capo, 1971.

Deutsch, Otto Erich. *Franz Schubert: Sein Leben in Bildern.* 2d ed. Munich: Georg Müller, 1913.

Deutsch, Otto Erich. "Zu Beethovens grossen Akademien von 1824." *Österreichische Musikzeitschrift* 19 (September 1964), 426–429.

Dorfmüller, Kurt, ed. *Beiträge zur Beethoven-Bibliographie: Studien und Materialen zum Werkverzeichnis von Kinsky-Halm.* Munich: G. Henle, 1978.

Drouot Richelieu (Laurin, Guilloux, Buffetaud, Cailleur). [*Auction Catalog.*] Paris, May 10, 1995.

Drouot Rive Gauche (Pierre Berès). *Autographes Musicaux.* Auction catalog. Paris, June 20, 1977.

Eismann, Georg. *Robert Schumann: A Biography in Words and Pictures.* Translated by Lena Jaeck. Leipzig: VEB, 1964.

Fecker, Adolf. "Die Beethoven-Handschriften des Kestner-Museums in Hannover." *Österreichische Musikzeitschrift* 26 (July 1971), 366–379; (November 1971), 639–641.

Fishman, Nathan. "Dva Avtografa Beethovena." *Sovetskaia Muzika* 8 (August 1958), 94–98.

Fishman, Nathan. "Obschii obzor i ukazateli vsekh avtografov Beethovena, viavlennikh i uchtennikh v SSSR na 1 yanvaria 1980 goda." In *Etudi i ocherki po Beethoveniane,* pp. 119–143. Moscow: Muzika, 1982. [For a German translation, see Fishman (1988).]

Fishman, Nathan. "Verzeichnis aller in der UdSSR ermittelten und registrierten Beethoven-Autographe — Stand: 1. Januar 1980." Translated by Christoph Hellmund. In *Zu Beethoven 3: Aufsätze und Dokumente,* ed.

Harry Goldschmidt, pp. 113–140. Berlin: Verlag Neue Musik, 1988. [Translation of Fishman (1982).]

Fojtíkova, Jana, and Tomislav Volek. "Die Beethoveniana der Lobkowitz-Musiksammlung und ihre Kopisten." In *Beethoven und Böhmen: Beiträge zu Biographie und Wirkungsgeschichte Beethovens,* ed. Sieghard Brandenburg and Martella Gutiérrez-Denhoff, pp. 219–258. Bonn: Beethoven-Haus, 1988.

Frimmel, Theodor. "Aus Beethovens Kreisen." *Beethoven-Jahrbuch* 2 (1909), 321–328.

Frimmel, Theodor. *Beethoven-Handbuch.* 2 vols. Leipzig: Breitkopf & Härtel, 1926.

Frimmel, Theodor. "Beethovenstellen aus zeitgenössischen Briefen im Besitz des Herrn Universitätsprofessors Dr. Gustav Riehl." *Beethoven-Forschung* 3, no. 10 (1925), 48–51.

[Frimmel, Theodor (?).] "Kaiser Franz und Beethovens Neffe." *Neue Freie Presse* (Vienna), December 25, 1907, p. 13.

Frimmel, Theodor. "Neue Beethovenstudien." *Deutsche Kunst- und Musik-Zeitung* 22, no. 2 (January 15, 1895), 17–18.

Frimmel, Theodor. "Ein ungedruckter Brief Zmeskalls an Beethoven." In his *Beethoven-Studien,* II, 83–90 (Munich: Georg Müller, 1906).

Frimmel, Theodor. "Ein unveröffentlichter Brief Hans Georg Nägelis an Beethoven." In his *Beethoven-Studien,* II, 121–134 (1906).

Frimmel, Theodor. "Verzeichnisse." *Beethoven-Jahrbuch* 1 (1908), 110–111.

Frimmel, Theodor, and Edward Speyer. "Verzeichnis. . . ." *Beethoven-Jahrbuch* 2 (1909), 310–312.

Fürstenau, M. "Zwei noch unbekannte Briefe Beethoven's." *Allgemeine musikalische Zeitung,* n.s., 1, no. 36 (September 2, 1863), 618–620, 631–633.

Geiser, Samuel. *Beethoven und die Schweiz.* Zürich: Rotapfel, 1976.

Gerstinger, Hans, ed. *Ludwig van Beethovens Stammbuch.* Facsimile. 2 vols. Bielefeld and Leipzig: Velhagen & Klasing, 1927.

Glossy, Karl. "Ein Gedenkblatt." *Österreichische Rundschau* 5 (1906), 131–133.

[Goethe, Johann Wolfgang von.] *Goethe und seine Freunde im Briefwechsel.* Edited by Richard M. Meyer. Berlin: Georg Bondi, 1911.

Goethe-Briefe mit Einleitungen und Erläuterungen. Edited by Philipp Stein. 8 vols. Berlin: Otto Eisner, 1905.

Goethes Briefe. Edited by Bodo Morawe. 4 vols. Hamburg: Christian Wegner, 1965.

Grasberger, Franz, ed. *Beethoven, the Man and His Time*. Exhibition catalog. University of Guelph, May 3–May 31, 1970.

Gutiérrez-Denhoff, Martella. " 'o Unseeliges Dekret': Beethovens Rente von Fürst Lobkowitz, Fürst Kinsky und Erzherzog Rudolph." In *Beethoven und Böhmen: Beiträge zu Biographie und Wirkungsgeschichte Beethovens*, ed. Sieghard Brandenburg and Martella Gutiérrez-Denhoff, pp. 91–145. Bonn: Beethoven-Haus, 1988.

Hadden, J. Cuthbert. *George Thomson, the Friend of Burns: His Life and Correspondence*. London: John C. Nimmo, 1898.

Hanson, Alice M. *Musical Life in Biedermeier Vienna*. Cambridge: Cambridge University Press, 1985.

Harmonicon. [See Schultz.]

Hase, Oskar von, and Hellmuth von Hase. *Breitkopf & Härtel: Gedenkschrift und Arbeitsbericht*. 3 vols. 1917. Reprint, 4 vols., Wiesbaden: Breitkopf & Härtel, 1968.

Hauschild, H. M. *Alte Bremer*. Bremen: H. M. Hauschild, 1905.

Hellinghaus, Otto, ed. *Beethoven (Bibliothek wertvoller Denkwürdigkeiten)*. Freiburg: Herder, 1922.

Helms, Marianne, and Martin Staehelin. "Bewegungen von Beethoven-Quellen, 1973–1979." *Beethoven-Jahrbuch* 10 (1983), 331–357.

Hess, Willy. "Ein Beethoven-Autograph in Kanada (Kanon 'Freu dich des Lebens,' WoO 195)." In *Beiträge zur Beethoven-Bibliographie: Studien und Materialien zum Werkverzeichnis von Kinsky-Halm*, ed. Kurt Dorfmüller, pp. 113–114. Munich: G. Henle Verlag, 1978.

Hess, Willy. *Verzeichnis der nicht in der Gesamtausgabe veröffentlichten Werke Ludwig van Beethovens*. Wiesbaden: Breitkopf & Härtel, 1957.

Hill, Cecil. *Ferdinand Ries: Briefe und Dokumente*. Bonn: Ludwig Röhrscheid, 1982.

Hilmar, Rosemary. *Der Musikverlag Artaria & Comp.: Geschichte und Probleme der Druckproduktion*. Tutzing: Hans Schneider, 1977.

Hitzig, Wilhelm. "Die Briefe Gottfried Christoph Härtels an Beethoven." *Zeitschrift für Musikwissenschaft* 9 (March 1927), 321–340.

Homburg, Herfried. *Louis Spohr: Bilder und Dokumente seiner Zeit*. Kassel: Erich Röth, 1968.

Hunziker, Rudolf. "Hans Georg Nägeli: Einige Beiträge zu seiner Biographie." *Schweizerische Musikzeitung* 76, no. 22 (November 15, 1936), 601–640.

International Autographs. *Autograph Letters, Manuscripts and Documents.* Catalog no. 18. New York, 1967.

Jäger-Sunstenau, Hanns. "Beethoven-Akten im Wiener Landesarchiv." In *Beethoven-Studien: Festgabe der Österreichischen Akademie der Wissenschaften, zum 200. Geburtstag von Ludwig van Beethoven,* ed. by Erich Schenk, pp. 11–36. Vienna: Hermann Böhlaus, 1970.

Jäger-Sunstenau, Hanns. "Beethoven als Bürger der Stadt Wien." In *Colloquium Amicorum, Joseph Schmidt-Görg zum 70. Geburtstag,* ed. by Siegfried Kross and Hans Schmidt, pp. 132–145. Bonn: Beethoven-Haus, 1967.

Jansen, E. Gustav. "Briefwechsel Beethoven's und Schumann's mit Cplm. G. Wiedebein." *Neue Zeitschrift für Musik* 76 (June 11, 1880), 69–70; (June 18, 1880), 279; (June 25, 1880), 289–290; (July 9, 1880), 308–310; (July 23, 1880), 328–329.

Johnson, Douglas. "Music for Prague and Berlin: Beethoven's Concert Tour of 1796." In *Beethoven, Performers and Critics: International Beethoven Congress, Detroit, 1977,* ed. Robert Winter and Bruce Carr, pp. 24–40. Detroit: Wayne State University Press, 1980.

[Johnson-Tyson-Winter.] Johnson, Douglas, Alan Tyson and Robert Winter. *The Beethoven Sketchbooks: History, Reconstruction, Inventory.* Berkeley and Los Angeles: University of California Press, 1985.

Kagan, Susan. *Archduke Rudolph, Beethoven's Patron, Pupil and Friend: His Life and Music.* Stuyvesant, N.Y.: Pendragon, 1988.

Kalischer, Alfred Christlieb. "Die Beethoven-Autographe der Königl. Bibliothek zu Berlin." *Monatshefte für Musik-Geschichte* 28 (1896), 41–53, 57–67, 73–80.

[Kalischer.] Kalischer, Alfred Christlieb. *Beethovens Sämtliche Briefe.* 5 vols. Berlin: Schuster & Loeffler, 1906–1908. 2d rev. ed. Vol. 1, ed. Alfred Christlieb Kalischer, 1909. Vol. 2, ed. Theodor Frimmel, 1910–1911. Berlin: Schuster & Loeffler.

[Kalischer-Shedlock.] Kalischer, Alfred Christlieb. *Beethoven's Letters: A Critical Edition.* Translated by John S. Shedlock. 2 vols. London: J. M. Dent; New York: E. P. Dutton, 1909. Reprint, Freeport, N.Y.: Books for Libraries Press, 1969.

Kalischer, Alfred Christlieb. "Clemens Brentanos Beziehungen zu Beethoven." *Euphorion* 2 (1895), Ergänzungsheft no. 1, 36–64. Reprinted in his *Beethoven und seine Zeitgenossen*, vol. 4, *Beethoven und Wien* (Berlin: Schuster & Loeffler, 1909–1910), pp. 215–248.

Kapp, Julius. *Carl Maria von Weber: Eine Biographie*. New ed. Berlin: Max Hesse, 1944.

Karbusicky, Vladimir. *Beethovens Brief "An die unsterbliche Geliebte."* Wiesbaden: Breitkopf & Härtel, 1977.

[Kastner.] Kastner, Emerich, ed. *Ludwig van Beethovens sämtliche Briefe: Nebst einer Auswahl von Briefen an Beethoven*. Leipzig: Max Hesse, 1910.

[Kastner-Kapp.] Kastner, Emerich, ed. *Ludwig van Beethovens sämtliche Briefe*. Revised by Julius Kapp. Leipzig: Hesse & Becker, 1923. Reprint, Tutzing: Hans Schneider, 1975.

Kerman, Joseph, Alan Tyson and William Drabkin. "Ludwig van Beethoven." In *The New Grove Dictionary of Music and Musicians*, ed. Stanley Sadie, 2:354–414. 20 vols. London: Macmillan, 1980. Reprinted in revised form as *The New Grove Beethoven* (New York: Norton, 1983).

Kerst, Friedrich, ed. *Die Erinnerungen an Beethoven*. 2 vols. Stuttgart: Julius Hoffmann, 1913.

King, Alec Hyatt. *The Mozart Legacy: Aspects of the British Library Collections*. Seattle: University of Washington Press, 1984.

[Kinsky-Halm.] Kinsky, Georg. *Das Werk Beethovens: Thematisch-bibliographisches Verzeichnis seiner sämtlichen vollendeten Kompositionen*. Completed by Hans Halm. Munich: G. Henle, 1955.

Klein, Rudolf. "Beethoven im 'Klepperstall': Ein unbekannter Brief von Zmeskall v. Domanovecz" and "Postscriptum." *Österreichische Musikzeitschrift* 26 (January 1971), 3–9; (July 1971), 380.

Klein, Rudolf. *Beethovenstätten in Österreich*. Vienna: Elisabeth Lafite, 1970.

Klimovitsky, A[vram] I. "Novoe o Beethovene." In *Pamyatniki kulturi: Novie otkritiya*, pp. 246–249. Leningrad: Nauka, 1980.

Kobald, Karl. *Beethoven, Seine Beziehungen zu Wiens Kunst und Kultur, Gesellschaft und Landschaft*. Zürich: Amalthea, 1927.

Köhler, Karl-Heinz, Grita Herre, Dagmar Beck, Günter Brosche et al., eds. *Ludwig van Beethovens Konversationshefte*. 12 vols. projected; 10 vols. to date. Leipzig: VEB Deutscher Verlag für Musik, 1968–.

"Krach im Leuchtturm: Die Bonner Beethoven-Pflege liegt darnieder: Das

Geburtshaus des Komponisten verfällt, Personalquerelen blockieren das Archiv." *Der Spiegel,* no. 34 (August 22, 1994), 164–165.

Kreissle von Hellborn, Heinrich. *Franz Schubert.* Vienna: Carl Gerold's Sohn, 1865.

Kreissle von Hellborn, Heinrich. *The Life of Franz Schubert.* Translated by Arthur Duke Coleridge. London: Longmans, Green, 1869. Reprint, New York: Vienna House, 1972.

Kroll, Erwin. *Carl Maria von Weber.* Potsdam: Akademische Verlagsgesellschaft Athenaion, 1934.

Kross, Siegfried, ed. *Beethoven: Mensch seiner Zeit.* Bonn: Ludwig Röhrscheid, 1980.

Küthen, Hans-Werner. "Letters to the Editor." *Beethoven Newsletter* (San Jose) 7, no. 1 (Spring 1992), 30.

Ladenburger, Michael, ed. *Zimelien aus den Sammlungen des Beethoven-Hauses: 21 ausgewählte Neuerwerbungen der letzten drei Jahrzehnte.* Bonn: Beethoven-Haus, 1991.

La Mara [Ida Marie Lipsius]. *Musikerbriefe aus fünf Jahrhunderten, nach den Urhandschriften. . . .* 2 vols. Leipzig: Breitkopf & Härtel, 1886.

Landon, H. C. Robbins, ed. *Beethoven: A Documentary Study.* New York: Macmillan, 1970.

Landon, H. C. Robbins, ed. *The Collected Correspondence and London Notebooks of Joseph Haydn.* Fair Lawn, N.J.: Essential Books, 1959.

Landon, H. C. Robbins. *Haydn, Chronicle and Works.* 5 vols. Bloomington: Indiana University Press, 1977–1980.

Landon, H. C. Robbins. "Two New Beethoven Letters." In *Festschrift Albi Rosenthal,* ed. Rudolf Elvers, pp. 217–220. Tutzing: Hans Schneider, 1984.

Ley, Stephan. "Aus Briefen an Beethoven." In *Aus Beethovens Erdentagen,* pp. 146–155. Bonn: Karl Glöckner, 1948.

Ley, Stephan. *Beethoven als Freund der Familie Wegeler–v. Breuning, nach dem Familien-Sammlungen und -Erinnerungen.* Bonn: Friedrich Cohen, 1927.

Ley, Stephan. *Beethovens Leben in authentischen Bildern und Texten.* Berlin: Bruno Cassirer, 1925.

[London Musicians' Company.] *An Illustrated Catalogue of the Music Loan Exhibition held by the Worshipful Company of Musicians at Fishmongers' Hall, June and July, 1904.* London: Novello, 1909.

Lühning, Helga. " 'Fidelio' in Prag." In *Beethoven und Böhmen: Beiträge zu Biographie und Wirkungsgeschichte Beethovens,* ed. Sieghard Brandenburg and Martella Gutiérrez-Denhoff, pp. 349–391. Bonn: Beethoven-Haus, 1988.

Lühning, Helga, and Sieghard Brandenburg, eds. *Beethoven: Zwischen Revolution und Restauration.* Bonn: Beethoven-Haus, 1989.

Lütge, Wilhelm. "Waldmüllers Beethovenbild." *Der Bär* (1927), 35–41.

MacArdle, Donald W. *Beethoven Abstracts.* Detroit: Information Coordinators, 1973.

MacArdle, Donald W. "Beethoven and George Thomson." *Music and Letters* 37 (1956), 27–49.

[MacArdle & Misch.] MacArdle, Donald W., and Ludwig Misch, eds. *New Beethoven Letters.* Norman: University of Oklahoma Press, 1957.

Marek, George. *Beethoven: Biography of a Genius.* New York: Funk & Wagnalls, 1969.

[Meredith, William.] "Miscellanea." *Beethoven Newsletter* (San Jose) 6, no. 3 (Winter 1991), 84–85.

Moore, Julia V. "Beethoven and Musical Economics." Ph.D. diss., University of Illinois, 1987.

Morrow, Mary Sue. *Concert Life in Haydn's Vienna: Aspects of a Developing Musical and Social Institution.* Stuyvesant, N.Y.: Pendragon, 1989.

Moscheles, Charlotte. *Life of Moscheles, with Selections from His Diaries and Correspondence.* Translated by Arthur Duke Coleridge. 2 vols. London: Hurst & Blackett, 1873.

Müller, Erich H. "Zur Geschichte des Hauses Simrock." *Simrock-Jahrbuch* 1 (1928), 3–23.

Müller, Erich H. "Beethoven und Simrock." *Simrock-Jahrbuch* 2 (1929), 11–62.

Nagel, Willibald. "Kleine Beethoveniana." *Sammelbände der Internationalen Musik-Gesellschaft* 12 (1911), 586–588.

Nettl, Paul. *Beethoven Encyclopedia.* New York: Philosophical Library, 1956. 2d ed. *Beethoven Handbook.* New York: Frederick Ungar, 1967. Reprint, Westport, Conn.: Greenwood, 1975.

Nettl, Paul. "Erinnerungen an Erzherzog Rudolph, den Freund und Schüler Beethovens." *Zeitschrift für Musikwissenschaft* 4 (1921–1922), 95–99.

The New Grove Dictionary of Music and Musicians. Edited by Stanley Sadie. 20 vols. London: Macmillan, 1980.

Nohl, Ludwig. *Beethoven's Leben.* 3 vols. Leipzig: Ernst Julius Günther, 1867–1877.

[Nohl-Wallace.] Nohl, Ludwig, ed. *Beethoven's Letters.* Translated by Lady Wallace. 2 vols. London, 1866; New York: Leypoldt & Holt, 1867.

Nohl, Ludwig, ed. *Briefe Beethovens.* Stuttgart: J. G. Cotta, 1865.

Nohl, Ludwig, ed. *Neue Briefe Beethovens.* Stuttgart: J. G. Cotta, 1867.

Nohl, Ludwig. "Die Briefe Galitzins." *Allgemeine Deutsche Musik-Zeitung* 6 (1879), 1–4.

Nohl, Walther. "Ludwig van Beethoven widmet die 'Neunte' dem preussischen König." *Die Musik* 30, no. 1 (October 1937), 38–44.

Nottebohm, Gustav. *Beethoveniana: Aufsätze und Mitteilungen.* Leipzig: C. F. Peters, 1872. Reprint, with an introduction by Paul Henry Lang. New York: Johnson Reprint, 1970.

Nottebohm, Gustav. *Ein Skizzenbuch von Beethoven aus dem Jahre 1803.* Leipzig: Breitkopf & Härtel, 1880. Included in *Two Beethoven Sketchbooks,* trans. Jonathan Katz (London: Victor Gollancz, 1979).

Nottebohm, Gustav. "Ein Stammbuch Beethoven's." In *Beethoveniana: Aufsätze und Mitteilungen,* pp. 138–144. Leipzig: C. F. Peters, 1872. Reprint, New York: Johnson Reprint, 1970.

Nottebohm, Gustav. *Zweite Beethoveniana: Nachgelassene Aufsätze.* Leipzig: C. F. Peters, 1887. Reprint, New York: Johnson Reprint, 1970.

Orel, Alfred. "Ein Verlegerbrief über eine Beethoven-Gesamtausgabe." In *Festschrift Adolph Koczirz zum 60. Geburtstag,* ed. Robert Haas and Josef Zuth, pp. 29–35. Vienna: Ed. Strache, 1930.

Orel, Alfred, ed. *Ein Wiener Beethoven-Buch.* Vienna: Gerlach & Wiedling, 1921.

Osthoff, Wolfgang. "Ein unbekannter Beethoven-Brief in Venedig." In *Ars Iocundissima, Festschrift für Kurt Dorfmüller zum 60. Geburtstag,* ed. Horst Leuchtmann and Robert Münster, pp. 245–255. Tutzing: Hans Schneider, 1984.

Pachler, Faust. *Beethoven und Marie Pachler-Koschak: Beiträge und Berichtigungen.* Berlin: B. Behr, 1866.

Plantinga, Leon. *Clementi: His Life and Music.* London: Oxford University Press, 1977.

Plevka, Bohumil. *Beethoven v Českých Láznich.* [Prague:] Severočeské Nakladatelství, 1975.

Plevka, Bohumil. "Ludwig van Beethoven und Joseph Franz Maximilian Lobkowicz." *Beethoven Jahrbuch* 10 (1983), 307–312.

Plevka, Bohumil. "Vztah Beethoven — Lobkovic ve Světle Nových Doku-mentu." *Hudebni Veda* 17, no. 4 (1980), 331–339.

Pohl, Carl Ferdinand. *Denkschrift aus Anlass des hundertjährigen Bestehens der Tonkünstler-Societät.* Vienna: Carl Gerold's Sohn, 1871.

Pohl, Carl Ferdinand. *Die Gesellschaft der Musikfreunde des österreichischen Kaiserstaates und ihr Conservatorium, auf Grundlage der Gesellschafts-Acten.* Vienna: Wilhelm Braumüller, 1871.

Pohl, Carl Ferdinand. "Zur C-dur-Messe von Beethoven." *Die Grenzboten* 27, pt. 2, no. 2 (1868), 245–248.

Prelinger, Fritz, ed. *Ludwig van Beethovens sämtliche Briefe und Aufzeich-nungen.* 5 vols. Vienna: C. W. Stern, 1907–1911.

Reinöhl, Fritz von. "Neues zu Beethovens Lehrjahr bei Haydn." *Neues Beethoven-Jahrbuch* 6 (1935), 45–47.

Russo, Anna Maria. "Una lettera sconosciuta di Beethoven." *Nuova rivista musicale italiana* 25, no. 1 (January–March 1991), 74–82.

Sandberger, Adolf. "Antonie Brentano an Johann Michael Sailer wegen Beethovens Neffen." *Jahrbuch der Musikbibliothek Peters* 21–22 (1914–1915), 43ff. Reprinted in his *Ausgewählte Aufsätze zur Musikgeschichte II*, pp. 251–257 (Munich: Drei Masken, 1924; reprint, Hildesheim: Georg Olms, 1973).

Sandberger, Adolf. "Beiträge zur Beethoven-Forschung." *Archiv für Musik-wissenschaft* 2 (1920), 394–410.

Sandberger, Adolf. "Franz Xaver Kleinheinz." In *Ausgewählte Aufsätze zur Musikgeschichte II*, pp. 226–247. Munich: Drei Masken, 1924. Reprint, Hildesheim: Georg Olms, 1973.

Sandberger, Adolf. "Zum Kapitel: Beethoven und München." In *Ausgewählte Aufsätze zur Musikgeschichte II*, pp. 258–262. Munich: Drei Masken, 1924. Reprint, Hildesheim: Georg Olms, 1973.

Schiedermair, Ludwig. "Neue Schriftstücke zu Beethovens Vormundschaft über seinen Neffen." *Neues Beethoven-Jahrbuch* 8 (1938), 59–64.

Schiedermair, Ludwig. "Ein unbekannter Opernentwurf für Beethoven." *Neues Beethoven-Jahrbuch* 7 (1937), 32–36.

[Schindler-MacArdle.] Schindler, Anton. *Beethoven as I Knew Him.* Trans-lated by Constance S. Jolly. Edited by Donald W. MacArdle. London: Faber & Faber; Chapel Hill: University of North Carolina Press, 1966. Reduced-size reprint, New York: W. W. Norton, 1972.

Schindler, Anton. *Beethoven in Paris: Nebst anderen . . . Mittheilungen: Ein Nachtrag zur Biographie Beethoven's.* Münster: Aschendorff, 1842.

[Schindler (1840).] Schindler, Anton. *Biographie von Ludwig van Beethoven.* Münster: Aschendorff, 1840.

[Schindler (1860).] Schindler, Anton. *Biographie von Ludwig van Beethoven.* 3d ed. 2 pts. Münster: Aschendorff, 1860.

[Schindler-Moscheles.] Schindler, Anton. *The Life of Beethoven, Including His Correspondence.* . . . Edited by Ignaz Moscheles. 2 vols. London: Henry Colburn, 1841. Altered reprint, Boston: Oliver Ditson, [1840s].

Schlosser, Johann Aloys. *Ludwig van Beethoven: Eine Biographie desselben, verbunden mit Urtheilen über seine Werke.* Prague: Buchler, Stephani & Schlosser, 1827. Rev. 2d printing, 1828.

Schmidt, Hans. "Addenda und Corrigenda zum Katalog 'Die Beethovenhandschriften des Beethovenhauses in Bonn.' " *Beethoven-Jahrbuch* 8 (1975), 207–220.

Schmidt, Hans. "Die Beethovenhandschriften des Beethovenhauses in Bonn." *Beethoven-Jahrbuch* 7 (1971). [Entire issue.]

Schmidt, Leopold, ed. *Beethoven-Briefe an Nicolaus Simrock, F. G. Wegeler, Eleonore v. Breuning und Ferd. Ries.* Berlin: N. Simrock, 1909.

Schmidt-Görg, Joseph, ed. *Beethoven: Dreizehn unbekannte Briefe an Josephine Gräfin Deym geb. v. Brunsvik.* Bonn: Beethovenhaus, 1957. Reprint, Bonn: Beethovenhaus, 1986.

Schmidt-Görg, Joseph. *Katalog der Handschriften des Beethoven-Hauses und Beethoven-Archivs Bonn.* Bonn: Beethoven-Haus, 1935.

Schmidt-Görg, Joseph. "Neue Schriftstücke zu Beethoven und Josephine Gräfin Deym." *Beethoven-Jahrbuch* 6 (1969), 205–208.

Schmidt-Görg, Joseph, and Hans Schmidt, eds. *Ludwig van Beethoven.* Hamburg: DGG, 1969; New York: Praeger, 1970.

Schmidtke, Gotthard. *Musikalisches Niedersachsen: Künstler aus Braunschweig und der Heide.* Braunschweig: Waisenhaus-Buchdruckerei, [ca. 1963].

Schneider, Hans. *400 Musikerautographen: Katalog Nr. 199.* Tutzing: Musikantiquariat Hans Schneider, 1976.

Schneider, Hans. *Musikerautographen: Katalog Nr. 225.* Tutzing: Musikantiquariat Hans Schneider, 1978.

Schneider, Hans. *Musikerautographen: Katalog Nr. 232.* Tutzing: Musikantiquariat Hans Schneider, 1979.

Schneider, Hans. *Musikalische Seltenheiten: Eine Auswahl aus 250 Katalogen.* . . . Tutzing: Hans Schneider, 1981.

Schönfeld, Johann Ferdinand von. *Jahrbuch der Tonkunst von Wien und Prag.* Vienna: Schönfeld, 1796. Reprint, with an afterword and an index by Otto Biba, Munich: Emil Katzbichler, 1976.

Schottländer, Johann Wolfgang. "Zelter und die Komponisten seiner Zeit." *Jahrbuch der Sammlung Kippenberg* 8 (1930), 175–211.

Schuler, Manfred. "Unveröffentlichte Briefe von Ludwig van Beethoven und Georg Friedrich Treitschke: Zur dritten Fassung des 'Fidelio.'" *Die Musikforschung* 35 (1982), 53–62.

Schultz, Johann Reinhold. "Beethoven's Last Illness and Death." *Harmonicon* 5 (May 1827), 84.

Schultz, Johann Reinhold. "Hopeless State of Beethoven." *Harmonicon* 5 (February 1827), 23.

Schünemann, Georg. "Beethovens 'Kanone.'" *Die Musik* 32, pt. 2 (August 1940), 377, plate facing p. 377.

Schwarz, Boris. "Beethoveniana in Soviet Russia." *Musical Quarterly* 47, no. 1 (1961), 15–21.

Schwarz, Boris. "More Beethoveniana in Soviet Russia." *Musical Quarterly* 49, no. 2 (1963), 143–149.

Schwarz, Ignaz. "Beethoven und Berlin." *Der Merkur* (Österreichische Zeitschrift für Musik und Theater) 3, no. 3 (February 1912), 88–90.

Shedlock, John S. "Beethoven Sketches Hitherto Unpublished." *Musical Times* 50 (November 1, 1909), 712–714.

Shedlock, John S. "Clementi Correspondence." *Monthly Musical Record* 32 (August 1, 1902), 141–144.

Smidak, Emil F. *Isaak-Ignaz Moscheles: The Life of the Composer, and His Encounters with Beethoven, Liszt, Chopin and Mendelssohn.* Aldershot: Gower; Brookfield, Vt.: Scolar, 1989. [Heavily based on Moscheles (1873).]

Smolle, Kurt. *Wohnstätten Ludwig van Beethovens von 1792 bis zu seinem Tod.* Bonn: Beethoven-Haus, 1970.

Solomon, Maynard. "Antonie Brentano and Beethoven." *Music and Letters* 58, no. 2 (1977), 153–169. Expanded in his *Beethoven Essays* (Cambridge, Mass.: Harvard University Press, 1988), pp. 166–189.

Solomon, Maynard. *Beethoven.* New York: Schirmer Books, 1977.

Solomon, Maynard. "A Beethoven Acquaintance: Josef von Hammer-Purgstall." *Musical Times* 124 (January 1983), 13–15.

Somfai, László. *Joseph Haydn: His Life in Contemporary Pictures.* New York: Taplinger, 1969.

Sonneck, Oscar George, ed. *Beethoven: Impressions by His Contemporaries.* New York: G. Schirmer, 1926. Reprint, New York: Dover, 1967.

Sotheby & Co. *Catalogue of Valuable Printed Books, Music, Autograph Letters and Historical Documents.* Auction catalog. London, June 13, 1966.

Sotheby & Co. *Catalogue of Valuable Printed Books, Music, Autograph Letters.* Auction catalog. London, May 11–12, 1970.

Sotheby & Co. *Music, Continental Manuscripts and Printed Books.* Auction catalog. London, May 9–10, 1985.

Sotheby & Co. *Music, Continental Manuscripts and Printed Books.* Auction catalog. London, November 26–27, 1987.

Sotheby & Co. *Continental Manuscripts and Music.* Auction catalog. London, May 18, 1995.

Sotheby Park Bernet. *Fine Books and Autograph Letters.* Auction Catalogue no. 4314. New York, November 27, 1979.

Staehelin, Martin. "Die Beethoven-Materialien im Nachlass von Ludwig Nohl." *Beethoven-Jahrbuch* 10 (1983), 201–219.

Staehelin, Martin. *Hans Georg Nägeli und Ludwig van Beethoven.* Zürich: Hug, 1982.

Staehelin, Martin, ed. "Unbekannte oder wenig beachtete Schriftstücke Beethovens." *Beethoven Jahrbuch* 10 (1983), 21–85.

Staehelin, Martin, Sieghard Brandenburg and the Beethoven-Haus, Bonn, eds. *Ludwig van Beethoven: Der Briefwechsel mit dem Verlag Schott.* Munich: G. Henle, 1985.

Stargardt, J. A. *Autographen aus verschiedenem Besitz: Katalog 577.* Marburg, November 29–30, 1966.

Stargardt, J. A. *Autographen aus allen Gebieten: Katalog 601.* Marburg, February 21–22, 1973.

Stargardt, J. A. *Autographen aus allen Gebieten: Katalog 602.* Marburg, November 27–28, 1973.

Stargardt, J. A. *Autographen aus allen Gebieten: Katalog 618.* Marburg, November 27–28, 1979.

Stargardt, J. A. *Autographen aus drei alten Schweizer Sammlungen: Auktion, Erasmushaus, Basel: Katalog 66/652.* Marburg, September 19, 1992.

Sterba, Editha, and Richard Sterba. *Beethoven and His Nephew: A Psychoanalytic Study of Their Relationship.* Translated by Willard Trask. New York: Pantheon, 1954.

[Thayer.] Thayer, Alexander Wheelock. *Ludwig van Beethoven's Leben.* Translated by Hermann Deiters. 3 vols. Berlin: Ferdinand Schneider; W. Weber, 1866, 1872, 1879. [Coverage only to 1816.]

[Thayer-Deiters-Riemann.] Thayer, Alexander Wheelock. *Ludwig van Beethovens Leben.* Translated by Hermann Deiters. Edited by Hugo Riemann. 5 vols. Leipzig: Breitkopf & Härtel, Vol. 1, 1901, 1917; Vol. 2, 1910; Vol. 3, 1911; Vol. 4, 1907; Vol. 5, 1908.

[Thayer-Krehbiel.] Thayer, Alexander Wheelock. *The Life of Ludwig van Beethoven.* Translated and edited by Henry Edward Krehbiel. 3 vols. New York: Beethoven Association, 1921. Reprint, London: Centaur, 1960.

[Thayer-Forbes.] *Thayer's Life of Beethoven.* Edited by Elliot Forbes. 2 vols. Princeton, N.J.: Princeton University Press, 1964. Rev. ed., 1967.

Tyson, Alan. "The 1803 Version of Beethoven's *Christus am Ölberge.*" *Musical Quarterly* 56, no. 4 (1970), 551–584. Reprinted in *The Creative World of Beethoven,* ed. Paul Henry Lang, pp. 49 82. New York: Norton, 1971.

Tyson, Alan. "An Angry Letter from Beethoven." *Musical Times* 112 (September 1971), 842–845.

Tyson, Alan. "Beethoven to the Countess Susanna Guicciardi: A New Letter." In *Beethoven Studies,* ed. Alan Tyson, pp. 1–17. New York: Norton, 1973.

Tyson, Alan. "New Beethoven Letters and Documents." In *Beethoven Studies 2,* ed. Alan Tyson, pp. 30–32. London: Oxford University Press, 1977.

Tyson, Alan. "Notes on Five of Beethoven's Copyists." *Journal of the American Musicological Society* 23 (Fall 1970), 439–471.

Tyson, Alan. "Prolegomena to a Future Edition of Beethoven's Letters." In *Beethoven Studies 2,* ed. Alan Tyson, pp. 1–19. London: Oxford University Press, 1977.

Unger, Max. "Beethoven und B. Schott's Söhne: Mit zwei ungedruckten Briefen des Verlags an den Meister." *Die Musik* 34 (June 1942), 285–295.

Unger, Max. "Die Beethovenbilder von Neugass." [*Neue*] *Zeitschrift für Musik* 102 (1935), 1211–1216.

Unger, Max. "Beethovens Konversationshefte als biographische Quelle." *Die Musik* 34 (September 1942), 377–386; 35 (November 1942), 37–47.

Unger, Max. *Ludwig van Beethoven und seine Verleger, S. A. Steiner und Tobias Haslinger in Wien, Ad. Mart. Schlesinger in Berlin: Ihr Verkeher und Briefwechsel.* Berlin: Schlesinger, 1921.

Unger, Max. "Muzio Clementi and His Relations with Gottfried Christoph

Härtel of Leipzig, as Shown in the Letters of Clementi." Translated by Kurt Krause. *Monthly Musical Record* 38 (November 1908), 246–247; (December 1908), 270–273.

Unger, Max. *Muzio Clementis Leben.* Langensalza: Hermann Beyer & Söhne, 1914.

Unger, Max. "Neue Briefe an Beethoven." *Neue Zeitschrift für Musik* 81, no. 28 (July 9, 1914), 409–413.

Unger, Max. "Neue Kunde vom Totenbette Beethovens." *Deutsche Musiker-Zeitung* 58 (1927), 276–280.

Unger, Max. "Nova Beethoveniana." *Die Musik* 12, pt. 3 (November 1912), 160–162.

Unger, Max. *Eine Schweizer Beethovensammlung: Katalog.* Zürich: Corona, 1939.

Unger, Max. "Ein unbekannter französischer Brief Ludwig van Beethovens." *[Neue] Zeitschrift für Musik* 103 (April 1936), 414–419.

Unger, Max. "Zur Entstehungs- und Aufführungsgeschichte von Beethovens Oper 'Leonore.'" *[Neue] Zeitschrift für Musik* 105, no. 2 (February 1938), 136–137.

Valentin, Erich. *Beethoven: Eine Bildbiographie.* Munich: Kindlers Klassische Bildbiographen, 1957. Translated by Norma Dean as *Beethoven and his World* (New York: Viking, 1958).

Van Hasselt, Luc. "Beethoven in Holland." *Die Musikforschung* 18 (1965), 181–184.

[Vienna.] *Die Flamme lodert: Beethoven Ausstellung der Stadt Wien . . . 26. Mai bis 30. August 1970.* Edited by Fritz Racek, Ernst Hilmar et al. Vienna: Rathaus, 1970.

[Vienna.] *Hof- und Staats-Schematismus der . . . Stadt Wien.* Vienna: Joseph Gerold, 1800, 1801, 1804, 1805, 1808.

[Vienna.] *Vollständiges Auskunftsbuch, oder enzig richtiger Wegweiser in . . . Wien, für Kaufleute, Fabrikanten, Künstler und Handwerker.* Vienna: Joseph Gerold, 1804, 1805.

Vienna. Historisches Museum. *Beethoven Zentenar-Ausstellung der Stadt Wien: "Beethoven un die Wiener Kultur seiner Zeit." Führer.* Vienna: Selbstverlag der Gemeinde Wien, 1927.

Virneisel, Wilhelm. "Kleine Beethoveniana." In *Festschrift Joseph Schmidt-Görg zum 60. Geburtstag,* ed. Dagmar Weise, pp. 361–376. Bonn: Beethovenhaus, 1957.

Volek, Tomislav, and Jaroslav Macek. "Beethoven und Fürst Lobkowitz." In *Beethoven und Böhmen: Beiträge zu Biographie und Wirkungsgeschichte Beethovens*, ed. Sieghard Brandenburg and Martella Gutiérrez-Denhoff, pp. 203–217. Bonn: Beethoven-Haus, 1988.

Volkmann, Hans. "Beethoven und die erste Aufführung des Fidelio in Dresden." *Die Musik* 15, no. 1 (December 1922), 177–184.

Volkmann, Hans. *Beethoven in seinen Beziehungen zu Dresden*. Dresden: Deutscher Literatur-Verlag, 1924.

Weber, Max Maria von. *Carl Maria von Weber: Ein Lebensbild*. 3 vols. Leipzig: Ernst Keil, 1864.

Wegeler, Franz Gerhard, and Ferdinand Ries. *Biographische Notizen über Ludwig van Beethoven*. Coblenz: Baedeker, 1838; *Nachtrag* by Wegeler, 1845.

Wegeler, Franz Gerhard, and Ferdinand Ries. *Biographische Notizen über Ludwig van Beethoven*. Edited by Alfred Christlieb Kalischer. Berlin: Schuster & Loeffler, 1906. Translated by Frederick Noonan as *Beethoven Remembered* (Arlington, Va.: Great Ocean, 1987).

Weissenbäck, Andreas. "Drei noch unveröffentlichte Briefe Albrechtsbergers an Beethoven." *Musica Divina* 9 (1921), 10–12.

Whistling, Carl Friedrich, and Friedrich Hofmeister. *Handbuch der musikalischen Litteratur*. Leipzig: [Whistling], 1817–1827. Reprint, with an introduction by Neill Ratliff, New York: Garland, 1975.

"Die Wiener internationale Ausstellung für Musik und Theaterwesen." By F.v.W. *Neue Zeitschrift für Musik* 88, no. 47 (November 23, 1892), 525–526.

Worgull, Elmar. "Ferdinand Georg Waldmüller. . . ." *Studien zur Musikwissenschaft (DTÖ)* 30 (1979), 107–153.

Zahn, Johannes. "Tucher, Gottlieb von." *Allgemeine deutsche Biographie*, 38:767–770. Leipzig, 1894. Reprint, Berlin: Duncker & Humblot, 1971.

[Zelter, Carl Friedrich.] "Drei Briefe, zwischen Beethoven und Zelter gewechselt." *Niederrheinische Musik-Zeitung* 5 (1857), 22–23.

Ziegler, Anton. *Addressen-Buch von Tonkünstlern. . . .* Vienna: Anton Strauss, 1823.

INDEX OF INCIPITS

Incipits beginning with articles (der, die, das, etc.) are alphabetized under that article rather than the following word, with no cross-reference to that second word. Readers should also consider potential variants in spelling when consulting this index. The citations refer to letter numbers.

INDEX OF CORRESPONDENTS

Citations refer to letter numbers. For letters to and from Beethoven himself, readers should consult the list of letters and documents at the beginning of each volume.

s = Senders of letters and authors of documents
r = Recipients of letters (and documents, when designated)
na = Primarily documents with no specific sender/author or recipient designated

INDEX OF BEETHOVEN'S WORKS

Works are grouped in the following order by genre. Listings within each genre are ordered in a way best suggested by the genre itself. The citations refer to letter numbers.

Instrumental

SYMPHONIES

CONCERTOS AND CONCERTED MOVEMENTS

DANCES

OTHER ORCHESTRAL WORKS

MILITARY BAND WORKS

STRING QUARTETS

SONATAS (NON-KEYBOARD)

OTHER CHAMBER MUSIC

PIANO WORKS

    General

    Sonatas

    Other Piano Music

OTHER KEYBOARD WORKS

Vocal (and Dramatic Non-Vocal)

DRAMATIC WORKS

OTHER WORKS FOR VOICE AND ORCHESTRA

CHORAL WORKS

    Completed

    Incomplete/Unrealized

SONGS

FOLKSONGS

    Alphabetical List

    Untitled (by Opus, WoO, and Hess)

    Arrangements, Collections, and Variations

    Hymns and Overtures

CANONS

Miscellaneous

GENERAL INDEX

This index of people, places, things, titles, and concepts contains no primary entries under "Beethoven, Ludwig van." To find references to Beethoven's health, look directly under Health. Similarly, streets and other geographical locations in Vienna and its environs are given their own entries rather than listed as subentries under Vienna. Many institutions (the Kärntnertor Theater, for instance) are found under Vienna, while more frequently cited organizations (such as the Gesellschaft der Musikfreunde) are given their own entry. In most cases, a system of cross-references will guide the user from one point in the index to another. Nevertheless, the careful researcher will want to search proper names, especially, under a variety of phonetic renderings used in Beethoven's time. This index includes few references to researchers, authors, and editors named in the *Sources* notes, most of whom are found alphabetically in the bibliography.

KEY: Arabic-numbered citations in this index refer to letter numbers, not page numbers. Roman numerals, however, refer to pages in the prefatory material. Under individuals' names, bold typeface indicates a letter where substantial background may be found. The term *illus.* at the end of an entry indicates the volume of this collection in which a pertinent illustration may be found.